Using Literature to Enhance Content Area Instruction

A GUIDE FOR K–5 TEACHERS

REBECCA OLNESS
Black Diamond, Washington, USA

INTERNATIONAL
Reading Association
800 BARKSDALE ROAD, PO BOX 8139
NEWARK, DE 19714-8139, USA
www.reading.org

The International Reading Association attempts, through its publications, to provide a forum for a wide spectrum of opinions on reading. This policy permits divergent viewpoints without implying the endorsement of the Association.

Executive Editor, Books   Corinne M. Mooney
Developmental Editor   Charlene M. Nichols
Developmental Editor   Tori Mello Bachman
Developmental Editor   Stacey Lynn Sharp
Editorial Production Manager   Shannon T. Fortner
Production Manager   Iona Muscella
Supervisor, Electronic Publishing   Anette Schuetz

Project Editors   Tori Mello Bachman and Rebecca A. Fetterolf

Cover   Design, Linda Steere; Photo, © Digital Vision/Getty Images

Copyright 2007 by the International Reading Association, Inc.

The publisher would appreciate notification where errors occur so that they may be corrected in subsequent printings and/or editions.

Library of Congress Cataloging-in-Publication Data

Olness, Rebecca.

  Using literature to enhance content area instruction : a guide for K-5 teachers / Rebecca Olness.
     p. cm.

  Includes bibliographical references and index.

  ISBN 978-0-87207-600-6

  1. Content area reading--United States. 2. Reading (Elementary)--United States. 3. Children's literature--Study and teaching (Elementary)--United States. I. Title.

  LB1573.75.O46 2007

  372.41--dc22

                                                                                    2007017500

Contents

About the Author

Rebecca Olness is a retired literacy specialist with more than 30 years of teaching experience. She also has been a staff developer and an adjunct professor at Seattle Pacific University and Seattle University, Washington, USA. Currently a private reading and writing consultant, Rebecca speaks at conferences and for school districts and individual schools. She has presented at literacy conferences throughout the United States and Canada, as well as in New Zealand and the Caribbean.

Rebecca received her bachelor's degree in music and education and master's degree in developmental reading from the University of Washington, Seattle, Washington, USA. An active member of her local and state reading councils, she has served on numerous International Reading Association committees, as well as on the Association's Board of Directors.

She has served on several children's literature awards committees and also reviews and annotates professional development materials. Rebecca's first book, *Using Literature to Enhance Writing Instruction* (IRA, 2005), combines her love of literature with writing instruction and is based on the Six-Trait Analytical Writing Model. This book extends that love of literature into the content areas.

Rebecca enjoys traveling, including yearly ski trips to Italy and taking cruises, reading, and playing the piano. She and her husband, Ron, live on Lake Sawyer in Black Diamond, Washington, USA, with their cat, Nicky, and dog, Daisy. They have two grown children: Michael, who lives in the Florida Keys, and Jennifer, who also lives in Black Diamond. Rebecca volunteers and serves on the board of the Black Diamond Community Center and was recently elected to the Black Diamond City Council.

Rebecca can be reached by e-mail at rolness@comcast.net.

Foreword

Becky Olness and I served as members of the International Reading Association's Board of Directors several years ago, and I quickly learned of her passion for teaching and her love of literature that could help energize reading instruction in elementary schools. I also learned, during a visit to her lovely home near the water in Washington state, that her passion for books, especially children's books, was clearly demonstrated by a huge library. I am pleased that Becky has used her vast knowledge of children's literature to prepare this well-researched and extremely helpful book for elementary teachers who have an interest in strengthening their instruction by infusing trade books into key content areas. From my perspective, the task Becky faced was gigantic, but she was more than equal to the challenge, and you can take her efforts to the next step: Use the research and practical ideas to help enhance your students' learning in the content areas.

In the pages that follow is a very readable and useful book that will help you integrate trade books into the content areas of social studies, science, mathematics, and the arts (music, dance, drama, and visual art). But don't overlook the two introductory chapters where you will learn much valuable information about trade books and *how* to successfully use them in your content area instruction. You'll also read some cautionary notes and possible pitfalls to avoid. In addition, there are several helpful descriptions of successful programs that used trade books to enhance student achievement.

Busy teachers (aren't we all?) will be especially pleased with the four chapters that help you integrate trade books into selected content areas in a meaningful and instructionally useful way. Each of the content area chapters has several common elements. After an introduction, there is in important presentation of the curriculum standards for that particular content area. There also are some general ideas for helping students acquire the standards. This information is useful, but you will be especially impressed with the sample lesson plans at selected grade levels. I believe that these lesson plans offer a point of departure for integrating trade books into the content areas. Expect to see the inclusion of specific content area texts that should be appropriate for that grade. Often, a week's lesson is included along with ideas for assessment. Additional books that can help meet the content standards are also included. Finally, there is a handy annotated bibliography of children's literature to use in each of the content areas that make up the core of the book.

I hope my words will stimulate teachers, especially those in the United States and Canada, to take the many ideas and resources in *Using Literature to Enhance Content Area Instruction* to do just that—enhance instruction, student engagement, and student learning with high-quality trade books. I'm sure Becky would be pleased to know that her hard work has made it easier for you to help your students achieve higher levels of literacy and content area mastery.

Jerry L. Johns
Distinguished Teaching Professor, Emeritus
Northern Illinois University
2002–2003 President
International Reading Association

Preface

Teachers are expected to reach unattainable goals with inadequate tools. The miracle is that at times they accomplish this impossible task.

—Dr. Haim Ginott

When I first started teaching, the typical school day looked something like this: one hour for reading; one hour for math; and various half-hour segments for spelling, penmanship, writing, social studies, science, and health (sometimes on alternate days). We had daily read-aloud storytime, taught art at least once a week, had physical education and music, and went to the library. Of course the schedule also had to allow for recess, lunch, assemblies, and special events. Times have changed!

Recent mandates in the United States that judge schools by how well students are doing in reading and math have reduced the time allocated to other subject areas (Jones et al., 1999). Many interpret the No Child Left Behind (NCLB) legislation of 2001, supported by the report of the National Reading Panel (National Institute of Child Health and Human Development, 2000), to mean that teachers must focus on basics: reading and math. Fortunately, writing has also begun to emerge to the forefront of the basics (National Commission on Writing in America's Schools and Colleges, 2003). But what has happened to the other subjects? Although there are many schools in which all subjects are being taught, there is growing concern that in some schools, they are being neglected.

In the June/July 2005 issue of *Reading Today*, Alan Farstrup, Executive Director of the International Reading Association (IRA), describes IRA's "mixed feelings" (p. 7), which reflect not only strong support for elimination of the achievement gap and for improvement of reading achievement through evidence-based teaching but also a growing frustration with how NCLB has been implemented. IRA is concerned that demands upon curriculum have the effect of reducing or weakening content instruction in areas such as science, social studies, math, and the language arts in general. And, because various professional content area associations are expressing concerns about reduced emphasis on vital school subjects other than reading and math, IRA has brought together representatives of these organizations, including the National Council of Teachers of English (NCTE), National Council for the Social Studies (NCSS), National Council of Teachers of Mathematics (NCTM), National Science Teachers Association (NSTA), American Association of School Librarians (AASL), and others. This group of professional organizations will issue a brief paper, titled *Making Every Moment Count*, to iterate their shared consensus on the effective use of instructional time through a comprehensive, integrated curriculum, to teach all subjects. (At the time this book went to press, the document was scheduled for release in June 2007.)

In Washington, USA, 37 local school districts have asked for delayed implementation of a new science requirement for the graduating class of 2010. Districts claim that they don't have the money to prepare students for the science portion of the Washington Assessment of Student Learning (WASL) standardized test, a test that students must pass in order to graduate. One district superintendent threatened a lawsuit, and one school board official stated, "In math, reading and writing we're very well trained. It's not that we're saying don't ever assess kids with a science WASL. We just need more time and money for resources" (Swift, 2005, p. A-14).

In Canada, because there is no national Department of Education, each province has its own standards, so teachers in Canada have not been told what or how much to teach beyond the provincial curriculum guidelines. However, there are two consortiums: Western Canada Protocol Partners (Alberta, British Columbia, Manitoba, Northwest Territories, Nunavut, Saskatchewan, and Yukon) and the Council of Atlantic Ministers of Education and Training, formerly the Atlantic Provinces Education Foundation (New Brunswick, Newfoundland and Labrador, Nova Scotia, and Prince Edward Island). These groups have common curriculum frameworks. Ontario and Quebec are not part of these groups, but they have curriculum guidelines within their own Ministries of Education. During the 1980s, curriculum reform across Canada resulted in a new commitment to resource-based learning (Ontario Ministry of Education, 1982). Other provinces soon joined this educational focus and prepared similar guides to facilitate the implementation of the resource-based model implicit in the curriculum guidelines. These documents recommend integration across all subject areas, although they are only advisory and do not *mandate* resource-based learning in schools. This emphasis on integration is important when one looks at the excellent performance on international tests by Canadian students (see Chapter 2).

I have great admiration, respect, and sympathy for today's teachers. They sometimes seem to have an impossible job. Scores must go up, but there is simply not enough time in the school day or the school year to teach all that must be taught. The emphasis on time on task has even done away with recess in some districts (Mills, O'Keefe, & Jennings, 2004). No one can dispute that literacy and math are vitally important, but we all know that in order to become productive citizens and have a well-rounded knowledge base, children must be exposed to history, geography, science, health, and the arts. Many teachers are faced with a conflict between what they are *expected* to teach and what they know in their hearts they *must* teach (Mills et al., 2004). It comes down to what you *have* to do versus what you *should* do. Therefore, with the time restraints and demands placed on teachers today, using literature to broach content area subjects is the wisest—and often the only—choice. Children's literature has long played a dominant role in teaching the language arts, and most would agree it is an established and essential element of any solid language arts program (Galda & Liang, 2003). The two areas of the curriculum in which children's literature is most often used as content are the language arts and social studies. But literature also has its place in the teaching of other content area subjects. According to Guthrie (1996), unifying reading, writing, science, and social studies through integrated studies fosters intrinsic motivation and sustains engagement in literacy. Literature of all genres can play an important role in such unification, and the values of fiction and nonfiction trade books in the classroom are numerous and well-documented.

It should be noted that in a literature-based curriculum, literary works, usually called trade books by the publishing industry, are the dominant materials for instruction instead of textbooks (Harris & Hodges, 1995). For some, the term *literature* connotes only fiction, but with the wide array of quality children's trade books available in all genres, most of us consider both fiction and nonfiction to be literature. For instance, children's literature courses include all genres, as do children's sections in libraries and bookstores. For this reason, I use the terms *literature* and *trade books* interchangeably throughout this book to encompass all genres of children's books other than textbooks.

Trade books of all genres can capture the attention of the reader by appealing to imagination and interest (Vacca et al., 2003). In other words, curiosity is a powerful motivator for reading (Baker & Wigfield, 1999). Children can read more about a topic of particular interest in informational text; autobiographies and biographies provide ways to learn about real people and their contributions to society, and historical fiction sets the stage for understanding a particular era in history. For some time, reading professionals have advocated using nonfiction trade books with older students, but the call to use nonfiction trade books in the early grades is relatively new (Palmer & Stewart, 2003). Because of this, there recently has been a multitude of quality books published in all subject areas for even the youngest children.

Reading from textbooks, many of which are often outdated, is not always the best or only way for children to gain knowledge. When I was in elementary school, my least favorite subject was social studies. I don't really know why, but I had absolutely no interest in it. But when I was in high school, I had a wonderful history teacher, Mr. Bemis. He told stories—stories full of personal anecdotes, descriptions, and colorful language that made the events come to life. I learned more about history in his class than I did in my previous 10 years of schooling. I was interested, and I sought out more information because I wanted to know more.

Trade books can do for children what Mr. Bemis did for me. They can be used in conjunction with textbooks to supplement content area instruction or they can be used exclusively. They also can be read aloud by the teacher. This is often the best way to introduce new subject areas and concepts to young children. As Moje and her colleagues (2004) explain, "To be literate in a content area involves learning the content associated with the area" (p. 45).

There has been widespread advocacy for using trade books in the social studies by professional organizations such as NCSS and by educators and researchers. Trade books can develop students' interests and give a wider perspective of particular events in ways not typically addressed in textbooks, and they can add flexibility to the curriculum so that different ability levels of students can be served. And picture books can help students visualize the place and time of historical events, especially in the last half of the 20th century.

Nonfiction trade books offer a source for answering specific questions children ask about science and for stimulating further questioning. Bosma and Brower (1995) field-tested an integrated literature-based science curriculum for first graders using children's trade books for a science unit on animals. Students exhibited evidence of critical thinking as a result of the literature-based science lessons. This study was built on assumptions made by Weaver (1988), who found that children's conceptual background is broadened and they display increased motivation in reading and learning when a variety of books is available.

Teaching mathematics with trade books has become increasingly popular in recent years for a variety of reasons. Some researchers suggest that literature not only motivates students (Usnick & McCarthy, 1998) and provokes interest (Welchman-Tischler, 1992) but also helps students connect mathematical ideas to their personal experiences, accommodates different learning styles, promotes critical thinking (Murphy, 2000), and provides a context for using mathematics to solve problems (Jacobs & Rak, 1997).

The fine arts also are supported in many ways through children's literature. For some children, seeing reproductions of paintings in a trade book is the introduction and often the only exposure they may have to famous artists. Reading or hearing a story about a musician can serve as a springboard for further study of a musical genre. Picture biographies of famous dancers define different types of dance, and some books invite dramatization and performance.

Because there is ample information available regarding the use of literature to teach reading and writing, this book focuses on the content areas of social studies, science, mathematics, and the arts. Chapter 1 focuses on the research evidence supporting the use of trade books for content area instruction. It also provides guidelines and criteria for choosing appropriate books. Chapter 2 explores integrated curriculum, themes, differentiated instruction, and assessment. Chapters 3 through 6 cover specific content areas: social studies, science, mathematics, and the arts. Each of these chapters includes curriculum standards for each subject area, rationale for integrating literature into content area study, ideas for choosing appropriate trade books in each area, sample lesson plans organized by grade level, and an annotated bibliography. The appendix contains a list of professional organizations, ideas for additional sources for books, and websites.

It is my aim in writing this book to give classroom teachers in kindergarten through grade 5 some tools and titles to integrate the "forgotten" content areas into the elementary school curriculum. Students deserve the best education possible—in *all* subject areas. I hope some of the ideas presented will assist teachers in providing this well-rounded education.

Acknowledgments

There are many friends and colleagues who have helped me throughout the writing of this book. Thank you to Lori Jamison Rog, who has "kept me honest" by reminding me to include Canada in my books. She has also been a great resource.

Thank you to Jerry Johns, who called to wish me a happy New Year and ended up writing the foreword to this book; to first-grade teacher Anne Veer, who provided many ideas and materials from her students at Springbrook Elementary in Kent; and to Billy and Sarah Wheeler and their teacher Liz White for sharing information about "Night of the Notables" at Lake Wilderness Elementary in Maple Valley.

I am grateful to the publications staff at the International Reading Association, especially Teresa Curto, who began this journey with me, for her support and encouragement, and Tori Mello Bachman, who guided me through the final portion with patience, understanding, and professional wisdom.

Finally, I want to thank my mother, Edith Lewis, for encouraging me, and my husband, Ron, for taking care of himself, the animals, and the house while I write.

CHAPTER 1

Trade Books in the Content Classroom

Books are the characters of civilization. Without books, history is silent, literature dumb, science crippled, thought and speculation at a standstill.

—Barbara Tuchman

According to *The Literacy Dictionary* (Harris & Hodges, 1995), "trade books" are books published for sale to the general public, as compared to "textbooks," which are used solely for instructional purposes. Many children's trade books present topics relating to content areas. Math facts and concepts can be better understood through literature. Biographies, both in picture book and longer form, can lead to better understanding of the subject's purpose, feelings, accomplishments, and contributions to society. Nonfiction trade books can give relevant information and also serve as a model for reports. Social studies and science trade books, as well as fiction, provide quality literature along with opportunities for reading and strengthening the language arts skills. For older students, fiction and historical fiction novels can be used to whet the appetite for significant events in history or explain a scientific theory or fact. And a better understanding and appreciation of art, music, and drama can be gained through literature.

Danielson and LaBonty (1994) list the value of using trade books in the classroom: Vocabulary and concepts are learned more efficiently and effectively, literature generates interest in the real world, literature provides models for writing while it nurtures the imagination, and literature allows students to enjoy reading while they learn. Trade books offer better coverage of topics, go deeper than the survey of information most common in textbooks, and can be easier for students to read (Vacca & Vacca, 1996). An added value of using literature in the content areas is that it is particularly useful for teaching children who are deemed at risk. Textbooks, if available, are often far above the reading level of many children in the classroom, making them nearly useless for these students. Good trade books are available on nearly any topic and at every reading level.

Textbooks vs. Trade Books

While there are many excellent textbooks for students, one of the biggest disadvantages of using textbooks in content areas is that they are written for one specific reading level. We all know that within a particular grade level, students exhibit a wide range of reading abilities. The density of dates, names, and places make social studies texts difficult to read (Beck & McKeown, 1991; Beck, McKeown, & Gromoll, 1989) and respond to (Person & Cullinan, 1992). Though textbooks have long dominated science instruction, children reaching the upper elementary grades often have a difficult time comprehending these texts (Armbruster & Anderson, 1988; Beck, McKeown, Hamilton, & Kucan, 1997; Casteel & Isom, 1994). And Walpole's (1998/1999) study indicated that newly published science basals' layout of text on pages, designed to be more eye-catching, caused confusion for child readers.

Many content area textbooks are written by experts in the field who use specialized vocabulary terms and concepts that are not reader-friendly (Miller, 1997). The amount of information and sheer volume of technical vocabulary can be overwhelming obstacles to student comprehension (Gunning, 2003). Both the writing style and format can make textbooks cumbersome (Afflerbach & VanSledright, 2001). The terseness of some textbooks, coupled with their cursory treatment of multiple topics, abbreviates or ignores the high drama and seductive detail that draw children to a historical period (Roser & Keehn, 2002).

And, unfortunately, sometimes textbooks are just unappealing to students, especially struggling readers. In grades 3 through 5, where there is more emphasis on content area subjects and more widespread use of textbooks, the reading ability gap widens. Using trade books makes it possible to have books at different readability levels available in the same classroom; the teacher may choose more difficult ones for a read-aloud, and students are given a choice. Struggling readers often find informational trade books more appealing because the content is mature, often even at a primer level. There are many accurate, colorful informational trade books written at easier reading levels that may appeal to these readers. And remember that every student does not have to read the same book at the same time.

Another disadvantage of textbooks in content area subjects is that they are almost always outdated. Most school districts adopt new texts every five to eight years. In our rapidly changing world, there are virtually no subject areas where a text that is at least three years old can have the most up-to-date, accurate information. Also, with the current emphasis on basics in American schools, money in the elementary school budget is often not allocated to content textbooks. If a school does have content area texts, there are rarely enough for each student to have one. Most often, there is a "classroom set" that must be shared with all classes in each grade level, which does not allow for access or use at all times. And few modern textbooks for children treat the humanities: music, dance, drama, and visual arts.

I am not saying that there is no value in using content area textbooks in the elementary school. If they are available, they often are the best way to introduce a subject or concept. But teachers need to be aware of their disadvantages, especially for beginning and struggling readers, and find ways to utilize both textbooks and trade books in order to give students maximum opportunities for learning.

Nor am I saying that trade books are always the answer. Trade books are not designed to cover a body of knowledge whose parameters are defined by curricula (Sebesta, 1989). For instance, *Frogs* (Gibbons, 1993) does not explain all life cycles, but it does give pertinent information about frogs, including their physical characteristics, reproductive cycle, and habitat. In the primary grades, it often is more effective to introduce several books about different species for the study of life cycles. And, of course, if a textbook is available, it can be the introduction to life cycles, with selected trade books used to reinforce and further study.

Trade books may also present a particular point of view, whereas quality textbooks strive to maintain an unbiased and objective account. This subjective point of view or bias is not a disadvantage but, rather, a means to show many perspectives of an issue or situation. For older students, *Yankee Girl* (Rodman, 2004) does not fully explore racism and civil rights in the American South, but it does look at events in Mississippi during 1964 through the eyes of a 12-year-old girl. Reading this book independently, or as a class read-aloud, offers a better understanding after reading a few paragraphs in the textbook.

Mathematics is one area where a text and/or curriculum series should certainly be used as the foundation, but there are many trade books that can enhance and further explain the concepts and skills being studied. *The Hershey's Kisses Addition Book* (Pallotta, 2001) is an excellent way to reinforce addition facts using candy that most children are familiar with. For older students, *Sir Cumference and the First Round Table* (Neuschwander, 1997) uses a fanciful tale of King Arthur and Camelot to explain geometric shapes. But this book cannot be fully appreciated if the reader doesn't have a basic understanding of geometry. In the other content areas, if you have access to quality textbooks, by all means, use them when they are appropriate. But be sure to supplement with trade books for group and independent reading, as read-alouds, for additional study, and to accommodate the different reading abilities in your classroom (see Appendix for ways to obtain trade books for the classroom).

Trade Books as Read-Alouds

Read-alouds often function as the foundation for the curriculum. And there is little that can compare to reading aloud to establish a motivation for further reading. Often, books that children are interested in are far too difficult for them to read independently. If they are not read aloud, the child will not experience them. As Sebesta (1989) points out, "Trade books serendipitous to a curricular topic can make the difference between a passive reader who quits when the bell rings and an active, lifelong, self-motivated reader/learner" (p. 114).

Trade books in the content area will most often be used for guided reading and as writing models—within the literacy block. They should be part of the classroom library and put in interest centers. But they should also be used as read-alouds. You can use trade book read-alouds to motivate students to read and to build their topical knowledge about a specific subject (Hoffman, Roser, & Battle, 1993). The read-alouds model fluent oral reading and animation and expression, and strategic use of book discussions can occur before, during, and after the reading. They also provide opportunities for students to ask questions about related subjects. British educators MacLure (1988) and Barnes (1992) found that read-alouds led to an improvement in language expression throughout all curriculum subjects. Expert teachers use read-alouds to coincide with a unit of study and connect to what has occurred in the classroom during the day (Fisher, Flood, Lapp, & Frey, 2004). For instance, in third grade, when life cycles are part of the science curriculum, your students may better understand their study of owl pellets and the substances hidden within each pellet when you include *Poppy* (Avi, 1995) as a read-aloud.

Informational trade books as read-alouds promote much interaction centered on meaning seeking, too. Roser and Keehn (2002) examined the kinds of inquiries children accomplish in a cross-curricular unit involving various kinds of texts. Fourth-grade students relied on biography, historical fiction, and informational trade books to enter and give complexity to a historical period within the universal themes of human rights, courage, ethics, and sacrifice. Teachers introduced the unit by reading aloud one chapter per day of a biography. Students were given brief introductions to three pieces of historical fiction, all within the same period, with each child choosing one of the three books to read and forming book clubs for discussion purposes. Children then met as a whole group, discussing questions and observations based on the read-aloud and their reading. There was an increase (on pre- and post-assessments) in children's accurate notions about this period of history; further, their misconceptions were reduced by half. There was an increasing willingness to work together, to sustain talk, to support ideas with evidence, and to acknowledge and build on others' talk. And some children continued to read on the subject after the unit was concluded. Therefore, choosing content area trade books to read aloud may not only increase children's knowledge about a topic but may also motivate them by activating curiosity.

Magazines and newspaper articles also can be used as read-alouds. It is a well-established fact that listening comprehension is typically better than reading comprehension, which provides another reason for reading aloud within the content area. Because time for reading aloud in the classroom is often difficult to find and sometimes to justify, teachers must carefully choose books that will meet the needs of both the curriculum and the students.

Trade Books for Reading Instruction

Nonfiction trade books also should be used for independent, group, and guided reading. These books can provide students with authentic reading experiences that connect with their lives and expand background knowledge needed to understand core content area concepts. They also can assist in building vocabulary by introducing technical words not often found in fiction. And most importantly, using nonfiction trade books for reading instruction can help students develop critical reading skills and strategies while extending content area knowledge. Basal reading anthologies now contain more nonfiction than ever before, and many publishing companies are producing affordable paperback sets of nonfiction readers suitable for guided reading and research.

Content area books also can be used in literature circles. Chappel (1998) adapted a strategy—literature circles—for science that she originally used for reading instruction. If students are already familiar with this strategy, they learn that it can be used in another setting. She used topics and issues from the science curriculum to integrate reading, writing, and science, putting emphasis on generating questions that lead to further study. After a short lesson and experimentation, the students listed conclusions and further questions. Then science-related trade books were made available. Students then formed groups, read their book, and developed questions about the book. After discussion, one member of each group explained their book to the rest of the class.

Picture Books in the Content Areas

The use of picture books to introduce and reinforce content areas is becoming increasingly popular in elementary school classrooms. By presenting information in a pleasing format, combining pictures and texts, picture books can present complex ideas and make content learning easier. Some of the most exciting picture books present topics relating to history, geography, and science (Tiedt, 2000). Picture books can create a response in readers that powerfully represents the events or topic, often through quality illustrations or photographs that add understanding to the information presented. For example, in *Iditarod: The Great Race to Nome* (Schultz & Sherwonit, 1993), although the text describes the origin and history of the race, the stunning photographs provide a visual reinforcement of the danger racers encounter and the bond between humans and dogs. Because of their shorter length, picture books can be read fairly quickly as both guided and independent reading, as well as read-alouds, to build on prior knowledge of the subject and connect to previous learning and/or textbook passages. They can be used as models for writing and contribute new information for class discussions. The illustrations and stories in picture books help students connect to the material on a more personal level, which adds to their involvement in learning and understanding of the content. And the interesting visuals in picture books encourage both reluctant readers and English-language learners.

Picture books are gaining popularity with older students, as well as younger ones. Albright and Vardell (2003) note that recent picture books treat complex subjects in a more complicated way that makes them "appropriate for older, more 'sophisticated' readers" (p. 21). It is important for educators, students, and parents to realize that picture books are not only for the very young. In fact, there are many picture books that are not even appropriate for younger students because of the subject, amount of text, and presentation of complex concepts. *A Prairie*

Alphabet (Bannatyne-Cugnet, 1992) is indeed for younger children because of its alphabet format and simple text; yet *Pearl Harbor Warriors* (Nicholson, 2001) has a more sophisticated format and text, intended for ages 10 and older.

Informational Trade Books in the Content Areas

The Literacy Dictionary (Harris & Hodges, 1995) defines an "information book" as a nonfiction book of facts and concepts about a subject or subjects. Traditionally, primary teachers refer to "informational books" and upper-grade teachers to "nonfiction," but recently that has changed; the two terms generally mean the same to most people and are used interchangeably. Informational text can be narrative, expository, or a combination of the two (Kletzien & Dreher, 2004). Many informational trade books for young children are presented in story or narrative format. Information is conveyed, but authors choose a story format that they feel will be more appealing to the reader. These books contain the story elements of character, setting, plot, and resolution. Examples of narrative-informational text include *Eliza and the Dragonfly* (Rinehart, 2004), a story with factual information about dragonflies, and *But No Candy* (Houston, 1992), a fictionalized account of the candy shortage during World War II. Many biographies for children also are written in narrative form, such as *Brave Harriet* (Moss, 2001), the story of the first woman to fly across the English Channel.

Expository-informational books do not include story elements. They are characterized as reports, using expository text structures such as cause–effect, compare–contrast, sequence, and description. Expository-informational books explain the natural and social world, including animals, places, and cultural groups. Examples are *Beacons of Light* (Gibbons, 1990) and *The Wright Brothers* (Freedman, 1991). Expository-informational books also serve as excellent models for student writing.

Many informational trade books combine both narrative and expository writing and are called *mixed text*. The Magic School Bus series by Joanna Cole is an example of this. The story is imaginary, but it is supported by facts in boxes, charts, reports, and illustrations. Another example is *The Popcorn Book* (dePaola, 1978), a story of brothers making popcorn. Facts about popcorn appear in speech bubbles as one brother reads from an encyclopedia.

Although all three of these types of informational books have a place in the classroom library, the majority of the books used for content area instruction should contain factual information and expository writing. Kletzien and

Dreher (2004) recommend that at least half the classroom library contain informational books, with narrative-informational or mixed-text books making up no more than a third of that number. Moss (2003) notes,

> About half the classroom library collection should be devoted to engaging informational books and biographies, and this percentage should increase as children move through the grades. Some books should be pertinent to classroom topics of study, while others should have a broader appeal. Students can use these books for voluntary reading, inquiry study, reference, or browsing. (p. 63)

Teaching Children to Read Informational Trade Books

Pairing fiction and nonfiction (especially informational) books is a popular way of introducing young children to concepts and content area texts. Camp (2000) calls this pairing of texts "teaching with Twin Texts" (p. 400). One of her suggestions is to pair *The Foot Book* (Dr. Seuss, 1968) with *What Neat Feet!* (Machotka, 1991). In fact, some publishing companies are producing twin-text sets. Sundance (2002) offers Little Reader Twin Texts, pairing fiction and nonfiction texts by topics, which support the following curriculum strands: life science, earth science, physical science, citizenship, America, people and places, math, and self-awareness. For older students, you might want to use *Snowflake Bentley* (Martin, 1998), a biography in narrative form that tells the story of Wilson Bentley, who spent his life finding a way to photograph snowflakes, with *Snow Crystals* (Bentley & Humphreys, 1962), which explains the fundamentals of crystallography and contains Bentley's actual photographs.

Because narrative is the most common type of literature used with very young children, most students know the parts of a book or story and know their functions (Snow, Burns, & Griffin, 1998). However, it is important to realize that because most informational books are written differently from narrative books, children must be taught to read them differently. Narrative books are meant to be read from beginning to end, but many informational books can be read one page, section, or chapter at a time because there is no story line. Often, one page may give the information that is sought. (The exception, of course, would be informational books about life cycles.)

Most informational trade books have common features, such as tables of contents, headings and subheadings in bold and larger print, glossaries, and indexes. Many also have charts, graphs, maps, and diagrams, which can present a great deal of information in a small amount of space. They provide visuals so readers can get information that would take much longer to read and understand if presented in text only. But students must be taught how to exploit all these features. I once heard a representative from a publishing company speak about teaching children how to read informational trade books. She told about working with a group of children who were all excellent readers and high achievers. She prepared them for reading by posing a few questions and then had the students read a short chapter in an informational book. When they were finished, there were a few unanswered questions. She assured the students that they would find the information in the text. Again, they could not find it. Some became argumentative and frustrated. These children were used to reading narrative text and had completely overlooked captions under illustrations, maps, and diagrams.

Read-alouds with big books, with class sets of books, or in a small-group setting are excellent ways to introduce children to the features of informational books. Or you could reproduce selected pages and place them on an overhead projector, then model the conventions that will help children use search features effectively and point out words in boldface and captions. Certainly all informational trade books, especially those for very young children, do not have all these features—and they are much simpler in some—but most have at least a table of contents and a glossary. When choosing books to use for content area instruction, it is important that some include search features.

Children need direct instruction in strategies for comprehending informational books, including modeling a strategy and providing guided practice, feedback, and time for independent practice (Flood & Lapp, 1991). The essence of this instruction is to help students understand how expository texts work differently from more familiar narrative texts and to give children the tools they need to create mental structures for understanding the texts (Greeno & Hall, 1997).

You can teach students to preview nonfiction by using a strategy called THIEVES (Manz, 2002): T stands for title, H for heading, I for introduction, E for every first sentence in a paragraph, V for visuals and vocabulary, E for end-of-chapter questions, and S for summary (see Figure 1). This mnemonic teaches children to gather the important facts in a book, chapter, passage, or article, and then read for additional information. You can demonstrate the activity until children are able to use it on their own. The acronym can be posted on the wall or each child can have a bookmark or card with the information.

K-W-L, a strategy developed by Donna Ogle (1986), is especially useful for identifying purposes for reading informational text. Create three columns on a page labeled What I **Know**, What I **Want** to Learn, and What I **Learned** and Still Need to Learn. Select a topic, then have students fill in the first two columns (What I Know and What I Want to Learn) prior to reading the selection (see Figure 2). Students should be reminded to look at special features, as well as text, when they read. After reading, students can fill in the third column (What I Learned). If there are still unanswered questions, provide additional resources.

FIGURE 1. THIEVES—A Strategy for Previewing Nonfiction

T—Title
H—Headings
I—Introduction
E—Every first sentence in a paragraph
V—Visuals and vocabulary
E—End-of-chapter questions
S—Summary

Reprinted from Manz, S.L. (2002). A strategy for previewing textbooks: Teaching readers to become THIEVES. *The Reading Teacher, 55,* 434–435.

FIGURE 2. K-W-L Chart

K-W-L strategy sheet

1. **K**—What I know	**W**—What I want to find out	**L**—What I learned and still need to learn

2. Categories of information we expect to use
    A.   E.
    B.   F.
    C.   G.
    D.

Reprinted from Ogle, D. (1986). K-W-L: A teaching model that develops active reading of expository text. *The Reading Teacher, 39,* 564–570.

Concept/definition mapping (Schwartz & Raphael, 1985) is a strategy that helps enrich student understanding of a word or concept in all content areas (see Figure 3). This graphic organizer focuses attention on the key components of a definition and encourages integration of personal knowledge. The key word or concept goes in the middle box. In the box labeled "What is it?" write the category; list properties in the boxes under "What is it like?"; and give examples in the bottom boxes.

Gregg and Sckeres (2006) offer a set of iterative strategies to support children's reading of expository text:

- Preview the organizational pattern for a variety of visual markers that denote important information (font, boldface, type, captions, diagrams, charts, or glossaries).

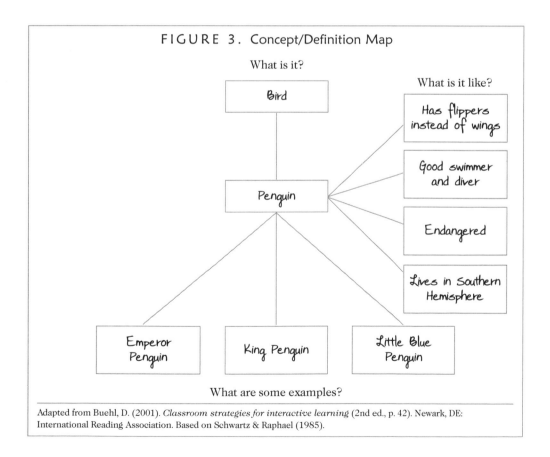

FIGURE 3. Concept/Definition Map

What is it?

Bird

What is it like?

Has flippers instead of wings

Good swimmer and diver

Penguin

Endangered

Lives in Southern Hemisphere

Emperor Penguin

King Penguin

Little Blue Penguin

What are some examples?

Adapted from Buehl, D. (2001). *Classroom strategies for interactive learning* (2nd ed., p. 42). Newark, DE: International Reading Association. Based on Schwartz & Raphael (1985).

- Summarize the information.
- Transform the text into a visual (map, picture, diagram, or web).
- Formulate questions about the content when previewing and reading.

Activities that invite children to revisit texts aid in their understanding. Even relatively accomplished readers may not be able to get meaning from the first or second reading. For this reason, it is advisable to encourage multiple readings and provide activities that encourage children to revisit texts to aid comprehension.

Selecting Trade Books

Teachers in grades 3 through 5 are often concerned with finding books appropriate for the reading levels of *all* their students, while primary grade teachers tend to be more concerned with the developmental appropriateness of the books for their students. But there are certainly other criteria to use in selecting informational trade books for content area instruction. Moss, Leone, and DiPillo (1997) identified "five A's" for selecting good nonfiction books for students: the **authority** of the author, the **accuracy** of the text content, the **appropriateness** of the book for its audience, the literary **artistry**, and the **appearance** of the book. Further, Kletzien and Dreher (2004) suggest several aspects to consider when making book choices: accurate content, appealing design and format, engaging writing style, and good organization. They also have developed a guide to help teachers evaluate informational trade books (see Figure 4). Further considerations for selection of books are the concepts presented, amount of information presented, and suitability of texts (readability and appeal).

As an example, let's look at the book *Recycle! A Handbook for Kids* (Gibbons, 1992). The cover is colorful, shows children recycling items, and has a subtitle that indicates child appeal. If you are not familiar with an author, you often can find his or her qualifications and background on the book jacket or at the end of the book. Sometimes authors list subject experts who have assisted them, or they will print sources of information as well. On the dedication page of *Recycle!* the author thanks a state recycling public outreach coordinator. This is a further indication of credibility and accuracy. Because this is a picture book, there are no chapters, but there are sections with headings. Simple, colorful illustrations take up most of each page. Pages contain information (such as definitions, labels, instructions, and cut-away views), but they are not too cluttered;

FIGURE 4. Guide for Choosing Informational Books

Name of Book_____ Type of Book_____

Characteristic	Notes	Possible Instruction
Content Accuracy		
Author's and illustrator's qualifications • Experts in field • "Insiders" (if multicultural book) • Award-winning		
References used • Consultants who are experts • Print sources		
Information current • Copyright date recent (if important) • Information up to date		
Distinguishes between fact and theory • Clear what is believed and what is known		
Text and illustrations clear		
Stereotypes not used in text or illustration		
Design		
Illustrations appropriate for content		
Illustrations well placed on page		
Clear about where to begin reading		
Illustrations labeled and explained		
Captions clear and informative		
Relative sizes indicated • Enlargements noted		
Style		
Lively, engaging language		
Accurate terminology used		
Appropriate for children's level		
Generalizations and concepts given (not just a collection of facts)		
Enthusiasm for topic evident		
Organization		
Informational book characteristics • Pagination, table of contents, index, glossary, additional reading list		
Headings and subheadings		
Clear pattern of organization		

Reprinted from Kletzien, S.B., & Dreher, M.J. (2004). *Informational text in K–3 classrooms: Helping children read and write.* Newark, DE: International Reading Association.

too many elements with not enough white space may cause vital information to be overlooked. The text on each page is relatively short (3–4 lines), making it appropriate for most grade levels in the elementary school. Key words, as well as uncommon vocabulary, are printed in boldface, and the most difficult are accompanied by a pronunciation key. At the end, there are two pages of interesting facts presented as pictures and vignettes titled "Can You Believe...?" The final page presents practical ways to recycle. Added endorsements appear on the book's back cover. There is a recommendation by *Booklist*, and the book has been named an NSTA–CBC Outstanding Science Trade Book for Children and an NCSS–CBC Notable Children's Trade Book in the Field of Social Studies. Upon examination, it is clear that this is a book that would certainly be useful in a study of the earth, environment, or Earth Day. As with most of Gibbons's books, it can be used in grades 1 through 3 but also is appropriate for fourth or fifth graders who read below grade level.

Now let's look at another book, *The Very Quiet Cricket* (Carle, 1990). Although Carle is a well-known and respected author/illustrator, his books are known more for their stories and illustrations than for informational content. This book has beautiful, colorful illustrations and certainly has child appeal—but only for very young children. There is no information about Carle's qualifications or expertise to write about crickets, but the illustrations certainly indicate that he has observed insects. This is a story with a small amount of information interspersed, so there are none of the search features one would expect in an informational book, but the title page gives a few facts about crickets. Although the illustrations are outstanding, the large scale of the insects and their ability to talk can be misleading to some young children. There is no doubt that this is an excellent book and can be found in many kindergarten and first-grade classrooms, but it would not be a good source of factual information about crickets or as a model for research and report writing. It would be useful, however, as an introduction or a supplement to a study of insects. Students could then compare it with an expository-informational book.

Students need to be taught how to select nonfiction trade books, especially if they are looking for specific information. For very young children or those who are unfamiliar with expository text, you should select a group of appropriate books and then give students a choice from that group. But, as children mature and become capable of choosing their own books for specific content, they need to be taught how to choose expository texts for themselves. When students recognize features such as the page numbers, table of contents, index, and glossary, it may become relatively easy for them to determine whether the information they are looking for is contained in a specific book. As mentioned, you can demonstrate on an overhead projector how to use these common features to find the desired information. Guided practice can then occur before students use this skill independently. Teach, also, that a book's publication date can be important for certain subjects where the most current information will be the most accurate. Often this knowledge is termed *library skills* in textbooks, workbook pages, and skill sheets. So, if you teach from a series that includes information-finding or library skills, you can occasionally use some of the included lessons or skill sheets to teach these skills to your students. Your school librarian also may be a useful resource in providing lessons on finding information.

Students might also use Questions to Monitor Information Searches (see Figure 5) as a guide to selecting expository books. Part of evaluation involves children deciding whether the information makes sense based on what they set out to

---

FIGURE 5. Questions to Monitor Information Searches

Question	Yes	No
What information do I need?		
Does this book (or website or magazine) have search features that would help me find what I want to know?		
Is the information that I need located here?		
Does the information I have located make sense?		
Is there anything in this book (or website or magazine) to help me decide if the information is correct?		
Does this information relate to things I already know?		
Do I have all the information that I need to answer my question? If not, I should continue searching.		

Reprinted from Kletzien, S.B., & Dreher, M.J. (2004). *Informational text in K–3 classrooms: Helping children read and write.* Newark, DE: International Reading Association; adapted from Dreher (1992).

find (Kletzien & Dreher, 2004). Using these questions can help students determine if the information can be found in their book or if they need to look further.

Let's look at some examples of how students might look at a book to determine if it has the desired information. You can demonstrate these examples as well. If a second or third grader is looking for specific information on bighorn sheep, she might choose *Faces in the Mountains* (Hirschi, 1997) because there is a photograph of a Bighorn sheep on the cover. However, the book jacket only contains information about watching wildlife in the mountains, and there is no table of contents or page numbers. The student must begin skimming through the pages, which contain photographs of a bear, marmot, hare, and weasel, before finding two pages with bighorn and Dall sheep. But there is very little information in the sparse text. The following pages feature moose, beaver, deer, fox, coyote, and several types of birds. The final pages are titled "Mountain Facts," but there are only two sentences about sheep; there is no index. This book would not be a good resource for a report on sheep. But if the child is interested in mountain animals, this would be a good choice for perusing.

Intended for grades 1 through 3, *Face-to-Face With the Cat* (Frattini, 2003) has no table of contents but has sections (two numbered pages) with headings, featuring photographs and text. Although there is no index, the last page features questions about cats, listing the page number where the answer can be found. A quick scan of the headings and the questions at the end can help a student discern whether he or she will find what they are looking for in this book. This book would be a good resource for general information about cats or for reports.

If a fifth-grade student is looking for information on U.S. or Texas history, he might choose *Inside the Alamo* (Murphy, 2003). This book has a table of contents, bibliography, index, and a notes section. Most pages include a brief vignette that explains an italicized word in the text. There are one-page biographies interspersed throughout, as well as photographs, maps, and reproductions of documents. This book offers a wealth of information, although it may appear overwhelming to some students unless they have good information searching skills.

Dorling Kindersley Eyewitness books are well-known for providing information and color photographs in a format that appeals to all ages. The *Question & Answer Book* (Farndon, 1993) is no exception. There is a table of contents, but it is quite simplistic, and the book is divided into three sections: What Do You Know About Nature? When Did It Happen? and Who Invented It? However, specific questions are listed, page numbers are given, and there is an index. This book is appealing to students because of the intriguing and unusual topics and photographs, but the information is so brief that it is unlikely to provide adequate information for a report or research project. But it has proven to be a favorite for acquiring general knowledge and for pleasure reading.

When choosing books to use for content area study, you must make sure these books contain the kind of information you wish students to learn. Select books that communicate messages about content and connect to concepts in the curriculum (such as electricity or body systems) or to particular units of study (such as civil rights; measurement; or state, province, or country history). There are also numerous sources to help you identify good informational trade books (see Appendix).

Many professional organizations give suggested titles to use in content areas (see Appendix for a list of professional organizations' contact information). Do an Internet search for possible titles. Ask colleagues if they have books or lists that you might borrow. Consider building your own database of all the books you own, or all the books that would be appropriate for your classroom, with *subject area* as one of the fields. As you build your collection and knowledge of trade books, this database will make it relatively easy to access a list of books for any topic. When choosing a read-aloud, think about current or upcoming content area to be studied and make your selection accordingly. Your students will benefit from your careful selection of books, and they also will learn more about content areas.

Conclusion

Although children's literature has long been used in teaching language arts, it is gaining popularity in other subject areas as well. Because the majority of time in the school day is devoted to literacy and mathematics, content area subjects must often be addressed during that time frame. Trade books can be used as read-alouds, as a supplement to textbooks, or exclusively for content area instruction. In order to use informational trade books effectively in the content area classroom, you must understand the different types of informational trade books available, know how to select appropriate ones, and teach children to use this genre's special features to gain information.

CHAPTER 2

Making a Case for Integrated Curriculum

I never teach my pupils; I only attempt to provide
the conditions in which they can learn.

—ALBERT EINSTEIN

Integrated curriculum is intended to bring into close relationship the concepts, skills, and values of separately taught subjects to make them mutually reinforcing. Perhaps the best known and most widely used example is *integrated language arts*, in which students study and use speaking, listening, reading, and writing as a unified core of concepts (Harris & Hodges, 1995). But integration does not only apply to language arts. Mathematics, science, social studies, and the arts can all be integrated through the use of themes, trade books, or in the language arts block. For example, fractions, ratio, and measurement can be reinforced while studying the relationship of musical whole notes, half notes, and quarter notes. An art lesson on perspective and other representational art can emphasize the use of scale. And students can convert feet, yards, and miles to millimeters and kilometers (and vice versa) when running on the playground or in physical education class. In Norfolk, Virginia, USA, teachers used dance, literature, vocabulary, geography, history, song, and other engaging activities that crossed disciplinary boundaries for a social studies unit about African studies and the nation of Mali (Reeves, 2005). As a result, students displayed improvements in their performance on state social studies tests.

Bosma and Guth (1995) define integrated learning as the incorporation of language development and content, with emphasis on the interrelatedness of subject and skill areas, concepts, and topics, within personal and shared contexts. They stress that integrated learning does not mean *adding* more subjects or activities but looking differently at what is already scheduled to be taught. Breaking learning into bits and pieces can actually make things more difficult for students. In fact, "individuals who are performing below their peers are *most* in need of opportunities to see how the discrete pieces of literacy learning cohere into a communicable whole" (Routman, 2003, p. 50). Routman (2003) recommends teaching reading skills in social studies and science, not just in reading and literature classes, because when students begin to connect subject areas under one type of lesson, it makes teaching in that subject more manageable, stimulating, and effective. Interdisciplinary curricula represent combinations of knowledge domains that are traditionally separated. With quality literature, curriculum objectives can be gradually integrated throughout weekly lessons. Additionally, because today's teachers must make the best possible use of instructional time, integration of subjects often is the most efficient way to include the content that must be taught. Instead of spending an hour on social studies and then another hour on language arts, it makes more sense to spend two or more hours on a combination of the two as they complement each other (Hawley & Spillman, 2003). When students read better, they write better, and the chain continues as good writing contributes to further achievement in reading and in other subjects (Calkins, 1994; Reeves, 2002). And one must realize that tests of science, social studies, and virtually every other subject area are, in fact, tests of reading and writing—so it is wise to teach these literacy skills at the same time.

Rationale Supporting an Integrated Curriculum

The concept of integrated curriculum is not new. Dewey (1938) proposed an integration of knowledge and experience. He recommended combining subject areas into theme studies and incorporating real-life activities into the classroom. But Dewey's ideal classroom was severely criticized by many, among them Edward L. Thorndike, an educational psychologist whose great hope was to develop a science of education. The Thorndike model of formal, content-based curriculum, including a fervor for accountability through formal testing, became dominant in the 1940s and 1950s (Chall, 2000). In the 1970s, Piaget's work on cognitive development influenced student-centered education, and when his work, and that of Vygotsky, was translated into English, there was a renewed interest in child-centered learning. Piaget emphasized providing a supportive learning environment to enhance children's cognitive development (Piaget & Inhelder, 1966/1969), and Vygotsky (1934/1978) stressed the importance of the social nature of human learning. Later, research on peer interaction (Forman & Cazden,

1985) encouraged teachers to use the social classroom environment for effective learning. More research followed (e.g., Caine & Caine, 1994; Fogarty, 1991; Fogarty, Perkins, & Barell, 1992; Gardner, 1982), offering a variety of basic principles of integrated curriculum.

The strongest support for integration comes from work by Morrow and Guthrie and their colleagues. Morrow, Pressley, and Smith (1995) conducted an extensive study of integrating curriculum in science and literature in third-grade classrooms. Children in the fully integrated group did significantly better on all literacy measures than children in the other two groups. They also performed better on a test of science concepts and indicated on a survey that they had better attitudes toward science than those in other groups. Another integration plan, Concept-Oriented Reading Instruction (CORI), designed by Guthrie, McGough, Bennett, and Rice (1996), integrated science and the language arts in a fifth-grade classroom; it was later replicated in both grade 3 and grade 5 classrooms. CORI was organized around broad, interdisciplinary conceptual themes with the goal to enable students to gain conceptual understanding that was flexible, transferable, and informed by multiple genres. Children in the CORI classroom read more frequently and widely than students in the same school who were in a basal, nonintegrated program. These students were able to express more sophisticated conceptual understanding through drawing and writing than students receiving traditional instruction. They also gained higher order knowledge of science content that exceeded the skills and content knowledge of children learning in nonintegrated instructional environments.

In Canada, commitment to resource-based learning is evident in policy documents developed by each province. Termed a *resource-based model*, this integrated curriculum strives to develop information-literate students who have "the ability to acquire, critically evaluate, select, use, create and communicate information in ways that lead to knowledge and wisdom" (Ontario Ministry of Education and Training, 1995, p. 4). These documents outline the rationale behind resource-based learning, how it fits into the curriculum, the benefits it offers, and the role of librarians and classroom teachers in its integration across all subject areas. According to the 2003 Programme for International Student Assessment (PISA), administered by the Organisation for Economic Co-operation and Development, Alberta students continue to achieve excellent results on international tests. Former Alberta Minister of Education Gene Zwozdesky credited the province's excellent teachers, high-quality centralized curriculum, outstanding learning and teaching resources, and standardized assessment program for these results (Alberta Government Online, 2004). In 2000, Alberta students scored the highest of all participants on the reading component of the PISA tests, which focused on reading and literacy. They had the third highest rankings in science (behind Korea and Japan) and mathematics (behind Japan and Quebec). PISA 2003 focused on mathematics and a new content area called *problem-solving skills*, which tests a student's ability to solve real-life situations requiring more than one subject area. On this test, Alberta students again had the highest scores in reading, improved from third to second in mathematics, and were fourth in science. These results certainly endorse the use of an integrated, resource-based curriculum.

In 1995, Douglas Reeves began research in high-poverty schools that also demonstrated high academic performance. He coined the term *90/90/90* based on schools in Milwaukee, Wisconsin, USA, that had the following characteristics: 90% or more of the students were eligible for free or reduced lunch, 90% or more of the students were members of ethnic minority groups, and 90% or more of the students met the district or state academic standards in reading or another areas (Reeves, 2000). Researchers sought to identify a set of characteristics common to all 90/90/90 schools and found

- a focus on academic achievement,
- clear curriculum choices,
- frequent assessment of student progress and multiple opportunities for improvement,
- an emphasis on nonfiction writing, and
- collaborative scoring of student work.

They also found clear, concise essays and outstanding math, science, and social studies projects. And, although there was a disproportionate emphasis on language arts and mathematics, these schools significantly outperformed peer schools on science tests as well.

These schools deliberately involved other subject areas in the language arts, resulting in the improvement of academic results for all students. Schools that had the greatest gains did not eliminate special area subjects such as music, art, physical education, and technology. Instead, these subject areas were explicitly part of the academic preparation of each student. Schools made a deliberate trade-off to devote more time to reading comprehension and nonfiction writing, even if it meant less time for social studies and science. But scores in social studies and science did not decline—they increased! One possible explanation might be the students' improved ability to read the questions on the tests, but the emphasis on nonfiction writing and written responses certainly must have had an effect.

Potential Dangers of an Integrated Curriculum

It is important to note that there are several potential hazards to instructional integration. One inherent danger is loss of integrity in one of the disciplines (Guthrie & McCann, 1997). In an integrated social studies and art lesson, for instance, drawing pictures of George Washington or Abraham Lincoln has little concept-building value unless the pictures are related to facts or incidents previously studied, as well as instruction on how to draw human figures. When integrating math and language arts, graphing or charting the frequency of words or parts of speech in a passage has little meaning unless the words or parts of speech also are being studied. Teachers need to be aware that merely adding an art project, performance, or assignment can be a superfluous or superficial attempt at real integration, where meaningful learning in all content areas occurs.

An attempt to integrate curriculum can sometimes provide in-depth learning in one area at the expense of broader knowledge. For this reason, you should use multiple methods of instruction—textbooks; teacher instruction; cooperative learning with group reading, discussion, and/or reports; independent reading; or read-alouds—to cover the necessary information. For a social studies and language arts lesson on World War II, you might read aloud the novel *Snow Treasures* (McSwigan, 1942), a story of Norwegian children protecting their town's gold during the German occupation of 1940. Then the class might read and discuss a chapter in a social studies text. Small groups could each read different trade books such as *No Pretty Pictures* (Lobel, 1998), which tells the author's experiences as a Polish Jew during World War II; *The Children of Topaz* (Tunnell & Chilcoat, 1996), a diary account of a Japanese American internment camp; *V Is for Victory* (Krull, 1995), a World War II scrapbook; *The Bomb* (Taylor, 1995), historical fiction about the aftermath of the bombings of Hiroshima and Nagasaki; or *Pearl Harbor Warriors* (Nicholson, 2001), the true story of a friendship between a U.S. Marine and his former enemy, a Japanese pilot. After reading and discussing the books, each group can then use the language arts skills of summarizing and synthesizing the information to share it with the rest of the class. This is a variation of the Jigsaw

Strategy (Aronson, 1978), which involves students in reading different selections and then sharing what they have learned with a group or whole class.

If poorly implemented, integrated instruction can sometimes lead to decline in skill. Meece, Blumenfeld, and Hoyle (1988) found that project-based science approaches may not assure fluency in basic skills of coordinating data with theory. To use the example from the previous paragraph, merely reading trade books about World War II will not suffice to explain the causes and effects of the war and its historical significance. But trade books can serve to aid and enhance understanding, through discussion and comparison, after initial instruction. Teacher planning, collecting books and other resources, scheduling activities, and designing authentic assessments are all necessary to implement an effective integrated program. And above all, you must be sure to incorporate curriculum requirements and guidelines into the instructional plan for each subject area within a grade level.

Models of Integrated Curriculum

One comprehensive proposal for integration is the *coherent curriculum* (Pate, McGinnis, & Homstead, 1995), which contains the following factors:

- goals of learning how to learn, problem solving, student responsibility, collaboration, deep content understanding, and risk taking;
- content integrations of science, social studies, math, language arts, and fine arts;
- multiple forms of assessment that exhibit student achievement;
- personalized learning in which student interests and skills determine learning activities;
- school scheduling to allow blocks of time for projects;
- communication to parents; and
- teacher reflection on instruction.

The desired outcome is for students to transfer problem-solving techniques and metacognitive skills across subject areas.

Several years ago I gave a presentation on integrated curriculum to teachers at a rural school in a remote area near Mt. Rainier, Washington, USA. At the break, a teacher told me that he had been integrating the curriculum without being aware of it. He invited me to look at his classroom, a room with high ceilings and

17 desks. Mounted on the walls, completely circling the room, were 17 deer and elk heads. The teacher explained that his class consisted of 17 boys for whom hunting and fishing were a way of life in this wilderness setting. Their project for the fall was learning taxidermy. He described how they read books about hunting and taxidermy, wrote about their hunting experiences, and used math and science to understand and apply the principles of taxidermy, which provided a finished product and a sense of accomplishment. He indeed was integrating the curriculum in a most meaningful way for his students.

In another example of integrated curriculum, teacher Liz White assigns her fourth- and fifth-grade students an integrated project at the beginning of each school year. Based on the reading of a biography of a famous person, each student must prepare for "Night of the Notables," which is held at the end of the first trimester. Students utilize note-taking and questioning for class interviews, write an autobiography of the person they choose to be, and prepare materials for a booth at the culminating event (see Figure 6 for a sample timeline for this multiweek, integrated lesson). Billy chose to be Beethoven. He read about the composer in trade books and encyclopedias. Because he takes piano lessons, he and his piano teacher performed and recorded a few Beethoven selections to be played at his booth. Billy researched clothing of Beethoven's time so he could provide authentic art work and a costume. He became an expert on Beethoven so he could answer questions as students and parents came to his booth.

Thematic Teaching

Thematic teaching is a way of organizing instruction around themes instead of around subject areas (Allen & Piersma, 1995). It is grounded in the notion that we learn best when things make sense. In thematic teaching, the subject areas are connected. Thematic teaching, centered on children's literature, provides integration of both activities and subject areas. It seeks to paint a big picture to look at the largest ideas embedded in the curriculum, the how and why of history, ecology, biology, and so on: "A thematic unit is the result of a process in which learning experiences are organized around a central focus" (Hepler, 1989, p. 31).

The potential of the conceptual theme-driven model depends on the selection of a generative topic that is educationally valuable for advanced learning of content and skills (Lipson, Valencia, Wixson, & Peters, 1993). The theme often serves as the hook for students to become motivated to learn. District, state/provincial, and national standards should be consulted when choosing themes, and

FIGURE 6. Timeline for Night of the Notables 2006

Week 1—September 5–8
- Acquire and begin reading biographies
- Review note-taking or outlining in class to begin notes
- Begin writing knowledge level questions for class interview (in class)

Week 2—September 11–15
- Continue notes, read most of biography
- Write comprehension and application level interview questions
- Biography comprehension activity—begin in class

Week 3—September 18–22
- Finish reading biography
- Biography comprehension activity continues
- Write upper-level interview questions
- Consider two free choice ideas for booth
- Begin draft: autobiography of notable in class

Week 4—September 25–29
- Draft free choice #1
- List timeline dates and events
- Costume sketch
- Finalize interview questions, begin interviews
- Draft autobiography of notable in class

Week 5—October 2–6
- Draft booth layout: 5 categories (autobiography, face, timeline, two choice sections)
- Interviews
- Draft free choice #2
- Complete timeline final copy
- Work on autobiography final copy in computer lab

Week 6—October 9–13
- Complete interviews
- Complete autobiography final copy
- Prepare art project for booth (in class)

Week 7—October 16–20
- Booth preparation: Finish final first free choice category
- Prepare an invitation in computer lab
- Assemble costume

Week 8—October 23–27
- Booth preparation: Finish final second free choice category
- Finalize costume
- Prepare and practice bio riddle

Week 9—October 30
- Final booth touches—booth due: October 31

Night of the Notables Evening Gathering—November 1—7:00, library themes should be broad enough to incorporate many types of books and materials but not so broad that connections within the topic are lost. Selection of themes should focus on what you believe will appeal to your students, such as holidays, animals, how other people live, transportation, hobbies, and natural phenomena such as wind and rain, as long as they fit within the standards for each grade level. For example, a science theme might be Earth. Then, for each grade level, the topic is defined more specifically: Kindergarten might focus on environmental awareness, grade 1 on seasons, grade 2 on temperature extremes, grade 3 on rocks and minerals, grade 4 on ecology, and grade 5 on weather stations.

An increasingly popular unit in the elementary grades is a study of the Iditarod, an annual dog sled race held in Alaska. This study integrates many subject areas: social studies (Alaskan geography and history; latitude and longitude, map skills, including topography and factors affecting the mushers and dogs), reading and language arts (independent and guided reading; research using textbooks, encyclopedias, and the Internet; written reports), math (graphing, temperatures, distances, cost involved), science (weather, animals, nutrition of dogs and mushers), and technology (research, finding race information and updates). It is important to note that the Iditarod is a *topic* (a specific idea or concept) that might fall under the *theme* (a major broad idea) of courage or adventure.

Santa (1997) described school change and transformation of teaching and curriculum in a Montana school district through the use of thematic integration and instruction. Teachers and administrators began the process of curriculum integration by examining the social studies and science curriculum, with the aim of covering less content but providing students with rich, in-depth studies relying primarily on hands-on activities, library materials, and fiction and nonfiction books, in order to acquire the literacy skills needed for continued learning. They believed that reading instruction must be incorporated and integrated within content areas using cross-curricular themes. Language arts skills, such as note taking, researching and writing reports, and giving oral presentations, were taught as part of the thematic studies as tools for learning and responding to content.

Differentiated Instruction

Differentiated instruction is an approach to teaching and learning that gives students multiple options for absorbing information and making sense of ideas. It is a process with which to approach teaching and learning for students of differing abilities in the same class (Hall, 2002). Many of its principles are compatible with integration and the use of themes. Tomlinson (2001) identifies three elements of the curriculum that can be differentiated—content, process, and products—where products are the culmination or evaluation (such as reports). The variation seen in a differentiated classroom is most frequently the manner in which students gain access to learning. Tasks must be aligned with instructional goals and objectives. Instructional concepts should be broad based and not focused on minute details or facts. The content should address the same concepts for all students but be adjusted by degree of complexity for the diversity of learners in the classroom. This is important to remember when selecting trade books for those reading below grade level. Easier books may bar access to concepts and ideas otherwise acquired by reading grade-appropriate trade books. When such books represent the only, or even the primary, material read routinely by students in classrooms, those children may develop what Fielding and Roller (1992) refer to as "knowledge handicaps" (p. 680). That is why the use of informational trade books in the content area can be so effective, providing the content meets instructional standards. When choosing trade books for struggling students, however, you must remember that every child is entitled to equal access to excellence. On the other hand, differentiating the content or topic can allow students who demonstrate an understanding of the concept to proceed beyond the instruction step. Often, they can accelerate their rate of progress and work independently or in small groups on some projects.

Differentiating the process means providing various learning activities or strategies for students to explore. It is important to remember that it is the *instruction* being differentiated, not the content. Although essential curricula goals may be similar for all students, the methodologies used in the classroom must meet the individual needs of the students. Flexible grouping is the process consistently used in differentiated classrooms. For instance, you may conduct whole-class introductory lessons to be followed by small group or pair work. Grouping of students is not fixed, but based on the content, projects, and ongoing evaluations. Initial and ongoing assessment of student readiness and growth are essential for differentiated instruction. Student responses may be differentiated for students to demonstrate or express their knowledge and understanding.

Differentiation is recognized to be a compilation of many theories and practices, but the "package" itself is lacking empirical validation. While there are a good number of testimonials and classroom examples provided by authors of several publications and websites, future research is warranted.

Effective Assessment

Many students are over-tested, but they are under-assessed. The distinction between testing and assessment must be clear. Testing implies a summative, evaluative process in which students take a test and the results—typically many months later—are used by newspapers and policymakers to render a judgment about education. And, in many areas, test results come back in the fall, when students are in a new grade and teachers have an entirely different class. In contrast, the best practice in assessment gives feedback to students quickly, and that feedback is designed and then used to improve student performance. Effective assessment is what great music educators and coaches routinely provide to their students (Reeves, 2005) when they give positive feedback and demonstrate or model specific behaviors or strategies designed to achieve improvement.

Consulting district, state/provincial, and national standards can assist you in planning effectively linked instruction and assessment practices at all levels across the curriculum. Effective assessment helps you figure out what students know and can do, not what they cannot do. Often, a simple discussion or checklist will inform you if students have grasped the content and/or skills presented. But teachers must give grades, and students are periodically required to take standardized tests, so we must prepare students for the different kinds of evaluation they will encounter throughout their school years.

If a textbook is used in the content area and there are accompanying tests, use them occasionally, but use these manufactured tests for instruction, not assessment. It is often helpful to do at least the first few items together as a class, so students will understand what is expected of them. Do these tests together so students learn how to respond to true–false, multiple-choice, matching, and short-answer questions because these are the types of responses required on most standardized tests. Reading the test questions and then finding the answer helps students glean the most important information presented. Teacher demonstration and repeated practice provide a learning experience and will help prepare students for those times when a formal test is required.

When instruction is based on trade books, group thinking activities, and projects, traditional assessments often fail to capture students' motivational development and higher order competencies (Guthrie, Van Meter, & Mitchell, 1994). Performance-based assessment often involves some type of student product that is planned, constructed, or developed, providing students opportunities to express or represent their knowledge in different ways (DeLain, 1999).

Performance-based assessment and rubrics are not new. They are frequently used, by both teachers and students, to identify key elements for levels of proficiency.

Writing as Assessment

The power of writing to learn in the content area is readily accepted by seemingly all members of the teaching community (Fisher, Frey, & Williams, 2002). Writing is a "way of knowing" (Santa, Havens, & Maycumber, 1996, p. 5). Students are more likely to remember information that they process at the inferential or conceptual level in writing (Ashcroft, 1994). Jacobs (2002) found that involvement with writing gives structure and sequence to ideas and enhances understanding of what is being studied. Students will not be able to produce a viable product if they don't understand the content presented. By far, the most common characteristic of the 90/90/90 schools mentioned previously was their emphasis on requiring written responses in performance assessment. Teachers in 90/90/90 schools placed a high emphasis on informative writing. Whether the student was writing a book report, lab report, social studies report, analysis of a sporting event, description of a piece of music, or a comparison of artists, the message was the same: This is the standard for good writing, and there are no compromises on these expectations for quality (Reeves, 2005). The association between writing and performance in other academic areas was striking. For instance, more than 80% of the 135 elementary schools in the study improved in science scores.

Student writing as a form of assessment can take many forms: response journals, reports, rewrites and innovations of alphabet or pattern books, or responses to specific questions. Students can also produce newspapers, brochures, plays, and advertisements.

A graphic organizer such as a paragraph frame (see Figure 7) can be used as another form of assessment that requires writing (Jones & Thomas, 2006). It provides students with a minimum framework for a well-written paragraph, which indicates to them what information is needed, and gives students prompting and direction. After reading a book together, introduce the technique by showing the frame on the overhead projector and have the class assist you in filling it out. Paragraph frames are especially helpful for students with writing difficulties or to introduce younger students to paragraph writing.

A report checklist (see Figure 8) can be used as an instructional tool to teach children to write reports. After reading an informational book together, put the checklist on the overhead projector and go over each of the steps. If

FIGURE 7. Paragraph Frames

Today's topic,_____, dealt with _____

_____

One of the key ideas was _____

_____

This is important because _____

_____

Another key idea was _____

_____

which was important because _____

_____

These ideas are useful when_____

_____

Reprinted from Jones, R.C., & Thomas, T.G. (2006). Leave no discipline behind. *The Reading Teacher*, 60, 58–64; based on Nichols (1980).

FIGURE 8. Report Checklist

1. My title tells what the report is about.

2. My first sentence tells what the report is about and has something interesting to make someone want to read it.

3. My facts are written in sentences and are in my own words.

4. I have enough facts in my report to make it interesting for someone else to read.

5. I have grouped my sentences into paragraphs that make sense.

6. I have a good ending that wraps up my report.

7. I have a picture, diagram, or chart to help make my report clear.

8. I have checked my spelling and punctuation.

9. The part I like best is _____.

Reprinted from Kletzien, S.B., & Dreher, M.J. (2004). *Informational text in K–3 classrooms: Helping children read and write*. Newark, DE: International Reading Association.

students are new to report writing, it will be helpful for you to demonstrate each step as you write an actual report. When students are familiar with this procedure, they should use the checklist to assess their own writing.

Assessing in Nontraditional Ways

Another useful way to assess if students have understood and acquired the intended information is through products, including models, dioramas, demonstrations, concept maps, time lines, oral reports, or performances. Nontraditional assessment also allows students to make the most of strengths they may have in music, drama, or art—especially useful with struggling readers or English-language learners (ELLs). Lenski, Ehlers-Zavala, Daniel, and Sun-Irminger (2006) offer methods of assessing English-language learners in mainstream classrooms, such as adopting a multidimensional approach that includes alternative assessments such as anecdotal records, checklists, rating scales, and portfolios.

Performance assessment tasks allow students to demonstrate their understanding by using Venn diagrams, charts, drawings, maps, or PowerPoint slides. These types of assessment are valuable tools for all students, and because many, if not most, classrooms include a number of mainstreamed students, they can be used with the entire class.

Conclusion

Integrating curriculum offers you the opportunity to be more efficient in your instruction. By merging content, learning is reinforced because new content connects to other areas. Trade books, both fiction and nonfiction, provide quality information as well as opportunities for reading and strengthening the language arts within the content areas. Integration also allows you to cover otherwise overlooked curriculum during the busy school day. Using themes often increases student interest in learning and provides an effective way to cover many areas of curriculum within a thematic framework. There are several ways to assess student understanding, as well. You can use informal methods on a daily basis, but you must also make sure that students are prepared for more formal testing procedures.

CHAPTER 3

Using Literature
to Teach Social Studies

The art of teaching is the art of assisting discovery.
—MARK VAN DOREN

In the past few years there has been increased concern about the lack of time spent on content area subjects, especially social studies, in U.S. elementary schools (Bryant, 2005; Manzo, 2005; Perkins-Gough, 2004). As Jones and Thomas (2006) write, "Preserving social studies instruction in the threatened arena of elementary curriculum may depend on the extent to which committed teachers employ survival skills that link the discipline to the accountability-favored subjects of reading and writing" (p. 58). In other words, the effective instructional practice of integration is one way to ensure that social studies gets enough attention in every classroom.

The National Council for the Social Studies (NCSS; 1994) defines social studies as the integrated study of the social sciences and humanities to promote civic competence. Social studies is not a singular discipline but a combination of many disciplines, with each competing for time in the curriculum. In 1994, a task force of NCSS published the *Curriculum Standards for Social Studies*, which provides an articulated K–12 social studies program that serves as a framework for the integration of other national standards in social studies, including U.S. and world history, civics and government, geography, global education, and economics. NCSS standards ensure that an integrated social science, behavioral science, and humanities approach for achieving academic and civic competence is available to guide social studies decision makers in K–12 schools. Although these standards are not mandated, because they are the product of a professional organization rather than the government, most school districts and publishing companies refer to these standards when setting curriculum and assessment guidelines.

The NCSS *Curriculum Standards for Social Studies* (1994) consists of ten themes incorporating fields of study that correspond with one or more relevant disciplines. The organization believes that effective social studies programs should include experiences that provide for the study of

1. culture;
2. time, continuity, and change;
3. people, places, and environments;
4. individual development and identity;
5. individuals, groups, and institutions;
6. power, authority, and governance;
7. production, distribution, and consumption;
8. science, technology, and society;
9. global connections; and
10. civic ideals and practices.

Zemelman, Daniels, and Hyde (1998) expanded on these standards by offering several recommendations for meeting them:

- Students of social studies need regular opportunities to investigate topics in depth.
- Students need opportunities to exercise choice and responsibility by selecting their own topics for inquiry.
- Social studies teaching should involve exploration and open questions that challenge students to think.
- Social studies must involve students in active participation in the classroom and the wider community.
- Social studies should involve students in both independent inquiry and cooperative learning, to build skills and habits needed for lifelong, responsible learning.
- Social studies learning should be built on students' prior knowledge of their lives and communities.
- Social studies should explore a full variety of cultures. (pp. 139–144)

Social studies instruction is not just a classroom activity. Principles of social studies are present in the entire community, such as democracy, government, and relations among social groups. When students actively participate in developing class rules or vote for class or student council officers they are learning social studies. Family history, customs, and heritage relate to history and geography. When parents or other community members share experiences about work, community groups, or political efforts, students learn the concept of community. Newspapers and news magazine articles foster awareness of local and national politics, social issues, and history. There are myriad trade books, both fiction and nonfiction, that illustrate these social studies concepts.

It is important to note that in the United States, each state has its own social studies curriculum guidelines, or scope and sequence, as does each Canadian province. But curriculum guidelines are all similar; the exceptions are grade 4, in which the emphasis is usually on the home state or province, and grade 5, which focuses on the home country. Most states and provinces include the following units in their social studies curriculum:

Kindergarten—Self

Grade 1—Family

Grade 2—Neighborhoods & Our Community

Grade 3—World Communities

Grade 4—Local History & Government

Grade 5—U.S./Canada History

Integrating Social Studies With Trade Books

There has been widespread advocacy for using trade books in the social studies by professional organizations such as NCSS and by educators and researchers. Davis and Palmer (1992) contend that children's literature extends the social studies curriculum, increases student participation, and draws on students' firsthand experiences. Trade books develop students' interest and give them a wider perspective by probing the complexity and ambiguity of particular events in ways not typically addressed in the standard textbook. Fortunately, there are many wonderful trade books available that fit within the social studies curriculum. These books can be used to supplement the text, providing more details and information; to accommodate many different reading levels; or solely to teach the curriculum. If textbooks are not available, most school districts have a list of appropriate trade books to use in the classroom.

Pairing fiction and nonfiction trade books in social studies helps students answer questions, build background knowledge, interact with stories, experience the lives and problems of characters, and compare fact and fiction. Historical fiction has long had a place in social studies, encompassing both history and geography. The personal voice of the author often provides a more interesting medium for students to be involved in the study of history.

Many teachers tell me they are using trade books, rather than a basal reader, for reading instruction. Most teachers have access to sets of fiction books, but it is important that nonfiction sets are available as well because reading more nonfiction can lead to higher reading achievement (Kletzien & Dreher, 2004; Routman, 2003). By using nonfiction for reading instruction, you can teach social studies content and reading skills simultaneously, so carefully choose books to correspond with the social studies curriculum at your grade level.

Many reading series anthologies contain nonfiction selections appropriate for the social studies curriculum at the particular grade level. Using such selections also can emphasize social studies content while teaching basic reading skills, and may even entice students to explore trade books on the same subject. Additionally, many basal readers provide suggestions of trade books on similar content and readability for further reading.

If social studies textbooks are available, there are ways to use them to accommodate the struggling or reluctant reader. For example, you or more able students can read aloud from the textbook, or students can read in pairs or small groups, helping one another. This also allows for questions, answers, and discussion, which aid comprehension. Of course the entire class will have to be taught how to be good listeners, helpers, etc. It is essential that you set guidelines so that all students are treated with respect. Providing students with a trade book that gives comparable information to the textbook is another way to meet the needs of various reading abilities and compare the information given. Pay attention to periodicals, too, which also make great supplementary resources for social studies information; see the Appendix for a list of periodicals.

As students read or listen to a selection, you can teach them to write an important piece of information or fact on an index card or piece of paper; some teachers suggest using one card for each piece of information. I also like to have students use the note card technique while they are reading independently. I instruct them not only to write down information, but also to write down questions they have. This note-taking technique must be taught, however. You can demonstrate it on the board or overhead projector by reading aloud a passage and asking students to help you decide what should be noted. This illustrates to students that note-taking is not simply copying, but it requires being able to glean the most important parts from a passage. Explain, too, that the notes can then be used as a study guide or to organize an oral or written report.

Choosing Appropriate Trade Books for Social Studies Instruction

Many publishing companies, such as Houghton Mifflin, Newbridge, Scholastic, Scott Foresman, and Sundance, offer nonfiction trade books to be used as group or class sets. They are relatively inexpensive and are designed to fit into the broad scope and sequence for social studies at each grade level in the United States and Canada. Most of these books are leveled, too, making it easy to match them with student reading ability. Harcourt leveled books include a "Think and Respond" section at the back of the book as well as a language arts activity and a suggestion for a school-home connection. Pebble Books (Capstone Press) include a table of contents, glossary, and an index, even at the earliest levels. They also have a "Read More" section with recommendations for further reading and a list of Internet sites related to the topic. National Geographic's Windows on Literacy series includes a literacy focus, with word count and vocabulary; decoding skills and phonemic awareness; comprehension/thinking skills; and ideas for writing, speaking, and listening. There is also a social studies focus, listing the content and thinking skills covered as well as ways to build social studies background, and there is an online teacher's guide. These types of books are excellent to use for guided reading in the literacy block because they cover content area during reading instruction. It's a good idea for schools to purchase these books and make them available to all grades.

When choosing trade books to use within your state/provincial curriculum guidelines, you might also consider the NCSS curriculum standards. Look for books that fit the subject area or time frame to be studied, yet cover different reading levels. Choose books that will be appealing to students, with colorful or interesting photographs, charts, maps, and diagrams (see Chapter 1 for suggestions on selecting informational trade books). Above all, the books must contain factual content. It can be time-consuming and sometimes difficult to peruse numerous trade books, but once you have a list of titles—and even better, obtain the books—

you can use most of them again. Ask your school or public librarian or literacy specialist for help. Consult lists of best books from the American Library Association or NCSS, too, and consider the annotated bibliography in this chapter, as well as the Literature Cited list and Appendix in this book.

Sample Lesson Plans

Teaching About Families (Grade K–1)

OBJECTIVE: Students will understand relationships in a family and be able to compare animal families with other animal families and human families (NCSS Standards 1, 4).

INSTRUCTIONAL MATERIALS

- *Animal Dads* (Collard, 1997)
- *A Mother's Journey* (Markle, 2005)
- *Animal Families* (Keys, 2002)
- Chart paper
- Templates: _____ live in families. They live and play _____. My family lives and plays in _____.

TIME: 3 days (approximately 20–30 minutes each day)

DAY 1

1. Read aloud *Animal Dads* (see Figure 9 for additional trade book suggestions for this topic). This simple text is appropriate for young children, and the information about each species can be discussed with the class.
2. Ask children to recall some of the things these animal dads do for their offspring (such as build homes, keep warm, bathe, protect, feed, teach, play, go away, stay, work, baby-sit, clean house). Record answers on a chart.
3. Ask students what their dads do that animal dads don't or can't (such as mow the lawn, drive a car, watch TV, get dressed, read the newspaper, etc.). Record answers on another chart.

> **FIGURE 9.** Other Books to Use to Study Families, Grades K–1
>
> dePaola, T. (1996). *The Baby Sister*. New York: Putnam.
> Joosse, B.M. (1991). *Mama, Do You Love Me?* (B. Lavallee, Illus.). San Francisco: Chronicle.
> Pelton, M.L. (2004). *When Dad's at Sea*. (R.G. Steele, Illus.). Morton Grove, IL: Albert Whitman.
> Russo, M. (1993). *Trade-In Mother*. New York: Greenwillow.
> Thiesing, L. (1998). *Me & You: A Mother–Daughter Album*. New York: Hyperion.
> Waddell, M. (1992). *Owl Babies*. (P. Benson, Illus.). Cambridge, MA: Candlewick.

4. Distribute copies of sentence starters or have students copy from the board:

> Animal dads _____.
> But my dad _____.

5. Have students complete the first sentence by choosing a word from the first chart. Have them choose a word from the second chart to complete the other sentence. Students can then illustrate the sentences.

DAY 2

1. Show students the book *Animal Dads* and ask them to recall some of the things the animal dads do. Display the first chart from the previous day.

2. Read *A Mother's Journey*. Ask students if the penguin family is like any of the families in *Animal Dads*. (There is a page about the father Emperor Penguin keeping the egg warm in *Animal Dads*, and two kinds of fish take care of the eggs before they hatch in *A Mother's Journey*.)

3. Have students finish their sentences and illustrations from Day 1, or complete another set of sentences and illustrations, based on the two books.

DAY 3

1. Read aloud *Animal Families*. This easy-to-read pattern book can be read aloud by some members of the class, depending on students' abilities. If multiple copies are not available, you may want to print the text on sentence strips or on a chart or overhead so the class can read along.

2. Have students create new sentences by inserting the names of animals they learned about in *Animal Dads* (such as fish, vole, gorilla, frog, beaver, bird, mongoose, tortoise, wolf, crocodile, sea horse).

3. After demonstrating several examples on the board or overhead, students can write and illustrate a page of their own. Have students copy, or provide a template:

_____ live in families. They live and play _____.

VARIATIONS

• Have students dictate, and you write the words.

• Have students write and illustrate about their own family, using the following template: People live in families. My family lives and plays in _____.

• Use completed sentences and illustrations to make a class book.

ASSESSMENT

Students should participate in a class discussion about each book. They should be able to fill out the template for Day 1, showing a basic difference between human and animal dads (some may have to dictate to the teacher or other adult). On Days 2 and 3, students should be able to recall pertinent information from the previous day's story and compare and contrast it to the new story.

Teaching About the Civil Rights Movement (Grades 2–3)

OBJECTIVE: Students will understand events leading up to the Civil Rights movement in the United States. They will be able to compare the contributions of various individuals who were instrumental in the movement (NCSS Standards 1, 5, 10).

INSTRUCTIONAL MATERIALS

• *Grandmama's Pride* (Birtha, 2005)

• *Happy Birthday, Martin Luther King* (Marzollo, 1993)

• K-W-L chart (see Figure 2 in chapter 2)—either one copy on transparency for the overhead projector or photocopies of individual charts for each student.

• Segregation chart for each student (see Figure 10)

TIME: 2 days, approximately 45 minutes per day

DAY 1

1. Ask students what they know about segregation and how African Americans were treated in the United States prior to the Civil Rights movement. Ask them, too, what they know about the Civil Rights movement: What was the time period? Who were some of the key people? What were some of the key events? How did things begin to change?

2. Have students help you fill out a K-W-L chart about what they know and what they want to know about segregation and the Civil Rights movement on the board or overhead. (Students might also have their own charts if they are familiar with this strategy.)

3. Read aloud *Grandmama's Pride* (see Figure 11 for additional trade book suggestions for this topic). Set in 1956, this picture book is a fictionalized account of segregation in the American South and the changes that occurred during the following year.

4. Ask students to help fill in the "learned" column on the K-W-L chart.

5. After the K-W-L chart has been revised, read aloud the author's note at the end of the book. This gives pertinent information about the Civil Rights movement. Make any additions to the chart.

6. Ask students to recall the places from the story where segregation existed (such as bus, restaurant, waiting room, water fountain, or bathroom). Create a segregation chart, such as the one shown in Figure 10, with a column for

---

FIGURE 10. Sample Segregation Chart

Places	People
Bus	Martin Luther King
Restaurant	Rosa Parks
Waiting room	
Water fountain	
Bathroom	

"places" and a column for "people." List answers in a column on the class segregation chart and have students write on their charts as well.

7. Ask students if they know the names of anyone who was instrumental in the Civil Rights movement. Record these names on the segregation chart.

8. Explain to students that they will be reading independently about some individuals who were influential in the Civil Rights movement. Introduce additional books and let them select the one they want to read. (Be sure to have enough books for the entire class. Duplicates are okay. You will probably have to set aside any books from your personal collection, borrow from other teachers, and also arrange with the librarian to get additional books or send students to the library.)

9. When students choose their books, they should record the name of their person on their segregation charts.

10. Give students time to read their books.

FIGURE 11. Other Books to Use to Study the Civil Rights Movement, Grades 2–3

Bray, R.L. (1995). *Martin Luther King*. (M. Zeldis, Illus.). New York: Greenwillow.

Cline-Ransome, L. (2000). *Satchel Paige*. (J.E. Ransome, Illus.). New York: Simon & Schuster.

Cline-Ransome, L. (2004). *Major Taylor: Champion Cyclist*. (J.E. Ransome, Illus.). New York: Atheneum.

Coles, R. (1995). *The Story of Ruby Bridges*. (G. Ford, Illus.). New York: Scholastic.

Davidson, M. (1986). *I Have a Dream: The Story of Martin Luther King*. New York: Scholastic.

Dingle, D.T. (1998). *First in the Field: Baseball Hero Jackie Robinson*. New York: Hyperion.

Grimes, N. (2002). *Talkin' About Bessie: The Story of Aviator Elizabeth Coleman*. (E.B. Lewis, Illus.). New York: Orchard Books.

Levine, E. (1990). *...If You Lived at the Time of Martin Luther King*. (A. Rich, Illus.). New York: Scholastic.

Livingston, M.C. (1992). *Let Freedom Ring: A Ballad of Martin Luther King, Jr.* (S. Byrd, Illus.). New York: Holiday House.

McWhorter, D. (2004). *A Dream of Freedom: The Civil Rights Movement From 1954 to 1968*. New York: Scholastic.

Robinson, S. (2004). *Promises to Keep: How Jackie Robinson Changed America*. New York: Scholastic.

Yoo, P. (2005). *Sixteen Years in Sixteen Seconds. The Sammy Lee Story*. (D. Lee, Illus.). New York: Lee & Low.

DAY 2

1. Read *Happy Birthday, Martin Luther King*, a picture biography with simple yet informative text.

2. Referring to the K-W-L chart from Day 1, ask students if they suggest any additions. Then, have students fill in their additions to the class segregation chart (i.e., schools, jobs, Rosa Parks).

3. Most students should have read their books. If not, allow an additional 10–15 minutes.

4. Instruct students to record any additional information from their reading on the segregation chart.

5. Have students prepare to give a brief oral summary of the book they read. Remind them to specifically look for pertinent information regarding segregation and what the person in their book did to overcome it. You also may want them to hand in a written report.

6. As students give their oral reports, the rest of the class should be adding additional information to their individual segregation charts.

7. After all students have given their reports, have the class help you complete the K-W-L chart.

VARIATIONS

• More capable students can write a paragraph, using the information from their segregation chart.

• Younger or less capable students can write a sentence from the chart and illustrate it.

ASSESSMENT

Students should be able to contribute orally in class to fill out the K-W-L chart. They should recall information from the first read-aloud story and begin to complete the segregation chart. After selecting and reading a book, students should summarize, giving pertinent information about their subject in an oral report. If you assign a written report, students should include the important ideas in an organized manner.

Teaching About Home Countries (Grades 4–5)

OBJECTIVE: Students will demonstrate a basic understanding of people, places, or historical events pertaining to their country. They will research for further information and write a summary (NCSS Standards 1, 2, 3, 4, 5, 6, 8).

INSTRUCTIONAL MATERIALS

- *A Is for America* (Scillian, 2001) or *M Is for Maple* (Ulmer, 2001)
- Reference materials, such as encyclopedias, trade books, social studies textbooks, and the Internet

TIME: 1–2 days, approximately 45–60 minutes per day

1. If you teach in the United States, read aloud *A Is for America*, or if you teach in Canada, read aloud *M Is for Maple* (see Figure 12 for additional trade book suggestions for this topic).

2. Have students (in pairs or alone) select a page (or letter of the alphabet) and further investigate one of the items listed (such as Klondike, Louisbourg, Philadelphia, Pike's Peak, Plymouth Rock, Rosa Parks).

3. Using the textbook, trade books, encyclopedias, or the Internet, students should gather important facts and information about the items they selected, then write a brief, single-page summary and draw an illustration of their chosen subject. If time permits, ask students to share their findings orally with the class.

4. Put together these new pages for each letter into a class book. If possible, make photocopies of each page so each student can have the entire book.

FIGURE 12. Other Books to Use to Study Canada
and the United States, Grades 4–5

Haugen, B. (2004). *Canada ABCs: A Book About the People and Places of Canada*. (D. Shaw, Illus.). Mankato, MN: Picture Window Books.
Schroeder, H. (2004). *The United States ABCs: A Book About the People and Places of the United States of America*. (J. Yesh, Illus.). Mankato, MN: Picture Window Books.
Discover America State by State series. (2006). Chelsea, MI: Sleeping Bear Press.
Discover Canada Province by Province series. (2006). Chelsea, MI: Sleeping Bear Press.

VARIATION

For younger students, ELLs, or students who struggle with reading, this same activity can be done using an alphabet book on the home state or province.

ASSESSMENT

Each student summary should be original, concise, and have pertinent and factual information about the subject. You also can assess students' writing and presentation of an oral report at this older grade level.

Conclusion

Because social studies combines so many disciplines, it is often advantageous to integrate topics into themes, using trade books as well as a textbooks. When you take a thematic approach to the subject, many of the concepts, skills, and topics in the social studies curriculum are covered with ease. When you provide a variety of trade books, students can choose their own topics for further inquiry after you give initial instruction. Using brief oral reports and allowing time for discussion and questions allows the entire class to benefit from individual research.

ANNOTATED BIBLIOGRAPHY—SOCIAL STUDIES

The following titles are organized by the thematic strands from Curriculum Standards for Social Studies: Expectations of Excellence (NCSS, 1994), although many of these books are applicable to more than one strand.

Culture and Cultural Diversity

Ammon, Richard. (2000). *An Amish Year*. (Pamela Patrick, Illus.). New York: Atheneum.

> Organized by seasons, fourth-grade student Anna describes the food, celebrations, chores, and games of Amish life. (Grades K–3)

Carrier, Roch. (1991). *A Happy New Year's Day*. (Gilles Pelletier, Illus.). Toronto, ON: Tundra.

> In the midst of World War II, the small Canadian village of Sainte-Justine celebrates the New Year. This book also includes details of daily life. (Grades K–3)

Ekoomiak, Normee. (1988). *Arctic Memories*. New York: Henry Holt.

> Through illustrations and simple text, Inuk artist Ekoomiak, from the James Bay region of arctic Quebec, explains various aspects of Inuit culture. Text is in both English and Inuit. (Grades 2–5)

Lewicki, Krys Val. (2001). *Thanksgiving Day in Canada*. (Ana Auml, Illus.). Toronto, ON: Napolean.

> Canadian history, traditions, and the story of Thanksgiving are covered in this colorful picture book, which also contains words and music to a lively, original song, and also is available in French. (Grades 3–5)

Maendel, Rachel. (1999). *Rachel, a Hutterite Girl*. (Hannah Marsden, Illus.). Scottdale, PA: Herald.

> This autobiographical picture book contains stories of work and play on a communal farm in Western Canada. (Grades K–3)

Marshall, Ingeborg. (1989). *The Beothuk of Newfoundland: A Vanished People*. St. John's, NL: Breakwater.

> The tragic story of extinction of the Red Indians of Newfoundland is told with both illustrations and text. Facts about housing, clothing, hunting, and social habits are included. (Grades 3–5)

Mercredi, Morningstar. (1998). *Fort Chipewyan Homecoming: A Journey to Native Canada*. (Darren McNally, Illus.). Markham, ON: Fitzhenry & Whiteside.

> This photographic essay follows a 12-year-old boy to the fort in Alberta where he learns about his Chipewyan, Metis, and Cree heritage. (Grades 3–5)

Podwal, Mark. (2003). *A Sweet Year: A Taste of the Jewish Holidays*. New York: Doubleday.

> Sights, smells, food, and history that are essential elements of each observation and rite are featured in this picture book. (Grades K–3)

Takabayashi, Mari. (2001). *I Live in Tokyo*. Boston: Houghton Mifflin.

> A colorful picture book introduction to the life and customs of Tokyo; each month of the year is highlighted with important traditions. (Grades K–2)

Wong, Janet S. (2000). *This Next New Year*. (Yangsook Choi, Illus.). New York: Farrar, Straus and Giroux.

> This fiction picture book about a family preparing for the Chinese New Year gives factual information about the lunar year and why it occurs at a different time each year. (Grades K–3)

Time, Continuity, and Change

Adler, David A. (2003). *A Picture Book of Lewis and Clark*. (Ronald Himler, Illus.). New York: Holiday House.

> At an easy reading level, this picture book captures significant moments as the Corps of Discovery made its way across the continent and back. (Grades K–2)

Allen, Thomas B. (2001). *Remember Pearl Harbor: Japanese and American survivors tell their stories*. Washington, DC: National Geographic Society.

> A balanced view of World War II is presented through first person oral histories. Also included are photographs, maps, timeline, and bibliography. (Grades 4–5)

Amis, Nancy. (2003). *The Orphans of Normandy: A True Story of World War II Told Through Drawings by Children*. New York: Atheneum.

> When Allied forces invaded Normandy, 100 girls were forced to leave their orphanage and walk 150 miles to safety in Beaufort-en-Vallee. Text and illustrations are based on journal entries, and a map and photographs also are included. (Grades 3–5)

Bradford, Karen. (2002). *With Nothing But Our Courage: The Loyalist Diary of Mary MacDonald*. Markham, ON: Scholastic Canada.

> Forced to leave New York because they support the British, a young girl and her family encounter hardships and tragedy on their dangerous journey to Quebec. (Grades 4–5)

Bruchac, Joseph. (2000). *Squanto's Journey: The Story of the First Thanksgiving*. (Greg Shed, Illus.). San Diego, CA: Harcourt.

> Picture book biography of the man who helped the Pilgrims survive the brutal winter. Young readers will appreciate this lesser known perspective of the first Thanksgiving. (Grades K–3)

Dalgliesh, Alice. (1956). *The Fourth of July Story*. (Marie Nonnast, Illus.). New York: Aladdin.

> Picture book history of the birth of the United States for younger readers. (Grades K–2)

Giff, Patricia Reilly. (2000). *Nory Ryan's Song*. New York: Random House.

> In this fictionalized account of the 1845 Irish potato famine, 12-year-old Nory Ryan refuses to give in to hunger and hopelessness. (Grades 4–5)

Hawk, Fran. (2004). *The Story of the H.L. Hunley and Queenie's Coin*. (Dan Nance, Illus.). Chelsea, MI: Sleeping Bear Press.

> Based on fact, the story of Lieutenant George Nixon and the mysterious disappearance of the Confederate submarine he commanded unfolds along with the modern-day discovery of the wreckage. (Grades 3–5)

Maestro, Betsy. (1986). *The Story of the Statue of Liberty*. (Giulio Maestro, Illus.). New York: HarperCollins.

> A history of the Statue of Liberty and its meaning to France, America, and America's immigrants. This picture book includes an appendix. (Grades K–2)

Maestro, Betsy. (1991). *The Discovery of the Americas: From Prehistory Through the Age of Columbus*. (Giulio Maestro, Illus.). New York: Scholastic.

> Clear, accurate text accompanies artistic maps and also includes diagrams of voyages and land routes in this picture history of the Americas. (Grades K–3)

Maestro, Betsy. (1996). *Coming to America: The Story of Immigration*. (Susannah Ryan, Illus.). New York: Scholastic.

> An exploration of the history of immigration to the United States from the Ice Age to the present, this informative book includes important dates and interesting facts about immigration. (Grades 2–4)

Prince, Bryan. (2004). *I Came as a Stranger: The Underground Railroad*. Toronto, ON: Tundra.

> This account of the Underground Railroad focuses on the role of Ontario as a refuge for fugitives from slavery. It includes a timeline, photographs, and a listing of heritage sites with a map of their locations. (Grades 4–5)

Turner, Ann. (1995). *Dust for Dinner*. (Robert Barrett, Illus.). New York: HarperCollins.

> An "I Can Read," easy chapter book (reading level 1–2) about an Oklahoma family living during the Dust Bowl during the Great Depression. (Grades K–2)

People, Places, and Environment (includes geography and life in other contexts)

Arbogast, Joan Marie. (2004). *Buildings in Disguise: Architecture That Looks Like Animals, Food, and Other Things*. Honesdale, PA: Boyds Mills Press.

> Unusual architecture in the United States is accompanied with the story of its origin, a description of how it was built, and photographs of the structures. This book also includes a map and can be used for geography and community lessons. (Grades K–5)

Bowers, Vivien. (1999). *Wow Canada! Exploring This Land From Coast to Coast to Coast*. (Dan Hobbs, Illus.). Toronto, ON: Owl Books.

> A 13-year-old boy and his younger sister travel by car across Canada with their parents. There is a chapter on each province and territory, accompanied by postcards and e-mails to friends back home. Illustrations, cartoons, photographs, and maps also are included. (Grades 3–5)

Curlee, Lynn. (1999). *Rushmore*. New York: Scholastic.

> A picture book describing the creation of this national monument from its inception in the 1920s by a state historian in South Dakota to its completion in 1941. (Grades K–3)

Ehrlich, Amy. (2003). *Rachel: The Story of Rachel Carson*. (Wendell Minor, Illus.). San Diego, CA: Harcourt.

> This picture book biography introduces young readers to the nature writer and activist who was instrumental in the environmental movement. (Grades 2–4)

Freedman, Russell. (1983). *Children of the Wild West*. New York: Clarion.

> Both pioneer and Native American children are documented through photographs in this account of life in the American West from 1840 to the early 1900s. (Grades 3–5)

Hughes, Susan. (2003). *Let's Call It Canada: Amazing Stories of Canadian Place Names.* (Clive & Jolie Dobson, Illus.). Toronto, ON: Maple Tree.

> Stories behind Canadian place names from coast to coast which were named for settlers, heroes, leaders, and renegades. (Grades 3–5)

Karim, Roberta. (1999). *Kindle Me a Riddle: A Pioneer Story.* (Bethanne Andersen, Illus.). New York: Greenwillow.

> This fictional picture book takes place in Utah in the 1850s. Each riddle explains the origin of a common element or aspect of frontier life. (Grades K–2)

Keller, Laurie. (1998). *Scrambled States of America.* New York: Henry Holt.

> This is a fanciful story about the states switching places. Facts about climate and other physical characteristics quickly convince the states to return to their original place. (Grades 2–5)

Knowlton, Jack. (1988). *Geography From A to Z: A Picture Glossary.* (Harriet Barton, Illus.). New York: Crowell.

> Geography terms from *archipelago* to *zone*, with definitions and descriptions, are explained in this picture alphabet book. (Grades 2–4)

Leedy, Loreen. (2000). *Mapping Penny's World.* New York: Henry Holt.

> A young girl makes a map of her bedroom for a school assignment. Then she decides to map the favorite places of her dog Penny. Good explanations of compass rose, scale, key, and symbols are included, as well as examples of the kinds of maps young students can understand and create. (Grades 1–3)

Major, Kevin. (2000). *Eh? to Zed: A Canadian Abecedarium.* (Alan Daniel, Illus.). Calgary, AB: Red Deer.

> Each letter of the alphabet is represented by four words linked to Canada, including people, places, animals, inventions, food, and words distinctly Canadian. (Grades K–3)

Say, Allen. (1993). *Grandfather's Journey.* Boston: Houghton Mifflin.

> In this account of his family's unique cross-cultural experience, Allen Say describes his own love for his two countries. (Grades 2–4)

Yin. (2001). *Coolies*. (Chris K. Soentpiet, Illus.). New York: Philomel.

> Thousands of Chinese fled to America in the mid-1800s to escape famine and the Taiping Rebellion. In the "land of opportunity," they were quickly employed to help build a great railroad across the West. This fictional picture book shows the hardships and prejudice they endured. (Grades 3–5)

Individual Development and Identity (includes family, community, school, and relationships to society)

Bannatyne-Cugnet, Jo. (1994). *A Prairie Year*. (Yvette Moore, Illus.). Toronto, ON: Tundra.

> Rural lifestyle on the prairies of Saskatchewan and Alberta is chronicled through a month-by-month anecdotal record. (Grades 3–5)

Caseley, Judith. (2002). *On the Town: A Community Adventure*. New York: Greenwillow.

> For a school assignment, Charlie and his mother walk through the neighborhood as he notes people and places in his notebook. (Grades K–2)

Citra, Becky. (1999). *Ellie's New Home*. Victoria, BC: Orca.

> In this novel, a young girl leaves England and struggles to adjust to life in the Canadian frontier in the 1880s. (Grades 3–4)

Debon, Nicolas. (2002). *A Brave Soldier*. Toronto, ON: Groundwood.

> Canada's involvement in World War I is presented through the viewpoint of one young Canadian soldier in this picture book. (Grades 2–5)

Freedman, Russell. (1994). *Kids at Work: Lewis Hine and the Crusade Against Child Labor*. (Lewis Hine, photos). New York: Clarion.

> Hine photographed underprivileged children working from 1908 to 1918. In this documentary of child labor, Freedman integrates the photographs with research. (Grades 4–5)

Geisert, Bonnie. (2001). *Desert Town*. (Arthur Geisert, Illus.). Boston: Houghton Mifflin.

> This picture book looks at life in a unique community over the course of a year. This is the fourth book in the Small Town U.S.A. series. (Grades K–3)

Haworth-Attard, Barbara. (1996). *Home Child*. Montreal, QC: Roussan.

> Thirteen-year-old Arthur is sent from an orphanage in England to work on a Canadian farm, paralleling the orphan trains in the United States (1854–1929) that sent orphans to the West. (Grades 4–5)

Kalman, Bobbie. (2000). *What Is a Community? From A to Z*. New York: Crabtree.

> This picture book explores the common aspects of most communities. Photographs accompany simple text. (Grades K–3)

Lunn, Janet. (2002). *Laura Secord: A Story of Courage*. (Maxwell Newhouse, Illus.). Toronto, ON: Tundra.

> This picture book chronicles the 19-mile journey of Laura, as she warns the British of an impending American attack in upper Canada during the War of 1812. (Grades 2–5)

Mochizuki, Ken. (1997). *Passage to Freedom: The Sugihara Story*. (Dom Lee, Illus.). New York: Lee & Low.

> Told by the young son of Chiune Sugihara, a Japanese diplomat in Lithuania in 1940, the story reveals how Sugihara risked his life and career by hand-writing visas for hundreds of Jewish refugees so they could escape the country. He and his family were thus imprisoned in a Soviet occupation camp for 18 months. (Grades 3–5)

Monk, Isabell. (1999). *Hope*. (Janice Lee Porter, Illus.). Minneapolis, MN: Carolrhoda.

> A young girl learns the story behind her name and to be proud of her biracial heritage when her aunt explains that she is generations of faith mixed with lots of love. (Grades K–3)

Rubin, Susan Goldman. (2000). *Fireflies in the Dark: The Story of Friedl Dicker-Brandeis and the Children of Terezin*. New York: Holiday House.

> Sent to Terezin Concentration Camp, art teacher Dicker-Brandeis brought art supplies and books and held secret classes for the children. Although only 100 children survived, their artwork and writings live on. (Grades 4–5)

Skrypuch, Marsha Forchuk. (2004). *Silver Threads*. (Michael Martchenko, Illus.). Markham, ON: Fitzhenry & Whiteside.

> This picture book, based on the author's grandparents, tells the story of a young couple fleeing the Ukraine to avoid war. When they arrive in Canada at the beginning of World War I, they are immediately confronted with prejudice and suffering, and when the young man tries to enlist in Canada's army, he is arrested and interned as an illegal alien. (Grades 2–4)

Sterling, Shirley. (1992). *My Name Is Seepeetza*. Toronto, ON: Groundwood.

> Based on the author's experience, this novel is written as the diary of a young girl during her sixth-grade year in the 1950s at the Kamloops Indian residential school in British Columbia. (Grades 4–5)

Takashima, Shizuye. (1989). *A Child in Prison Camp*. Toronto, ON: Tundra.

> This autobiography tells the story of an 11-year-old Japanese Canadian girl who is interned in the Canadian Rockies during World War II. (Grades 4–5)

Wallace, Ian. (1999). *Boys of the Deeps*. Toronto, ON: Groundwood.

> Set in Cape Briton, Nova Scotia, this picture book describes a boy's first day as a miner at the turn of the century. (Grades 2–4)

Warren, Andrea. (2001). *We Rode the Orphan Trains*. Boston: Houghton Mifflin.

> Warren interviewed eight orphan train-riders to tell their childhood experiences during "the largest children's migration in history" between 1854 and 1929. (Grades 4–5)

Individuals, Groups, and Institutions

Beil, Karen Magnuson. (1999). *Fire in Their Eyes: Wildfires and the People Who Fight Them*. San Diego, CA: Harcourt.

> This picture book with photographs and text describes the training, equipment, and real-life experiences of firefighters. (Grades 2–5)

Brown, Fern G. (1996). *Daisy and the Girl Scouts: The Story of Juliette Gordon Low*. (Marie De John, Illus.). Morton Grove, IL: Albert Whitman.

> This book is a biography of Low, but it is also about the Girl Scouts organization itself. After organizing the British Girl Guides, Low brought the idea to Georgia and formed the Girl Scouts of America. (Grades 3–5)

Duncan, Alice Faye. (1995). *The National Civil Rights Museum Celebrates Everyday People*. (J. Gerard Smith, Illus.). Mahwah, NJ: Bridgewater.

> A photo essay on the Civil Rights movement in the United States between 1954 and 1968, the narrative provides a historical framework, demonstrating that heroes can be everyday people. (Grades 3–5)

Fritz, Jean. (1999). *Why Not, Lafayette?* (Ronald Himler, Illus.). New York: Putnam.

> This book is a biography of the French nobleman who not only fought in the American Revolution but also advanced freedom in his own country. (Grades 4–5)

Garnett, Sammie, & Pallotta, Jerry. (2004). *U.S. Navy Alphabet Book*. (Rob Bolster, Illus.). Watertown, MA: Charlesbridge.

> This alphabet book describes the personnel, ships, equipment, weapons, and history of the United States Navy. The authors also have alphabet books on U.S. Marines, Army, Air Force, and Coast Guard. (Grades K–5)

Gibbons, Gail. (1995). *Knights in Shining Armor*. New York: Little, Brown.

> This picture book describes and illustrates the armor and weaponry knights used in battle during the Middle Ages, as well as the training and skills required to become a knight. (Grades K–3)

Gibbons, Gail. (1998). *Yippee-Yay! A Book About Cowboys and Cowgirls*. New York: Little, Brown.

> Life in the Old West, clothing, equipment, and lifestyle, as well as historical facts, are told through text, illustrations, and diagrams. Famous cowboys and cowgirls are featured at the end of the book, as well as other interesting facts. (Grades K–3)

Hamilton-Barry, Joann. (1998). *Boldly Canadian: The Story of the RCMP*. (Frances Clancy, Illus.). Toronto, ON: Kids Can Press.

> In six chapters, this story of the Royal Canadian Mounted Police covers its history, uniform, use of police dogs and horses, training, and assignments. (Grades 3–5)

Hopkins, Lee Bennett. (1999). *Lives: Poems About Famous Americans*. (Leslie Staub, Illus.). New York: HarperCollins.

> Sixteen famous Americans from various fields and centuries are profiled through poetry. (Grades 3–5)

Krull, Kathleen. (2000). *Lives of Extraordinary Women: Rulers, Rebels (and What the Neighbors Thought)*. (Kathryn Hewitt, Illus.). San Diego, CA: Harcourt.

> This book highlights 20 of the most influential women in history, with private interests and personalities. (Grades 3–5)

Marx, Trish. (2000). *One Boy From Kosovo*. (Cinda Karp, Illus.). New York: HarperCollins.

> This book is a pictorial essay of 12-year-old Edi Fejzullahus and his family who are driven from their home by Serbian soldiers and sent to a refugee camp in Macedonia. (Grades 4–5)

Newhouse, Maxwell. (2004). *The RCMP Musical Ride*. Toronto, ON: Tundra.

> This picture book features the expertly groomed and trained horses of the Royal Canadian Mounted Police. Rooted in the cavalry drills in the late 1800s, the modern-day Musical Ride features dance-like steps and riders maneuvering against different Canadian backdrops. (Grades K–4)

Oberle, Lora Polack. (2001). *The Canadian Forces Snowbirds: 431 Air Demonstration Squadron*. Mankato, MN: Capstone.

> Photos and simple text explore the history, missions, and equipment of this elite force, as well as the necessary qualifications and training required. (Grades 3–5)

Power, Authority, and Governance

Blumenthal, Karen. (2005). *Let Me Play: The Story of Title IX—The Law That Changed the Future of Girls in America*. New York: Atheneum.

> This chronological account of the women's movement for fair treatment at school and in the workplace includes profiles of women activists, politicians, and athletes. (Grades 4–5)

Catrow, David. (2002). *We the Kids: The Preamble to the Constitution of the United States*. New York: Dial.

In this picture book, political cartoonist Catrow shows the ideas and ideals in present-day, humorous illustrations. There is also a glossary of terms. (Grades 2–4)

Freedman, Russell. (2000). *Give Me Liberty! The Story of the Declaration of Independence*. New York: Holiday House.

This book examines events leading up to the Continental Congress and the writing of the famous document. The complete text of the Declaration of Independence and information about its preservation, storage, and display is also included. (Grades 4–5)

Granfield, Linda. (1990). *Canada Votes: How We Elect Our Government*. (Craig Terlson, Illus.). Toronto, ON: Kids Can Press.

For Canadians and non-Canadians alike, this book presents facts about voting (such as rights, who can vote, registration) and Parliament. (Grades 4–5)

Harness, Cheryl. (1998). *Ghosts of the White House*. New York: Simon & Schuster.

On a school tour of the White House, the ghost of George Washington takes a young girl on a personal tour, introducing her to other ghost presidents, who tell her what it was like to live in the White House and face the problems of their times. The book includes a timeline and information about presidents who are still alive. (Grades 4–5)

Kuitenbrouwer, Peter. (2004). *Our Song: The Story of "O Canada," the Canadian National Anthem*. (Ashley Spires, Illus.). Montreal, QC: Lobster Press.

The evolution of the anthem, from its composition in 1880 to when it was proclaimed the national anthem of Canada in 1980, is shown through text and illustrations in this picture book. The lyrics to the song are in both official languages. (Grades K–4)

Maestro, Betsy. (1987). *A More Perfect Union: The Story of Our Constitution*. (Giulio Maestro, Illus.). New York: Lothrop, Lee & Shepard.

An introduction to the U.S. Constitution, text and pictures tell how the Constitution was drafted and ratified. (Grades K–3)

McCain, Becky Ray. (2001). *Nobody Knew What to Do: A Story About Bullying*. (Todd Leonardo, Illus.). Morton Grove, IL: Albert Whitman.

> This picture book focuses on the feelings of powerlessness in the presence of a bully. It also addresses the importance of confiding in an adult, even if you are not the focus of the intimidation. (Grades K–3)

Murphy, Patricia J. (2002). *Canada Day*. New York: Children's Press.

> This simple picture book explains the history, importance, and celebration of Canada Day. (Grades K–3)

O'Neill, Alexis. (2002). *The Recess Queen*. (Laura Huliska-Beith, Illus.). New York: Scholastic.

> Mean Jean is the recess queen, but when Katie Sue, who is unaware of the playground hierarchy, comes to school, things change! This book is a humorous look at the serious problem of bullying. (Grades K–3)

Sandler, Martin W. (1995). *Presidents*. New York: HarperCollins.

> The lives of presidents from George Washington to Bill Clinton are not divided into each term but by their political achievements, families, pets, hobbies, and how they lived as ordinary people. Photographs and illustrations from the Library of Congress and various presidential libraries present a fresh view at the lives of these leaders. (Grades 4–5)

St. George, Judith. (2000). *So You Want to Be President?* (David Small, Illus.). New York: Philomel.

> Simple text and humorous illustrations look at interesting facts about 41 U.S. presidents. (Grades 1–3)

Thimmesh, Catherine. (2004). *Madam President: The Extraordinary, True (and Evolving) Story of Women in Politics*. (Douglas B. Jones, Illus.). Boston: Houghton Mifflin.

> Brief biographies of both famous and lesser known women show how these brave and tenacious women have paved the way for the leaders of tomorrow. A timeline is included. (Grades 3–5)

Production, Distribution, and Consumption

Ancona, George. (1991). *Bananas: From Manolo to Margie*. Boston: Houghton Mifflin.

> Both color and black and white photographs combined with text show how bananas are grown, harvested, and transported from a plantation in Honduras to the United States. (Grades 2–4)

Blumenthal, Karen. (2002). *Six Days in October: The Stock Market Crash of 1929*. New York: Atheneum.

> A comprehensive review of the events behind the stock market crash of 1929, this book contains photographs and newspaper articles. Information inserts are interspersed to aid the reader's understanding. (Grades 4–5)

Hughes, Susan. (2002). *Canada Invents*. Toronto, ON: Owl Books.

> Achievements in technology from early Inuit inventions to the present are highlighted along with the people who invented them. (Grades 3–5)

Jones, George. (1995). *My First Book of How Things Are Made: Crayons, Jeans, Peanut Butter, Guitars, and More*. New York: Scholastic.

> Colorful photographs and detailed yet easy-to-read text explain the manufacturing and distribution of crayons, peanut butter and jelly, footballs, orange juice, jeans, guitars, and books. (Grades 2–5)

Krull, Kathleen. (2001). *Supermarket*. (Melanie Hope Greenberg, Illus.). New York: Holiday House.

> Beginning with the early history of farming, this picture book shows how food gets from farm to shelf. Electric eye doors and shopping carts, as well as food marketing strategies, are also explained. There is information about the most famous crops of each state, including a U.S. map. (Grades K–3)

Paulsen, Gary. (1995). *The Tortilla Factory*. (Ruth Wright Paulsen, Illus.). San Diego, CA: Harcourt.

> Lyrical text and paintings describe the chronology of the life of a tortilla, from seed to plant, to delivery to the store. (Grades K–3)

Radford, Derek. (1994). *Building Machines and What They Do*. Cambridge, MA: Candlewick.

> Text and pictures describe machines, their parts, and functions, and answer questions young children have about the machines they see every day. (Grades K–2)

Rose, Sharon, & Schlager, Neil. (2003). *How Things Are Made: From Automobiles to Zippers*. New York: Black Dog & Leventhal.

> Each page of this book has informative text with detailed illustrations, diagrams, and sidebars. (Grades 2–5)

Wulffson, Don. (2000). *Toys! Amazing Stories Behind Some Great Inventions*. (Laurie Keller, Illus.). New York: Henry Holt.

> From dolls and checkers to pinball and video games, the stories behind classic and commercial toy inventions are told in this volume. (Grades 3–5)

Science, Technology, and Society

Ballard, Robert D. (1988). *Exploring the Titanic*. New York: Scholastic.

> Although the building of and the first fateful voyage of the Titanic are discussed in this text, the focus is on the team that located the shipwreck in 1985 and explored it in 1986. Photographs, diagrams, a timeline, and glossary are included. (Grades 2–5)

Bildner, Phil. (2004). *Twenty-One Elephants*. (LeUyen Pham, Illus.). New York: Simon & Schuster.

> When the Brooklyn Bridge was built, a number of New York City residents questioned its safety. This fictionalized account tells the true story of how P.T. Barnum paraded Jumbo and 20 of his other circus elephants across the bridge to prove it safe. (Grades K–3)

Bingham, Caroline. (2000). *Big Book of Rescue Vehicles*. New York: Dorling Kindersley.

> With colorful photographs, labels, and descriptions, rescue vehicles (ambulances, planes, boats, and helicopters) are profiled in this large volume. (Grades 2–4)

Cole, Joanna. (1999). *The Magic School Bus Gets Programmed: A Book About Computers*. (Bruce Degan, Illus.). New York: Scholastic.

> In this Magic School Bus series book, Miss Frizzle's class finds out how to use computers, how they work, and why it is important to know about them. (Grades 2–3)

Cook, Peter, & Manning, Scott. (1999). *Why Doesn't My Floppy Disk Flop? And Other Kids' Computer Questions Answered by the CompuDudes*. (Ed Morrow, Illus.). New York: Wiley.

> The history of computers and their various parts and uses are explained in this kid-friendly book that also includes a glossary, bibliography, and index. (Grades 2–5)

Gibbons, Gail. (1995). *Bicycle Book*. New York: Holiday House.

> Through colorful illustrations and diagrams, Gibbons gives a brief history of bicycles as well as how they work and how they are used. Safety tips and maintenance guidelines are also included. (Grades K–3)

Harness, Cheryl. (1995). *The Amazing Impossible Erie Canal*. New York: Simon & Schuster.

> This picture book follows the Erie Canal from conception and building to the 10-day parade down the canal led by the Seneca Chief. It also explains the canal's effects on a developing nation. (Grades 2–4)

Hodge, Deborah. (2000). *The Kids Book of Canada's Railway and How the CPR Was Built*. (John Mantha, Illus.). Toronto, ON: Kids Can Press.

> The decision to build the cross-country railroad shaped Canada's history by preventing the United States from taking the Canadian West. Accurate illustrations and readable text cover the construction of the Canadian Pacific Railway (CPR) as well as issues and consequences of blazing a trail through unknown and unfriendly terrain. (Grades 3–5)

Lord, Trevor. (1999). *Big Book of Cars*. New York: Dorling Kindersley.

> This large picture book emphasizes the features, facts, and performance of various cars, both rare and common. (Grades 3–5)

Matthews, Tom. (1999). *Always Inventing: A Photobiography of Alexander Graham Bell*. Washington, DC: National Geographic Society.

> Authentic photographs illustrate Bell's amazing life and inventions. (Grades 3–5)

Pallotta, Jerry, & Stillwell, Fred. (1997). *The Airplane Alphabet Book*. (Rob Bolster, Illus.). Watertown, MA: Charlesbridge.

> This picture alphabet book features informative text on planes, ranging from the Wright brother's first plane to the modern Ultralight. (Grades K–3)

Ready, Dee. (1998). *School Buses*. Mankato, MN: Bridgestone.

> Each part of the school bus, as well as safety features, is explained in this colorful picture book. (Grades K–2)

Simon, Seymour. (2000). *Seymour Simon's Book of Trucks*. New York: HarperCollins.

> Colorful photographs accompany each description of a type of truck and its intended use. (Grades K–2)

Spencer, Bev. (2003). *Made in Canada: 101 Amazing Achievements*. (Bill Dickson, Illus.). Markham, ON: Scholastic Canada.

> This book details 101 inventions, including the biggest, the best, the first, and wackiest in Canada. (Grades 3–5)

Thimmesh, Catherine. (2000). *Girls Think of Everything: Stories of Ingenious Inventions by Women*. (Melissa Sweet, Illus.). Boston: Houghton Mifflin.

> Through brief descriptions, this book describes ingenious inventions of women that have made our lives simpler and better. A timeline, diagrams, and illustrations are included. (Grades 3–5)

Global Connections

Baer, Edith. (1990). *This Is the Way We Go to School: A Book About Children Around the World*. (Steve Björkman, Illus.). New York: Scholastic.

> This picture book explores children from different countries traveling to school in different ways (such as on skis, by bicycle, by horse and buggy). At the end of the book is a list of names of children and the country where they live. The book also includes a world map. (Grades K–2)

Dorling Kindersley Publishing. (2002). *A Life Like Mine: How Children Live Around the World*. New York: Author.

> Using the tenets of UNICEF, this pictorial profiles the lives of 18 children in four sections: survival, development, protection, and participation, and it includes charts, maps, and children's quotes. (Grades 4–5)

Fox, Mem. (1997). *Whoever You Are*. (Leslie Staub, Illus.). San Diego, CA: Harcourt.

> Children all over the world may look different and speak different languages, but they are all alike in many ways. (Grades K–1)

Freeman, Dena. (2003). *How People Live*. New York: Dorling Kindersley.

> This cultural atlas, organized by continent, looks at countries, geography, and cultural and ethnic groups. (Grades 3–5)

Kindersley, Barnabas, & Kindersley, Anabel. (1995). *Children Just Like Me: A Unique Celebration of Children Around the World*. New York: Dorling Kindersley.

> Although their cultures are different, in many ways the daily lives of children all over the world are similar, as are their hopes, fears, dreams, and beliefs. (Grades 3–5)

Menzel, Peter, Mann, Charles C., & Kennedy, Paul. (1994). *Material World: A Global Family Portrait*. San Francisco: Sierra Club.

> Photographs offer a visual portrait of life in 30 nations, featuring one "statistically average" family in each country, and describe their work, attitudes toward possessions, and hopes for the future. Sidebars include statistics and a brief history of each country. (Grades 4–5)

Morris, Ann. (1992). *Houses and Homes*. (Ken Heyman, Illus.). New York: Lothrop, Lee & Shepard.

> Photographs and sparse text tell the story of housing around the world. Each photo is clearly labeled, and there is a map of each location. (Grades K–3)

Morris, Ann. (2000). *Families*. New York: HarperCollins

> This book shares that "all children are part of families." Families come in all sizes, nationalities, and configurations. A map is included, as well as an index identifying each group and nationality. (Grades K–3)

Ruurs, Margriet. (2005). *My Librarian Is a Camel: How Books Are Brought to Children Around the World.* Honesdale, PA: Boyds Mills Press.

>This book explores how librarians in 13 countries provide services using everything from boats to wheelbarrows to elephants. A map and basic facts are provided for each country. (Grades 3–5)

Smith, David J. (2002). *If the World Were a Village: A Book About the World's People.* (Shelagh Armstrong, Illus.). Toronto, ON: Kids Can Press.

>The global village is described in terms that children can relate to. Instead of 6 billion, the imaginary world village has just 100 inhabitants, allowing young readers to find out more about the real world and problems we may face in the future. (Grades 2–5)

Civic Ideals and Practices

Grodin, Elissa. (2004). *D Is for Democracy: A Citizen's Alphabet.* (Victor Juhasz, Illus.). Chelsea, MI: Sleeping Bear Press.

>This alphabet book describes U.S. government structure, components, and concepts. Pictures and text are appropriate for younger students (grades K–2), while older students (grades 3–5) will enjoy the more complex and detailed descriptions on inserts on each page. (Grades K–5)

Kielburger, Marc, & Kielburger, Craig. (2002). *Take Action! A Guide to Active Citizenship.* Toronto, ON: Gage Learning.

>Easy-to-follow guidelines show readers how they can change the world by making a difference in the lives of people all over the globe. (Grades 4–5)

Martin, Ann M. (1992). *Rachel Parker, Kindergarten Show-Off.* (Nancy Poydar, Illus.). New York: Holiday House.

>Two young girls, new neighbors, want to be friends, but one of them is a show-off! Children will relate to the civics lesson learned about getting along with others and making friends. (Grades K–1)

Russell, Joan Plummer. (2001). *Aero and Officer Mike: Police Partners.* (Kris Turner Sinnenberg, Illus.). Honesdale, PA: Boyds Mills Press.

>Photographs and easy-to-read text describe the partnership, skills, and demanding work of a police officer and his police dog. (Grades K–2)

Stephens, Edna Cucksey. (2002). *Rock U.S.A. and the American Way! A Freedom Handbook*. (Mark J. Herrick, Illus.). Auburn Hills, MI: EDCO Publishing.

This patriotic alphabet book highlights American events, places, people, and concepts. It emphasizes American civic responsibility. (Grades 1–3)

CHAPTER 4

Using Literature to Teach Science

The important thing in science is not so much to obtain new facts as to discover new ways of thinking about them.

—Sir William Bragg

T he broad goal of a school science program should be to foster under-standing, interest, and appreciation of the world in which we live. Lectures, demonstrations, and rote memorization have given way to the constructivist approach, which activates children's prior knowledge about a phenomenon, encourages questions about it, and helps them gather informa-tion and build their own concepts (Zemelman, Daniels, & Hyde, 1998). The National Science Teachers Association (NSTA) supports the notion that inquiry science must be basic to the daily curriculum of every elementary school stu-dent at every grade level (2002). Although NSTA and the *National Science Education Standards* (*NSES*; 1996) emphasize inquiry, this should not be in-terpreted as a recommendation for a single approach to teaching science. Teachers should use different strategies to develop the knowledge, understand-ings, and abilities described in the content standards. Conducting hands-on science activities does not guarantee inquiry nor is reading about science in-compatible with inquiry. A combination of both is essential in a good science program. Anderson (1998) found that students participating in an experimen-tal treatment group using both science observations and interesting texts gained more conceptual knowledge than any of the other groups. As in most good teaching, a variety of methods and materials will better meet the learn-ing styles and the needs of students.

The *NSES* were produced by NSTA in 1995 and published in 1996. The de-velopment of these standards was guided by certain principles, including the fol-lowing:

- Science is for all students.

- Learning science is an active process.

- School science reflects the intellectual and cultural traditions that characterize the practice of contemporary science.

- Improving science education is part of systemic education reform.

The standards describe the essential science content that all students must have the opportunity to learn, and that inquiry provides a context within which the content is to be learned. NSTA is now part of an ongoing effort to implement the following eight standards in classrooms throughout the United States:

1. Unifying concepts and processes (measurement, measurement tools)

2. Science as inquiry (asking questions, planning and conducting investigations, using appropriate tools and techniques to gather data)

3. Physical science (properties of objects and materials; position and motion of objects; light, heat, electricity, energy and magnetism)

4. Life science (organisms, life cycles of organisms, organisms and environments, structure and function in living systems, reproduction and heredity, regulation and behavior, populations and ecosystems; diversity and adaptations of organisms)

5. Earth and space science (properties of Earth materials, objects in the sky, changes in Earth and sky, structure of the Earth system, Earth's history, Earth in the solar system)

6. Science and technology (distinguish between natural objects and objects made by humans, abilities of technological design, understanding about science and technology)

7. Science in personal and social perspectives (personal health, characteristics and changes in populations, types of resources, changes in environments, science and technology in local challenges)

8. History and nature of science (science as a human endeavor, nature and history of science)

It is important to note that the content described in these standards is not a science curriculum. Content is what students should learn. Curriculum is the way content is organized and emphasized. These standards envision change, with less emphasis on memorization of scientific facts and information, subject matter disciplines, coverage of many science topics, investigations confined to one class period, and individual process skills, and more emphasis on integration of all aspects of science content, coverage of a few fundamental science concepts, inquiry as an instructional strategy, investigations over extended periods of time, and public communication of student ideas and work to classmates.

As in social studies, each U.S. state and Canadian province has its own science curriculum guidelines. But these guidelines are similar, although some provinces in Canada do not have a kindergarten curriculum other than Community and Environmental Awareness. In most states and provinces the curriculum centers on life science, physical science, and Earth science. For example, in life science, all grades K–5 study plants and animals. Kindergarten may focus on different types of plants and animals, grade 1 on plants' and animals' needs, grade 2 on life cycles, grade 3 on physical structure and behavior, grade 4 on growth and changes, and grade 5 on structure of the human body. The emphasis for physical science in grades K–5 is usually on the properties of objects and materials, which includes measurement, solids, liquids, gases, energy and matter, light, electricity, magnetism, and elements. Earth science in grades K–5 covers land, air, and water; rocks and minerals; seasons; weather; natural resources; and space.

Integrating Science With Trade Books

Bruning and Schweiger (1997) write,

> Science learning heavily depends on students' abilities to comprehend expository materials. Observation and experimentation engage students with scientific phenomena, but reading—especially comprehending expository materials—is needed for students to fully understand scientific concepts. Science programs that do not contain literacy activities provide an impoverished form of science learning. (p. 149)

For this reason, expository text, or nonfiction, must be emphasized in the primary grades. Nonfiction trade books offer a source for answering the specific questions children ask about science and for stimulating further questioning. Children's perceived disinterest and poor achievement in science led to the American Association for the Advancement of Science's Project 2061 (1989), which recommended integrating children's literature into the science curriculum.

According to NSTA's position statement on elementary school science (2002), elementary school students best learn science when instruction builds directly on the students' conceptual framework, content is organized on the basis of broad conceptual themes common to all science disciplines, and mathematics and communication skills are an integral part of science instruction. The paper also states that students most value science when other subject areas are infused into science instruction. An effective science program involves a wide range of language and mathematics skills. For instance, while working on a scientific investigation, students read whenever they compare written data and explanations. They may also read information from textbooks, trade books, and periodicals. They use writing to list what they know, generate questions, keep track of data, or write letters. And they use mathematics when measuring, tallying, graphing, and averaging.

A science journal is a wonderful place for students to develop informational writing skills (Akerson & Young, 2005). Students can record observations and write inferences based on their observations. Learning logs also involve journal writing, but this strategy calls for informal, reflective writing that stimulates thinking about how and what is being learned (Fulwiler, 1980). A learning log is an ongoing record of learning activity. Because it is very similar to a science journal, you should choose one for the class to avoid confusion. Students can also research and write their own book on a science theme. For younger students, an alphabet or counting book can be written. Books by Jerry Pallotta, like *The Icky Bug Alphabet Book* (1986) and *Ocean Counting* (2005), provide a model for writing. Students will be learning how to gain information from nonfiction text and group it into categories. And, of course, report writing is a more traditional method of integrating writing and science. Many of Gail Gibbons's nonfiction books are excellent examples for report writing. These types of writing activities help students develop an understanding of science content while providing opportunities for teachers to assess student understanding.

First-grade teacher Anne Veer uses *FOSS: Full Option Science System* (Regents of the University of California, 2005). Like many published curricula, it includes investigation kits, teacher guides, and equipment. But also included are a Big Book and student books for each kit, assessment and duplication masters, interdisciplinary extensions, and an additional listing of student books and websites. While studying mealworms, Ms. Veer's class observes mealworms change from larvae to pupae to adults. Students draw and write their observations in journals. For guided and independent reading, they read and discuss nonfiction trade books such as *Lifetimes* (Mellonie, 1983), *A Ladybug's Life* (Himmelman, 1998), and *Beetles* (Coughlan, 1999), adding new words to the class word bank. They do math activities about the number of legs, arms, heads, and antennae and chart the number of larvae, pupae, and adult mealworms; they also make three-dimensional beetles from construction paper with the appropriate characteristics.

Fourth/fifth-grade teacher Ed Barrett uses hands-on science discovery and scientific inquiry in his classroom, supported by nonfiction trade books. Mr. Barrett reports that his students use a variety of strategies to increase their understanding, including vocabulary exercises and setting a purpose for their reading. When students read with a partner, they stop at the end of each page and discuss what they have learned. As a class, students study the features of nonfiction texts, such as subtitles, illustrations with captions, sidebars, indexes, tables of content, glossaries, and lists of supporting resources. Students make connections, use background knowledge, ask questions, determine importance, and use mental imaging. Sometimes they draw pictures or graphs to demonstrate their understanding of the material.

In such instances where fiction and nonfiction are integrated into the curriculum, Buehl (2001) recommends using a graphic organizer such as a Fact Pyramid to differentiate essential from supportive details (see Figure 13). A Fact Pyramid spotlights what is important and worthy of being remembered over time

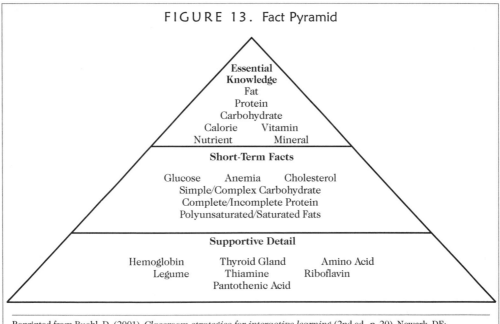

FIGURE 13. Fact Pyramid

Essential Knowledge
Fat
Protein
Carbohydrate
Calorie   Vitamin
Nutrient   Mineral

Short-Term Facts

Glucose   Anemia   Cholesterol
Simple/Complex Carbohydrate
Complete/Incomplete Protein
Polyunsaturated/Saturated Fats

Supportive Detail

Hemoglobin   Thyroid Gland   Amino Acid
Legume   Thiamine   Riboflavin
Pantothenic Acid

Reprinted from Buehl, D. (2001). *Classroom strategies for interactive learning* (2nd ed., p. 20). Newark, DE: International Reading Association.

by organizing information into three levels. The "tip" of the pyramid is for essential knowledge, the middle for short-term facts, and the base for supportive details.

Choosing Appropriate Trade Books for Science Instruction

There has been concern about the accuracy of the information in literature used for science instruction. Mayer's (1995) study of the fictional read-aloud *Dear Mr. Blueberry* (James, 1991) and its influence on science knowledge acquisition emphasized this growing concern. In Mayer's study, children did not demonstrate retention of much new information presented in the story and some even picked up misinformation, leading Mayer to caution against the use of fictional children's literature that has not been carefully considered for accuracy and presentation. Rice and Rainsford (1996) examined 300 trade books that included informational books, fantasy, and realistic fiction. They found misconceptions primarily in the stories, but they noted informational books also could lead readers astray.

Donovan and Smolkin (2001) studied the effect of genre and other factors that influence teachers' book selections for science instruction. They found that, in choosing books, teachers mentioned content as a major consideration in their selections, with a particular concern for accuracy of information. But Donovan and Smolkin also found that many teachers, when given the choice of non-fiction versus fiction, chose fiction because of their concern with children's enjoyment in their encounters with science. They write, "The presence of stories in science instruction may not only provide children misinformation and missed opportunities with science terms and text structures, but also cause them confusion in the stances we assume in reading different types of texts" (p. 437). The use of *Mr. Blueberry*, noted in the previous paragraph, is an example of this confusion. Another example is the misuse of the word *cocoon* in *The Very Hungry Caterpillar* (Carle, 1969). Authors of fiction sometimes choose words for aesthetic value or to suit the text, rather than focusing on content correctness. Teachers must realize that fictional stories that relate to science concepts must contain accurate information. Acknowledging that motivation is a major factor, Donovan and Smolkin are concerned simply that those who choose fictional stories are cognizant of the limitations of fiction for science instruction. For young children it can sometimes be effective to introduce a concept with a story, followed by an informational book. For instance, in grade 1, a study of penguins might begin with the teacher reading *Tacky the Penguin* (Lester, 1988). Although there is some authentic information in this story, it is fanciful, with Tacky wearing clothes and talking. A discussion should follow on what in the story is true about penguins and what is not. Then, a book such as *Welcome to the World of Penguins* (Swanson, 2003) should be read and discussed.

Donovan and Smolkin (2001) also found that teachers, who had no particular training in selecting science books, seemed to have many good ideas about features in their selections of trade books to enhance science instruction. The teachers addressed content in two ways: science concepts (including information and vocabulary) and accuracy of information. The other factor considered was suitability of texts, most specifically readability, strategies, and entertainment value.

Humor in children's books often helps spark the interest of reluctant readers and encourages their involvement with books. And the humor in some literature offers a light-hearted approach to science and engages the interest of the less curious in the group. Scholastic's The Magic School Bus series, which began in 1986 and is written by Joanna Cole and illustrated by Bruce Degen, uses the humorous adventures of Ms. Frizzle and her class to introduce science and health topics to children. Each book contains a wealth of information for children to respond to and extend in various ways (Freeman, 1995). Readers follow Ms. Frizzle's class to the waterworks, inside the Earth and the human body, into the solar system, on the ocean floor, and back to the time of dinosaurs. The text tells the story of the class's journeys. The speech bubbles can be read aloud by individual students, inserts of student reports can be read or further investigated, and students can make a timeline and/or map of the journey. But it is important to point out to students that these books are indeed fictional stories with scientific content and then proceed by introducing appropriate nonfiction.

Content remains the primary factor to consider when choosing books to enhance and further explain science instruction. As with social studies, many publishing companies offer affordable and appealing books on a variety of science topics at various readability levels. For younger readers, Sundance offers the AlphaKids Plus series for emergent readers and Little Green Readers for grades 1 and 2. For example, *The Pond* (Reed, 2002), part of the AlphaKids Plus series, contains simple sentences, such as "This is a pond. Lots of things live in the pond," accompanied by photographs. The book also includes a word count and a graphic of the food chain in a pond. Children's Press publishes a Rookie Read-About Science series that includes a vocabulary section, photographs, and an index.

Newbridge's Discovery Links, Houghton Mifflin's Little Readers, and National Geographic's Windows on Literacy series also offer books for emergent and early readers on science topics. National Geographic's Reading Expeditions, The Wright Group's Kids Discover Reading series, HarperCollins's Time for Kids: Science Scoops, Kidsbooks's Eyes on Nature series, and Parachute Press's Explorer Books are suitable for older readers.

When choosing trade books to use within your state/provincial curriculum guidelines, you might also consult the Science Content Standards. As with all good nonfiction books, those to use for science content should be factual, appealing, and appropriate for both the reading level and interest of your students. If you have a science textbook, select trade books that will support and supplement its content.

Sample Lesson Plans

Teaching About Bears (Grades K–1)

OBJECTIVE: Students will understand the characteristics, needs, life cycles, and differences of black bears, grizzly bears, and polar bears (NSTA Standard 4).

INSTRUCTIONAL MATERIALS

- *Goldilocks and the Three Bears* (Langley, 1993, or any other version of this story you have)
- *Bears, Born to Be Wild* (Ward, 2003)
- *The Adventures of Baby Bear* (Lang, 2001)
- *Grizzly Bears* (Gibbons, 2003)
- *Ice Bear: In the Steps of the Polar Bear* (Davies, 2005)
- *Bears: Polar Bears, Black Bears and Grizzly Bears* (Hodge, 1996)
- Wall chart, divided into three sections, one for each kind of bear
- Pictures of black, grizzly, and polar bears for students to color. Coloring pages can be found on the following websites:

    http://www.dep.state.ct.us/burnatr/wildlife/kids/bearcol.htm (black bear)

    http://www.first-school.ws/t/cpbeargrizzly.htm (grizzly bear)

    http://www.preschoolcoloringbook.com (polar bear)

- Wooden tongue depressors
- Additional books for independent reading

TIME: 4–5 days; 20–30-minute sessions each day to include a read-aloud and discussion

DAY 1

1. Read aloud *Goldilocks and the Three Bears* (see Figure 14 for additional trade book suggestions for this topic).
2. Explain that this is a folk tale. Ask students if there is anything in the story that tells factual information about bears (i.e., bears live in woods, walk).
3. Ask students what is not factual (i.e., bears talk, wear clothes, eat porridge, have furniture, live in house, etc.).
4. Read aloud *Bears, Born to Be Wild*, a nonfiction book that gives information about black, grizzly, and polar bears.
5. Introduce a large wall chart, divided into three sections for each kind of bear (or create a separate chart for each bear).
6. Ask students to recall information about each type of bear and write it in the appropriate column.
7. Have additional nonfiction trade books on bears available for students to read for independent reading.

FIGURE 14. Other Books to Use to Study Bears, Grades K–1

Bour, L. (1992). *Bears*. New York: Scholastic.
Cotton, J.S. (2004). *Polar Bears*. Minneapolis, MN: Lerner.
Eaton, D. (1997). *What Bear Cubs Like to Do*. New York: Sadlier-Oxford.
Fair, J. (1991). *Bears for Kids*. (L. Rogers, Illus.). Minocqua, WI: NorthWord.
Greene, C. (1993). *Reading About the Grizzly Bear*. Hillside, NJ: Enslow.
Kendell, P. (2003). *Grizzly Bears*. Austin, TX: Raintree.
Kenney, D.E. (1995). *Klondike & Snow: The Denver Zoo's Remarkable Story of Raising Two Polar Bear Cubs*. Niwot, CO: Roberts Rinehart.
Klingel, C., & Noyed, R.B. (2002). *Grizzly Bears*. Chanhassen, MN: The Child's World.
Lind, A. (1994). *Black Bear Cub*. (K. Lee, Illus.). Norwalk, CT: Soundprints.
Miller, D.S. (1997). *A Polar Bear Journey*. (J. Van Zyle, Illus.). New York: Little, Brown.

DAY 2

1. Refer to chart from previous day's lesson and ask students to recall information about each bear. Record any additional information students may have gained from independent reading.

2. Read aloud *The Adventures of Baby Bear*, a nonfiction account of the early life of two black bear cubs.

3. Ask students for additional information to record on the chart for the black bear.

4. Distribute copies of the black bear coloring sheet, and ask students to color it, cut it out, and attach it to a tongue depressor. Although they can be other colors, have students color it black to avoid confusion. These will be used on Day 5 for the Bear Facts game.

DAY 3

1. Review chart from previous day's lessons and ask students to add or revise any additional information.

2. Read aloud *Grizzly Bears*, a nonfiction book with facts about grizzly bears.

3. Ask students to give additional information to record on the chart for the grizzly bear.

4. Distribute copies of the grizzly bear coloring sheet for students to color, cut out, and attach to a tongue depressor. Ask them to color the grizzly bear brown.

DAY 4

1. Review chart from previous day's lesson and ask students to add or revise any additional information.

2. Read aloud *Ice Bear! In the Steps of the Polar Bear*. This is a book that is generally categorized as nonfiction yet written from the perspective of a fictional Inuit speaker.

3. Ask students for additional information to be recorded on the chart for the polar bear.

4. Distribute copies of the polar bear coloring sheet to cut out, and attach to a tongue depressor. (Note: It may be easier to simply cut out the polar bear from

white paper than to color it, though students may enjoy coloring facial features on the bear.)

DAY 5

1. Review chart from previous day's lesson and ask students to add or revise any additional information.
2. Read aloud *Bears: Polar Bears, Black Bears and Grizzly Bears*, a clearly written look at three North American bears.
3. Ask students for additional information to be added to the chart.
4. Play the Bear Facts game (see Figure 15). Students will need their colored bears on tongue depressors. When you read a fact, they should hold up the appropriate bear(s). If there are disputes, consult the chart for correct information. To vary this game, call on individual students or groups of students to answer each fact.

FIGURE 15. Bear Facts Game

Read each statement, and ask students to hold up the picture of the bear(s) that the fact describes. Appropriate answers appear in parenthesis.

This is the largest bear. It can weigh up to 1500 pounds. (Polar)
This bear has a large, muscular hump on its shoulders. (Grizzly)
This bear can weigh up to 500 pounds. (Black)
This bear is also called the Brown or Kodiak bear. (Grizzly)
These bears can be black, brown, or occasionally blonde. (Black and Grizzly)
This bear lives in the U.S., Canada, Russia, Greenland, and Norway. (Polar)
This bear is the smallest of the three. (Black)
This is the only true hibernator among bears. (Grizzly)
These bears eat both vegetation and animals. (Black and Grizzly)
The tips of this bear's fur are lighter in color. (Grizzly)
Each hair of this bear's fur are actually a clear, hollow tube. (Polar)
This bear can be found in North America, including Florida and Mexico. (Black)
These bears can climb trees. (Black & Grizzly)
Only the pregnant females of this type of bear hibernate. (Polar)
This bear prefers to eat nuts, fruit, insects, and greens. (Black)
This bear only eats meat. (Polar)
This bear has longer claws than other bears. (Grizzly)
This bear is very unlikely to attack humans, even in defense of cubs. (Black)

VARIATIONS

• Include pandas and koalas, emphasizing that the koala is actually a marsupial, rather than a bear.

• Use this lesson format to study toads and frogs.

ASSESSMENT

Students should hold up the correct bear while playing the Bear Facts game. Depending on students' abilities, have them dictate or write a few sentences and illustrate their favorite fact(s) about the black bear, grizzly bear, or polar bear. Students should provide a different and correct fact about each type of bear. The illustrations should show the characteristics of each bear.

Teaching About Butterflies (Grades 2–3)

OBJECTIVE: Students will observe and understand the complete metamorphosis in the butterfly and compare it to other insects. Students will understand that insects need air, water, food, and space (NSTA Standard 4).

INSTRUCTIONAL MATERIALS

• *Butterfly House* (Bunting, 1999)

• *Waiting for Wings* (Ehlert, 2001)

• *Becoming Butterflies* (Rockwell, 2004)

• Butterfly cage (A cage can be purchased, or it can be made with two end trays and four dowels and a net bag pulled over it. The net bag allows access to the interior once the cage is assembled.)

• Butterfly pupae (These can be purchased from a biological supply house. Your district science coordinator or local Department of Agriculture agent can provide sources.)

• Fresh leaves (For instance, painted lady butterflies feed on the mallow weed; for other types, you will need to find out what kind of plant works best for the type of butterfly pupae you have purchased.)

• K-W-L chart (You can create one copy for wall and/or copies for each individual student.)

- Student learning log for each student (The learning log can be spiral bound and used for various lessons.)
- Butterfly Life Cycle chart (see Figure 16)
- Small vial for sugar water
- Sugar
- Paper towel
- Red or orange paper flower

TIME: Because the average butterfly life cycle is over 30 days, this lesson will take place over a period of several weeks. Observations, activities, and assessment should occur at each stage (larva, pupa, adult). Each class period should be 30–45 minutes to allow for a read-aloud, discussion, and observation as well as recording observations and independent reading.

DAYS 1–18: INTRODUCTION & PUPA STAGE

1. Ask students what they know about caterpillars and butterflies. Record on a K-W-L chart in the "What I Know" and "What I Want to Learn" columns.

FIGURE 16. Butterfly Life Cycles Chart

Stage	Characteristic	Behavior
Larva	Bristles Segments	Eats leaves Molts Spins silk Hides in leaves
Pupa	Chrysalis	Sheds skin one last time Wiggles
Adult	Head Thorax Abdomen Antennae	Flies Sips nectar Lays eggs Migrates

2. Read aloud *Butterfly House* (see Figure 17 for additional trade book suggestions for this topic). In this story, grandfather helps a little girl make a butterfly house to keep a rescued caterpillar safe. Although this is fiction, there is factual information about the life cycle of butterflies.

3. Discuss and record information from the story on the K-W-L chart.

4. Explain that the class will observe larvae, which will then transform to pupae before they emerge as adult butterflies. This is a good time to consult your science textbook, if you have one, or one of the books listed in Figure 17 to make sure students get correct information.

5. Start a life-cycle vocabulary chart like the one Figure 16 (on wall or on individual student lists). Be sure to include words such as *egg*, *larva*, *pupa*, *adult*, *metamorphosis*, and *chrysalis*. Add to chart throughout the lesson.

6. Introduce the larvae in the container. (They usually arrive in a container of food and can stay in the container throughout their entire larval stage.)

7. Have students observe the larvae and record and date an entry in their student learning logs. Entries should include quantity, size, color, shape, structure, and behavior.

8. Make several books on butterflies available for students to read for further information (see additional titles in Figure 17 and in the annotated bibliography at the end of this chapter for title ideas). Encourage students to add information to their K-W-L chart in the "What I Learned" column as they read.

FIGURE 17. Other Books to Use to Study Butterflies, Grades 2–3

Allen, J. (2000). *Are You a Butterfly?* (T. Humphries, Illus.). New York: Kingfisher.

Gibbons, G. (1989). *Monarch Butterfly*. New York: Holiday House.

Hamilton, K. (1997). *The Butterfly Book: A Kid's Guide to Attracting, Raising, and Keeping Butterflies*. Santa Fe, NM: John Muir.

Heiligman, D. (1996). *From Caterpillar to Butterfly*. (B. Weissman, Illus.). New York: HarperCollins

Legg, G. (1998). *Lifecycles: From Caterpillar to Butterfly*. (C. Scrace, Illus.). Danbury, CT: Franklin Watts.

Lerner, C. (2002). *Butterflies in the Garden*. New York: HarperCollins.

Ryder, J. (1989). *Where Butterflies Grow*. (L. Cherry, Illus.). New York: Lodestar.

Sandved, K.B. (1996). *The Butterfly Alphabet*. New York: Scholastic.

Wallace, K. (2000). *Born to Be a Butterfly*. London: Dorling Kindersley.

Zemlicka, S. (2003). *From Egg to Butterfly*. (S. Knudsen, Illus.). Minneapolis, MN: Lerner.

9. During the next few weeks (12–18 days) make sure students have an opportunity to observe and record data in their journals daily, especially noting change. You may want to assign a small of group of students to observe and record for a few days. Be sure that there is time allotted every two or three for a report to be given to the class.

ASSESSMENT OF DAYS 1–18

- Student learning log entries should include notes about growth, molts and droppings, and random silk spinning in the container. Students should note that when ready to pupate, the larvae moved to the top of the container and hang upside down.
- Have students make a comparison chart noting the similarities and differences between butterfly larvae and other insect larvae.

DAYS 19–24: PUPA STAGE

1. Read aloud *Waiting for Wings*, a colorful celebration of butterfly metamorphism.
2. Ask students what they learned about the butterfly larvae during their observations and reading. Record on the K-W-L chart in the "What I Learned" column. Be sure to include any information they still want to learn in the "What I Want to Learn" column.
3. Show students the butterfly cage and explain how the net fabric will allow access to the cage.
4. Place a small amount of leaves in a cup of water inside the cage. Explain that this is food and also a place for females to lay eggs.
5. Explain that the larvae have all pupated and are now in a chrysalis hanging from the paper at the top of the original container. Carefully remove the paper and tape it to the top of the butterfly cage, before securing the netting.
6. Have students record this and any other new information in their learning logs, add it to the K-W-L chart, and add any new words to the life-cycle vocabulary chart.
7. Ask students to predict what will happen next and how long it might take. This information might be recorded in their learning logs or on the board to check later.
8. Again, assign small groups or individual students to observe the butterfly cage daily and report on changes to the class.

ASSESSMENT OF DAYS 19–24

Students should be able to demonstrate an understanding of the differences and similarities of butterfly pupae and those of other insects studied.

DAYS 25–30: ADULT STAGE

1. Read aloud *Becoming Butterflies*, a story about a classroom observing the metamorphism of caterpillars into butterflies.

2. Ask students to add any new information to the K-W-L chart and the life-cycle vocabulary chart.

3. Encourage discussion on the changes in the butterfly cage observed over the past week. Some students might read from their learning logs.

4. Ask students what butterflies eat (nectar).

5. Make a feeding station by filling a small vial with sugar water (1 tsp. sugar to 1/2 cup water). Make a hole in the cap of the vial. Roll up a 3" square of paper towel and insert it through the hole in the cap, making a wick. Attach a red or orange paper flower to the cap to attract the butterflies and give them a place to land.

6. Encourage students to observe the characteristics of the butterflies and record these in their learning logs.

7. Keep fresh leaves and water in the cage. The female butterflies should start laying eggs in about a week.

8. Explain that it is natural for the butterflies to die after about 3 weeks. Make sure students know that this is not a result of poor care or captivity.

ASSESSMENT OF DAYS 25–30

- Students should be able to fill in correct information in the Butterfly Life Cycle Chart (see Figure 16 on page 76). Depending on the ability of students, the form can be blank or you can provide the words at the bottom of the page to use to complete the chart.

- For younger or struggling students, reproduce diagrams or illustrations of the butterfly life cycle and have students cut them out and paste them in the correct sequence.

- Learning logs should describe the egg, larva, pupa, and adult stages.

VARIATION

Students can make a butterfly timeline, numbering squares from 1 to however many days it took for the adult stage to occur. Pictures or drawings of each observed change can be placed in the appropriate numbered square.

Teaching About Extreme Weather (Grades 4–5)

OBJECTIVE: Students will understand the effects of severe weather and the natural disasters they sometimes cause (NSTA Standard 5).

INSTRUCTIONAL MATERIALS

- *Twister* (Beard, 1999)
- *Hurricane Hunters! Riders on the Storm* (Demarest, 2006)
- *Monsoon* (Krishneswami, 2003)
- Map of the world to record where recent weather events have occurred. (One large map and individual small copies for students.) A good source for maps is http://www.nationalgeographic.com/xpeditions/atlas.
- Copies of Weather Research Questions for each student (see Figure 18)

FIGURE 18. Weather Research Questions

Using books, encyclopedias, and/or the Internet, each group must include information about their extreme weather topic using the following questions as guidelines:

- What part of the world experiences this type of weather? (Student must point out on the world map during presentation.)
- How does it begin?
- How long does it usually last?
- Is there any type of warning? If so, how long is there between the warning and the event?
- How do people protect themselves and their homes and property?
- What usually happens at the end of the storm?
- What kind of damage can occur (to crops, industry, animals, buildings, roads, etc.)?
- Is there more than one name for the storm (for example, hurricane and typhoon)?
- Give at least one historical example of this kind of weather event and its effect.

• Fact Pyramid (see Figure 13 on page 68) or other organizational chart for each student

TIME: This lesson will take at least five days, perhaps even a few weeks. Ample time must be given for groups to work together, although individuals will be doing some of the research on their own.

DAY 1

1. Ask students what they know about tornadoes. Distribute a Fact Pyramid to each student and have them label it "Tornadoes," explaining that they will fill it out after hearing and reading about tornadoes.

2. Read aloud *Twister* (see Figure 19 for additional trade book suggestions for this topic), a fictional story based on the author's experience as a young child during a tornado.

3. Have students locate the area of the tornado in the story on the map.

4. Allow time for students to add information to the Fact Pyramid and remind them to keep it in their notebook or folder.

5. Ask students to name other types of violent storms (hurricane, monsoon, blizzard, etc.). Record on a chart or transparency.

6. Explain that they will be reading and researching about extreme weather and storms. (Be sure to have enough books available so that each student has access to at least one. Provide books with varying readability levels to accommodate both competent and struggling readers.) Briefly show students the books you have gathered for independent reading and ask them to think about what type of weather they would like to explore. Allow time for students to view the books.

7. Divide the class into groups based on the type of storm chosen by each student. It is advisable to allow students a choice, but you may have to exert some influence so that a variety of storms are covered. If several students choose the same topic, there could be more than one group for that topic, providing there are enough books available. Each group of four or five students will be responsible for researching and presenting an oral report on tornadoes, hurricanes, blizzards, floods, lightning, or drought.

FIGURE 19. Other Books to Use to Study Extreme Weather, Grades 4–5

Nonfiction

Berger, M., & Berger, G. (2000). *Do Tornadoes Really Twist? Questions and Answers About Tornadoes and Hurricanes.* (H. Bond, Illus.). New York: Scholastic.

Berger, M., & Berger, G. (2004). *Hurricanes Have Eyes But Can't See: And Other Amazing Facts About Wild Weather.* New York: Scholastic.

Bramwell, M. (1987). *Weather.* London: Franklin Watts.

Ceban, B.J. (2005). *Floods and Mudslides: Disaster & Survival.* Berkeley Heights, NJ: Enslow.

Challoner, J. (2000). *Hurricane & Tornado.* London: Dorling Kindersley.

Chambers, C. (2001). *Drought.* Chicago: Heinemann Library.

Editors of *Time For Kids.* (2006). *Storms!* New York: HarperCollins.

Grace, C.O. (2004). *Forces of Nature: The Awesome Power of Volcanoes, Earthquakes, and Tornadoes.* Washington, DC: National Geographic Society.

Graf, M. (1998). *Lightning! And Thunderstorms.* New York: Simon Spotlight.

Harris, C. (2005). *Wild Weather.* (W. Faidley, Illus.). London: Kingfisher.

Hopping, L.J. (2003). *Tornadoes!* (J. Wheeler, Illus.). New York: Cartwheel.

Jennings, T. (2000). *Floods and Tidal Waves.* London: Belitha.

Keller, E. (1999). *Floods!* (Weather Channel). New York: Simon Spotlight.

Kramer, S.P. (1992). *Lightning.* (W. Faidley, Illus.). Minneapolis, MN: Carolrhoda.

Lauber, P. (1996). *Hurricanes: Earth's Mightiest Storms.* New York: Scholastic.

London, J. (1998). *Hurricane!* (H. Sorensen, Illus.). New York: HarperCollins.

Mann's Miracles. (2005). *When the Hurricane Blew.* Gulf Breeze, FL: Clear Horizon.

Morris, A. (2005). *Tsunami: Helping Each Other.* (H. Larson, Illus.). Minneapolis, MN: Lerner.

Murphy, J. (2000). *Blizzard! The Storm That Changed America.* New York: Scholastic.

Osborne, W., & Osborne, M.P. (2003). *Twisters and Other Terrible Storms.* New York: Random House.

Pitt, S. (2004). *Rain Tonight: A Story of Hurricane Hazel.* (H. Collins, Illus.). Toronto, ON: Tundra.

Rosado, M. (1999). *Blizzards! And Ice Storms.* New York: Simon Spotlight.

Rupp, R. (2003). *Weather!* North Adams, MA: Storey.

Simon, S. (1989). *Storms.* New York: William Morrow.

Stewart, G. (2005). *Catastrophe in Southern Asia: The Tsunami of 2004.* Farmington Hills, MI: Lucent.

Thomas, R. (2005). *Eye of the Storm: A Book About Hurricanes.* (D. Shea, Illus.). Minneapolis, MN: Picture Window.

Thompson, L. (2000). *Tornadoes.* New York: Children's Press.

Wasserman, R. (Ed.). (2003). *Extraordinary Wild Weather.* New York: Scholastic.

Fiction

Capeci, A. (2002). *Electric Storm.* (H. Gangloff, Illus.). New York: Scholastic.

Flaherty, M. (2004). *The Great Saint Patrick's Day Flood.* Pittsburgh, PA: Local History Co.

George, J.C. (1986). *One Day in the Prairie.* (B. Marstall, Illus.). New York: Crowell.

(continued)

FIGURE 19. Other Books to Use to Study Extreme Weather, Grades 4–5
(continued)

Gross, V.T. (1993). *The Day It Rained Forever: A Story of the Johnstown Flood*. (R. Himler, Illus.). New York: Viking.

Janke, K. (2002). *Survival in the Storm: The Dust Bowl Diary of Grace Edwards, Dalhart, Texas, 1935*. New York: Scholastic.

Lake, J. (2003). *Galveston's Summer of the Storm*. Fort Worth: Texas Christian University Press.

Naylor, P.R. (2002). *Blizzard's Wake*. New York: Atheneum.

Ruckman, I. (1984). *Night of the Twisters*. New York: Crowell.

Sanders, S. (1998). *Hurricane Rescue*. New York: Avon.

8. Distribute copies of Weather Research Questions to each student. Allow time for questions and discussion.

9. Each group will give a presentation to the class, with each member participating in some way. Explain that every group must include at least one visual aid (map, model, timeline) and a demonstration. Demonstrations might include a tsunami made in a plastic bottle, a readers theatre presentation explaining a monsoon, or a model showing the destruction caused by a violent storm.

10. Allow time for students to meet in groups. Remind them that they must have a plan, and assign tasks to each member of the group.

DAY 2

1. Distribute a new Fact Pyramid for "Hurricanes."

2. Read aloud *Hurricane Hunters! Riders on the Storm*, which explains the work of the large, converted cargo planes that fly into violent storms to collect weather data.

3. Have students add information to their Fact Pyramid.

4. Have students locate the area(s) described in the book on a map, then discuss these areas. (Are they near, far away from, or similar to where students live? Are there any areas listed that surprise students?) This is also a good opportunity to tie in social studies by simultaneously studying these areas.

5. Allow time for groups to meet to discuss their presentations and work on their projects.

DAY 3

1. Distribute a new Fact Pyramid for "Monsoons."

2. Read aloud *Monsoon*, a fictional picture book about a family awaiting the monsoon season.

3. Have students add information to their Fact Pyramid.

4. Have students locate the area of the monsoon on the map, then discuss this region (see #4 in Day 2).

5. Allow time for groups to meet to discuss their presentations and work on their projects.

DAY 4 (and subsequent days, as determined by needs of class)

1. Read aloud a selection about a type of extreme weather each day, following the above procedures. A variation is to select a class read-aloud novel about one of the storms.

2. As students work in groups, circulate and monitor as necessary. You may want to ask questions about things that you think might need clarification.

VARIATIONS

• Have students color portions of the world map using a different color for each type of weather event.

• You could assign written reports, instead of or in addition to the oral presentations.

ASSESSMENTS

• Group presentations should address all of the Weather Research Questions. As each group is presenting, the other students should be adding information to their Fact Pyramids. (New Fact Pyramids should be distributed for each new weather event covered.)

• Because the entire class will have heard all presentations, you may want to include a written quiz or test about the information on each weather event to assess their understanding. Students should use their completed Fact Pyramids as a study guide.

Conclusion

The use of trade books, both fiction and nonfiction, can enhance science learning. Colorful, appealing books with accurate content can be used to explain and elaborate many scientific concepts. Books should be used in conjunction with hands-on investigation and texts. Using trade books with science content for reading and writing activities provides integration of science and the language arts. Studying creatures' life cycles and habitats—and studying natural disasters, their effects, and the areas affected—provides a tie-in to many social studies lessons. By carefully choosing trade books for science, teachers can show students how many subjects and events are interrelated, thus providing a more comprehensive curriculum.

ANNOTATED BIBLIOGRAPHY—SCIENCE

The following titles are organized by the Science Content Standards (NSTA, 1996), although many of these books are applicable to more than one area.

Unifying Concepts and Processes

Arnosky, Jim. (2000). *Wild and Swampy*. New York: HarperCollins.

> Detailed paintings of a mangrove swamp create an account of life webbing through unique relationships. The poetic text inspires both respect and reverence for nature. (Grades 2–5)

Collard, Sneed B., III. (2000). *The Forest in the Clouds*. (Michael Rothman, Illus.). Watertown, MA: Charlesbridge.

> Through a look at a rain forest in the mountains of Costa Rica, Collard focuses on the delicate balance of the flora and fauna in this ecosystem. A bibliography, websites, maps, and a glossary are included, as well as suggestions about what can be done to protect the forest. (Grades 2–4)

George, Lindsey Barrett. (1999). *Around the World: Who's Been Here?* New York: Greenwillow.

> A teacher circles the globe to search for wildlife in its natural habitat. Her letters and pictures to her students encourage the reader to examine the pictures and discover "Who's Been Here?" Detailed information about the animals is at the end. (Grades 1–4)

Glaser, Linda. (2000). *Our Big Home: An Earth Poem*. (Elisa Kleven, Illus.). Brookfield, CT: Millbrook.

> A rhyming celebration of our commonalities and the interconnectedness of all living things, this picture book emphasizes that sun, rain, air, animals, and people are all part of the Earth, our big home. (Grades K–2)

Goodman, Susan E. (2001). *Seeds, Stems, and Stamens: The Ways Plants Fit Into Their World*. (Michael J. Doolittle, Illus.). Brookfield, CT: Millbrook.

> Illustrations and text describe plant adaptations: how they fit into the environment; getting sun, water, and food; inherent defenses; and propagating. Inquiry pages will inspire readers to investigate further. (Grades 3–5)

Hiscock, Bruce. (2001). *Coyote and Badger: Desert Hunters of the Southwest*. Honesdale, PA: Boyds Mills Press.

> Although a fictional account, the instinctive predatory nature of the coyote and badger is accurately described, including their cooperative relationship that allows them to hunt successfully. (Grades 2–4)

Horowitz, Ruth. (2000). *Crab Moon*. (Kate Kiesler, Illus.). Cambridge, MA: Candlewick.

> In this fictional picture book, Daniel and his mother observe the seasonal spawning of horseshoe crabs during the full moon. A page of facts about *limulus* (horseshoe crabs) is included as well as information about the preservation of the species. (Grades K–2)

Swinburne, Stephen R. (1999). *Once a Wolf: How Wildlife Biologists Fought to Bring Back the Gray Wolf*. (Jim Brandenburg, Illus.). Boston: Houghton Mifflin.

> A history of the relationship between wolves and humans, the value of wolves to the ecosystem, and the conservation effort to reintroduce wolves to the American landscape are all described in this book for older students. Color photographs, maps, a bibliography, websites, and an index are included. (Grade 5)

Science as Inquiry

Bradley, Kimberly Brubaker. (2001). *Pop! A Book About Bubbles*. (Margaret Miller, Illus.). New York: HarperCollins.

How bubbles are made, why they are always round, and why they pop are explained through simple text and photographs in this picture book. Directions for making a bubble solution and bubble experiments are also included. (Grades K–1)

Davies, Jacqueline. (2004). *The Boy Who Drew Birds: A Story of John James Audubon.* (Melissa Sweet, Illus.). Boston: Houghton Mifflin.

Historical information is combined with the description of the process a naturalist goes through to investigate a mystery of nature in this book about Audubon's interest in migrating birds. (Grades 2–4)

Goodman, Susan E. (2001). *Claws, Coats and Camouflage: The Ways Animals Fit Into Their World.* (Michael J. Doolittle, Illus.). Brookfield, CT: Millbrook.

Adaptation is grouped into four broad categories (Fitting In, Staying Safe, Getting Food, and Making a New Generation) in this book. Photographs and text pose questions that promote careful observation, critical analysis, and more inquiry. (Grades 4–5)

Hirschfeld, Robert. (1995). *The Kids' Science Book: Creative Experiences for Hands-On Fun.* (Nancy White, Illus.). Charlotte, VT: Williamson.

Experiments, games, and activities for science, which includes information about making and recording observations, are included in this book. (Grades 2–4)

Hoban, Tana. (1995). *Animal, Vegetable, or Mineral?* New York: Greenwillow.

Colorful photographs invite the reader to categorize the subject into the animal, plant, or mineral kingdom. Since there is no text, this book requires further research or investigation on the part of the reader. (Grades K–5)

Hurst, Carol Otis. (2001). *Rocks in His Head.* (James Stevenson, Illus.). New York: Greenwillow.

Hurst tells the story of her father, who had a fascination for rocks from an early age. His determination and study led to a career as the director of a science museum. Information about different types of rocks is included. (Grades 2–4)

Logan, Claudia. (2002). *The 5,000-Year-Old Puzzle: Solving a Mystery of Ancient Egypt*. (Melissa Sweet, Illus.). New York: Farrar, Straus and Giroux.

> Told in diary form, this fictionalized account of a young boy in Egypt tells of the actual discovery and excavation of a secret tomb in Egypt in 1925. Sidebars and historical fact sheets accompany this adventure/mystery. (Grades 3–5)

Pratt-Serafini, Kristin Joy. (2001). *Salamander Rain: A Lake & Pond Journal*. Nevada City, CA: Dawn.

> This book is a lesson in how keen observations can lead to a deeper understanding and appreciation in a temperate pond community. Journal notes, maps, and news articles provide a model for student journals. (Grades 2–5)

Rhatigan, Joe, & Newcomb, Rain. (2003). *Out-of-This-World Astronomy: 50 Amazing Activities & Projects*. New York: Lark.

> Facts, clear explanations, and easy-to-do activities for beginning sky watchers are presented through charts, diagrams, and photographs, as well as a glossary, index, and websites. (Grade 5)

Rockwell, Anne. (2001). *Bugs Are Insects*. (Steve Jenkins, Illus.). New York: HarperCollins.

> Physical characterizations of insects, their habitats, and their means for getting food are described through text and illustrations in this picture book. The distinction between insects and animals, as well as among different insects such as bugs and beetles, is also discussed. (Grades K–2)

Romanek, Trudee. (2001). *The Technology Book for Girls and Other Advanced Beings*. (Pat Cupples, Illus.). Toronto, ON: Kids Can Press.

> This book shows the relevance of science and technology while trying to entice girls to explore science. Explanations are accompanied by drawings, diagrams, photographs, activities, and ideas for projects. A bibliography and index are also included. (Grades 3–5)

Webb, Sophie. (2000). *My Season With Penguins: An Antarctic Journal*. Boston: Houghton Mifflin.

Journal entries and watercolor paintings describe the author's two-month stay in Antarctica studying Adelie penguins. This is a personal view of scientists at work, explained through the unique webs and relationships of Antarctic animals. A glossary is included. (Grades 3–5)

Physical Science

Bang, Molly. (2004). *My Light*. New York: Blue Sky.

This picture book shows the many ways we obtain energy from the sun's light: weather cycle, dams, turbines, electricity, windmills, fossil fuels, and solar cells. (Grades 1–3)

Berger, Melvin. (1989). *Switch On, Switch Off*. (Carolyn Croll, Illus.). New York: HarperCollins.

Readers find out how electricity is produced and transmitted and how generators, light bulbs, and electrical plugs work. Directions are also included to produce an electric current using wire, a bar magnet, and a compass. (Grades K–3)

Bradley, Kimberly Brubaker. (2005). *Forces Make Things Move*. (Paul Meisel, Illus.). New York: HarperCollins.

Simple language and humorous illustrations explain force, reaction, inertia, friction, and gravity. (Grades 1–3)

Cobb, Vicki. (2004). *I Fall Down*. (Julia Gorton, Illus.). New York: HarperCollins.

This basic introduction to gravity, and its relationship to weight, includes playful experiments and illustrations. (Grades K–1)

Glover, David. (2001). *Batteries, Bulbs, and Wires*. New York: Kingfisher.

This book discusses magnetism and electricity and explains how they are connected. Each concept introduced has at least one activity provided, linking to a scientific principle. (Grades 3–5)

Graham, Joan Bransfield. (1999). *Flicker Flash*. (Nancy Davis, Illus.). Boston: Houghton Mifflin.

Vivid illustrations accompany 23 concrete poems about the many shapes and forms of light. Candles, fireflies, lighthouses, and fireworks are among the light sources featured. This book is an excellent source for integrating science, art, and literature. (Grades K–3)

Parker, Steve. (2002). *Fantastic Facts: Magnets*. London: Southwater.

> Different kinds of magnets and their uses are featured, as well as activities and experiments. (Grades 3–5)

Pipe, Jim. (2002). *What Does a Wheel Do? Projects About Rolling and Sliding*. (Jo Moore, Illus.). Brookfield, CT: Copper Beech.

> Questions about how and why things move are answered by simple investigations and explanations of "Why It Works." Steps and materials are outlined for projects about rolling and sliding. (Grades K–2)

Stillinger, Doug. (2003). *Battery Science: Make Widgets That Work and Gadgets That Go*. Palo Alto, CA: Klutz.

> This fun book tells about electricity and how circuits work. Projects, from snow machines to lie detectors, have complete directions. (Grades 4–5)

Swinburne, Stephen R. (1999). *Guess Whose Shadow?* New York: Scholastic.

> The foreword briefly explains shadows and how they are made, as does the text and photographs. The last part of the book is a guessing game. The shadow is shown and the reader must guess whose shadow it is and turn the page to see the answer. (Grades K–2)

Walker, Sally M. (2006). *Electricity*. (Andy King, Illus.). Minneapolis, MN: Lerner.

> Through explanation, examples, and experiments, readers learn about different kinds of electricity, including static electricity, currents, and circuits. Experiments require common things usually found in the home, and a safety warning is given. (Grades 3–5)

Zoehfeld, Kathleen Weidner. (1998). *What Is the World Made Of? All About Solids, Liquids, and Gases*. (Paul Meisel, Illus.). New York: HarperCollins

> The three states of matter are explained in this picture book. Examples, attributes, and simple activities are also provided. (Grades K–2)

Life Science

Collard, Sneed B., III. (2002). *Beaks!* (Robin Brickman, Illus.). Watertown, MA: Charlesbridge.

> Simple text tells all about beaks of various birds and how they are used for eating, hunting, and gathering food. The book also includes a quiz. (Grades K–3)

Micucci, Charles. (1997). *The Life and Times of the Peanut*. Boston: Houghton Mifflin.

> Information includes where the peanut was first grown, what it has been used for, and how it has traveled around the world. This picture book also has a table of contents, color illustrations, and graphs. (Grades 2–4)

Pallotta, Jerry. (1996). *The Freshwater Alphabet Book*. (David Biedrzycki, Illus.). Watertown, MA: Charlesbridge.

> Each letter of the alphabet is represented by a fish in this book of freshwater biology. (Grades 1–3)

Pomeroy, Diana. (1997). *Wildflower ABC*. San Diego, CA: Harcourt.

> Wildflowers represent each letter of the alphabet. Younger readers will enjoy the acrylic potato print illustrations; older readers will appreciate the additional information on each flower at the end of the book. (Grades K–4)

Powell, Consie. (1995). *A Bold Carnivore: An Alphabet of Predators*. Niwot, CO: Roberts Rinehart.

> A predator represents each letter of the alphabet, accompanied by a brief statement explaining where it lives, how it hunts, and what it preys on. The illustrations offer clues about other prey. More information about each predator and its prey is given in the glossary. (Grades 2–5)

Rathmell, Donna. (2005). *Carolina's Story: Sea Turtles Get Sick Too!* (Barbara J. Bergwerf, Illus.). Mt. Pleasant, SC: Sylvan Dell.

> Photographs tell the story of Carolina, a critically ill loggerhead sea turtle, as she is nursed back to health at the Sea Turtle Hospital at the South Carolina Aquarium. A supplement at the end of the book includes turtle trivia, conservation issues, math games, and a craft. (Grades 1–3)

Ruurs, Margriet. (2003). *Wild Babies*. (Andrew Kiss, Illus.). Toronto, ON: Tundra.

> A simple statement and a sketch are accompanied by a photograph of baby animals featured. Children who look closely will find animals hiding and a clue about the animal on the next page. Additional information about each animal is included at the end of the book, as well as a listing of baby, male, female, and group names for each. (Grades K–2)

Sill, Cathryn. (2006). *About Marsupials: A Guide for Children*. (John Sill, Illus.). Atlanta, GA: Peachtree.

> Easy-to-understand language and illustrations inform readers about marsupials, how they look, how they move, what they eat, and where they live. This "About" book series also features guides about amphibians, arachnids, birds, crustaceans, fish, insects, mammals, mollusks, and reptiles. (Grades K–2)

Simon, Seymour. (2003). *Eyes and Ears*. New York: HarperCollins.

> The first part of this book is devoted to eyes and how they operate. The second is about the three parts of the ear. Clear text, photographs of eye and ear parts, and diagrams help clarify the information presented. (Grades 4–5)

Stewart, Melissa. (2003). *Maggots, Grubs, and More: The Secret Lives of Young Insects*. Brookfield, CT: Millbrook.

> Nymphs and larvae are explained, as well as the life cycles of a variety of insects through informative text and large, close-up photographs. Features of this book also include a glossary, an index, and suggestions for further reading. (Grades 4–5)

Urbigkit, Cat. (2005). *Brave Dogs, Gentle Dogs: How They Guard Sheep*. Honesdale, PA: Boyds Mills Press.

> Photographs enhance the text in this picture book about dogs that guard sheep. Complicated concepts such as socialization and bonding are clearly defined. (Grades K–2)

Earth and Space Science

Aillaud, Cindy Lou. (2005). *Recess at 20 Below*. Anchorage, AK: Alaska Northwest.

> Color photographs accompany text that tells of the impact of winter weather on attending school in the far North. (Grades K–2)

Asch, Frank. (1995). *Water*. San Diego, CA: Harcourt.

> Water is rain, dew, ice, and snow. This book is a simple introduction to one of the earth's most valuable resources. (Grades K–1)

Branley, Franklin M. (1990). *Earthquakes*. (Richard Rosenblum, Illus.). New York: HarperCollins.

> This Let's-Read-and-Find-Out series book explains the causes of earthquakes, how scientists predict and measure them, and how to protect yourself during one. (Grades K–2)

Branley, Franklin M. (1998). *Floating in Space*. (True Kelley, Illus.). New York: HarperCollins.

> Weightlessness, food, exercise, and work of astronauts in space are explained in this picture book. (Grades K–2)

Collard, Sneed B., III. (1998). *Our Wet World*. (James M. Needham, Illus.). Watertown, MA: Charlesbridge.

> Thirteen different aquatic ecosystems are featured in this colorful picture book. A world map and glossary are also included. (Grades 2–4)

Eagen, Rachel. (2005). *Flood and Monsoon Alert!* New York: Crabtree.

> Floods and monsoons are explained in this picture book, including warning signs and what to do in case of flood. A glossary, an index, and instructions for making a barometer are also included. (Grades 3–5)

Gibbons, Gail. (1995). *The Reasons for Seasons*. New York: Holiday House.

> Earth and its relationships to the sun are explained for each season. Diagrams and illustrations of each season are included. (Grades 1–3)

Gibbons, Gail. (1997). *The Moon Book*. New York: Scholastic.

> Phases of the moon, solar and lunar eclipses, and moon landings are explained in this picture book with diagrams and captions. The section at the end includes moon milestones, moon legends and stories, and more moon facts. (Grades 1–3)

Hilliard, Richard. (2005). *Neil, Buzz, and Mike Go to the Moon*. Honesdale, PA: Boyds Mills Press.

> Informative sidebars complement this picture book account of Apollo 11 and the three men who made the historic flight to the moon. (Grades K–4)

Kampion, Drew. (2005) *Waves: From Surfing to Tsunami*. Salt Lake City, UT: Gibbs Smith.

> Photographs, drawings, and diagrams accompany this study of wave action, lunar and wind influence, and the anatomy of a wave. (Grades 4–5)

O'Meara, Donna. (2005). *Into the Volcano*. Toronto, ON: Kids Can Press.

> This book of photographs and facts about volcanoes all over the world includes the types of volcanoes, lava, and explosions, as well as diagrams, a table of contents, a glossary, and an index. (Grades 4–5)

Paulauski, Patrick. (2005). *W Is for Wind*. (Melanie Rose, Illus.). Chelsea, MI: Sleeping Bear Press.

> This alphabet book explains weather terms (atmosphere, barometer, cloud). Additional, detailed information is included as an inset on each page, making it suitable for all ages. (Grades K–5)

Peddicord, Jane Ann. (2005). *Night Wonders*. Watertown, MA: Charlesbridge.

> Poetry about the galaxy is accompanied by illustrations, photographs, and factual information. A glossary and website addresses for additional information are included. (Grades K–3)

Simon, Seymour. (2003). *Hurricanes*. New York: HarperCollins.

> One of nature's most powerful forces is explained through dramatic photographs and well-organized text. Also included are facts about recent hurricanes and safety tips. (Grades 3–5)

Wick, Walter. (1997). *A Drop of Water*. New York: Scholastic.

> Stop-action photography and magnification allow the reader to examine a drop of water in its many transformations. Evaporation, condensation, capillary attraction, and surface tension are explained. (Grades 3–5)

Science and Technology

Editors of *YES Mag*. (2004). *Fantastic Feats and Failures*. Toronto, ON: Kids Can Press.

> Twenty notable highs and lows of engineering, from genius design to fatal flaws, are featured in this book. Short chapters are accompanied by photographs, and there is a table of contents, glossary, and index. (Grades 4–5)

Gibbons, Gail. (1990). *How a House Is Built*. New York: Holiday House.

> Through colorful illustrations and explicit text, Gibbons gives general information about the building process. Construction terms and workers are defined, and the appendix compares a modern frame house to simple houses of the past. (Grades K–3)

Goodman, Susan E. (2004). *Skyscraper*. (Michael J. Doolittle, Illus.). New York: Knopf.

> Facts and photographs describe the design and construction of this architectural wonder. (Grade 5)

Hampton, Wilborn. (2001). *Meltdown: A Race Against Nuclear Disaster at Three Mile Island*. Cambridge, MA: Candlewick Press.

> Human error and technical failure triggered the worst nuclear power accident in the United States. The author, a reporter, relives his hour-by-hour coverage on Three Mile Island. (Grades 4–5)

Kinmont, Ritchie. (2005). *Every Kid Needs Things That Fly!* Layton, UT: Gibbs Smith.

> Twenty amazing building projects include questions, ideas, and Internet and library search topics, with color illustrations and photographs. Directions for a hot-air balloon, parachute, UFO, water rocket, and jet pack projects are included. (Grades 4–5)

Mathews, Tom. (1999). *Always Inventing: A Photobiography of Alexander Graham Bell*. Washington, DC: National Geographic Society.

> This photobiography of the life and work of Alexander Graham Bell focuses not only on his inventions but also on his dedication to the advancement of science. (Grades 4–5)

Morris, Ann. (1992). *Tools*. (Ken Heyman, Illus.). New York: Lothrop, Lee & Shepard.

> Colorful illustrations and simple text describe tools used throughout the world and how they make life easier for everyone. (Grades K–2)

Petersen, Christine. (2004). *Wind Power*. New York: Children's Press.

> Diagrams and captions show how the wind as a natural force can be used in windmills, turbines, and wind farms. (Grades 3–5)

Snyder, Inez. (2002). *Home Tools*. New York: Children's Press.

> A young boy helps his mother clean the house and explains each tool (feather duster, vacuum, sponge, etc.) through simple text and photographs. This easy reader has a table of contents, index, section on new words, and suggestions for further information. (Grades K–1)

Vanderwarker, Peter. (2001). *The Big Dig: Reshaping an American City*. New York: Little, Brown.

> A chronicle of the building of Boston's underground expressway, the largest and most complex construction project any U.S. city has ever undertaken, this book includes photographs, maps, and illustrations. Sidebars introduce some of the men and women who are contributed to the renovation. (Grade 5)

Personal and Social Perspectives

Ehrlich, Amy. (2003). *Rachel: The Story of Rachel Carson*. (Wendell Minor, Illus.). San Diego, CA: Harcourt.

> This chapter biography, with full-page illustrations, tells of Rachel's love of nature as a small child, her work as a biologist, and the writing of *Silent Spring*. Also included are a bibliography and epilogue. (Grades 3–5)

Fleming, Denise. (1996). *Where Once There Was a Wood*. New York: Henry Holt.

> Simple text and colorful illustrations show how wildlife can be displaced if their environment is destroyed by human development. (Grades K–1)

Hyde, Margaret O., & Forsyth, Elizabeth H. (2003). *Diabetes*. Danbury, CT: Franklin Watts.

> Important topics related to the disease (history, types, causes, treatment, and research) are explained. Charts and fact boxes are included, as well as a glossary, an index, websites, and suggestions for further reading. (Grades 4–5)

Keller, Laurie. (2000). *Open Wide*. New York: Henry Holt.

> A whimsical tale, in which teeth are students in the classroom, this colorful book provides information about the structure and care of teeth and the services provided by dentists. (Grades 2–4)

Rockwell, Lizzy. (2004). *The Busy Body Book: A Kid's Guide to Fitness*. New York: Crown.

> Simple text and diagrams explain how various body systems function. Artwork shows youngsters engaged in various physical activities. (Grades K–1)

Quinn, Patricia O., & Stern, Judith M. (2001). *Putting on the Brakes: Young People's Guide to Understanding Attention Deficit Hyperactivity Disorder (ADHD)*. (Michael Chesworth, Illus.). Washington, DC: Magination.

> Short chapters, photographs, and drawings make this book appealing to children who have the disorder and those who may know someone who has it. Suggestions for managing the disorder and gaining control are practical and clear. (Grades 3–5)

Simon, Seymour. (2005). *Guts: Our Digestive System*. New York: HarperCollins.

> Simon clearly explains the role of each part of the digestive system and how it functions through colored X-rays, computer-generated pictures, and microscopic photographs. (Grades 4–5)

Stewart, Melissa. (2006). *A Place for Butterflies*. (Higgins Bond, Illus.). Atlanta, GA: Peachtree.

> The text gives basic information about the life cycle of butterflies, but sidebars contain information on human action that has harmed butterflies and ways people can protect certain butterfly populations. (Grades 1–4)

Swanson, Diane. (2001). *Burp! The Most Interesting Book You'll Ever Read About Eating*. (Rose Cowles, Illus.). Toronto, ON: Kids Can Press.

> Facts about food, eating, and functions of human body parts are explained using thoroughly researched information and anecdotes. Cartoon-like illustrations are accompanied by "try-it" activities. (Grades 3–5)

Wadsworth, Ginger. (2003). *Benjamin Banneker: Pioneering Scientist*. (Craig Orback, Illus.). Minneapolis, MN: Lerner.

> This On My Own Biography series book chronicles the life of America's first black man of science who was famous for his love of learning and his desire for an end to slavery. Banneker wrote almanacs, played a role in surveying the streets of Washington, DC, and built a clock out of wood. (Grades K–2)

Ziefert, Harriet, & Ehrlich, Fred. (2004). *You Can't Take Your Body to a Repair Shop: A Book About What Makes You Sick*. (Amanda Haley, Illus.). Maplewood, NJ: Blue Apple.

> Information about maladies that children can relate to (colds, earaches, blisters, warts, headaches, insect bites) is presented with both facts and humor. (Grades 2–4)

History and Nature of Science

Adler, David A. (1999). *A Picture Book of George Washington Carver*. (Dan Brown, Illus.). New York: Holiday House.

> This easy biography demonstrates the vastness and significance of Carver's many contributions to science. A bibliography, important dates, and a brief explanation of the peanut tariff of 1921 are included. (Grades 2–4)

Chorlton, Windsor. (2001). *Woolly Mammoth: Life, Death, and Rediscovery*. New York: Scholastic.

> New discoveries and old theories are emphasized in this account of a project to excavate and remove a frozen woolly mammoth in Siberia. Color photographs and illustrations enhance the text. (Grades 4–5)

DeCristofano, Carolyn Cinami. (2005). *Big Bang! The Tongue-Tickling Tale of a Speck That Became Spectacular*. (Michael Carroll, Illus.). Watertown, MA: Charlesbridge.

> This picture book offers a scientific explanation of how the universe began. A glossary is included. (Grades 2–4)

Dendy, Leslie, & Boring, Mel. (2005). *Guinea Pig Scientists: Bold Self-Experimenters in Science and Medicine*. (C.B. Mordan, Illus.). New York: Holt.

> Brief stories of men and women scientists involved with self-experimentation are presented through text, photographs, reproductions, and sidebars of additional information. (Grade 5)

Kramer, Stephen P. (2001). *Hidden Worlds: Looking Through a Scientist's Microscope*. (Dennis Kunkel, Illus.). Boston: Houghton Mifflin.

> Microscopic images and text offer a wealth of information about how scientists study the world. The author also discusses how a scientist

becomes interested in microscopes, how he uses them in his work, and what he has discovered in his research. An index and suggestions for further reading are included. (Grades 4–5)

Lyon, George Ella. (2003). *Mother to Tigers*. (Peter Catalanotto, Illus.). New York: Atheneum.

A picture biography of Helen Delaney Martini, who raised wild animal babies in her New York apartment until she founded the Bronx Zoo's animal nursery and consequently became the zoo's first woman zookeeper. (Grades 1–3)

McCutcheon, Marc. (2004). *The Kid Who Named Pluto: And the Stories of Other Extraordinary Young People in Science*. (Jon Cannell, Illus.). San Francisco: Chronicle.

Short profiles are given of young scientists, some famous, some not. (Grades 3–5)

Schanzer, Rosalyn. (2003). *How Ben Franklin Stole the Lightning*. New York: HarperCollins.

Although there is an overview of Franklin's various inventions and scientific experiments, the focus is on his discovery of lightning's electrical power. (Grades 1–3)

Thimmesh, Catherine. (2002). *The Sky's the Limit: Stories of Discovery by Women and Girls*. (Melissa Sweet, Illus.). Boston: Houghton Mifflin.

This book presents stories of past and present women and girls and 20 discoveries in astronomy, biology, anthropology, paleontology, and medicine. A timeline, index, and suggestions for further reading are included. (Grades 4–5)

CHAPTER 5

Using Literature to Teach Mathematics

The essence of mathematics is not to make simple things complicated but to make complicated things simple.

—S. GUDDER

The National Council of Teachers of Mathematics (NCTM) developed its *Principles and Standards for School Mathematics* (2000) to identify and describe features of mathematics education for today's world. They provide a vision for mathematics education built on high achievement for all students in the classroom. The principles highlight the basic characteristics of a high-quality mathematics instructional program and provide guidance for making education decisions. The six principles are as follows:

1. Equity—Excellence in mathematics education requires equity—high expectations and strong support for all students.

2. Curriculum—A curriculum is more than a collection of activities: it must be coherent, focused on important mathematics, and well articulated across the grades.

3. Teaching—Effective mathematics teaching requires understanding what students know and need to learn and then challenging and supporting them to learn well.

4. Learning—Students must learn mathematics with understanding, actively building new knowledge from experience and prior knowledge.

5. Assessment—Assessment should support the learning of important mathematics and furnish useful information to both teachers and students.

6. Technology—Technology is essential in teaching and learning mathematics; it influences the mathematics that is taught and enhances students' learning. (NCTM, 2000, n.p.)

The standards describe the mathematical knowledge, understanding, and skills that students should acquire from prekindergarten through grade 12. Five standards describe the mathematical content that students should learn to be successful in mathematics, and five highlight the mathematical processes that students draw on to acquire and use their content knowledge.

Content Standards

1. **Numbers and Operations**—Students in grades K–2 should count with understanding and recognize "how many" in sets of objects, understand various meanings of addition and subtraction of whole numbers and the relationship between the two operations, and develop and use strategies for whole-number computations using a variety of methods and tools. Students in grades 3–5 should understand the place-value structure of the base-ten number system and be able to represent and compare whole numbers, decimals, and fractions; understand various meanings of multiplication and division; develop fluency in adding, subtracting, multiplying, and dividing whole numbers; and use strategies to mentally compute problems and estimate the results of computations.

2. **Algebra**—Students in grades K–2 should sort, classify, and order objects by size, number, and other properties; recognize, describe, and extend patterns; use objects, pictures, and symbols to model addition and subtraction; and describe qualitative change. Students in grades 3–5 should describe, make generalization about, and analyze geometric and numeric patterns using words, tables, and graphs; express mathematical relationships using equations and a letter or symbol to represent an unknown quantity; and investigate how a change in one variable relates to a change in a second variable.

3. **Geometry**—Students in grades K–2 should recognize, name, build, draw, compare, and sort two- and three-dimensional shapes, and they should be able to relate ideas in geometry to ideas in number and measurement. Students in grades 3–5 should identify, compare, analyze, and classify two- and three-dimensional shapes and develop vocabulary to describe their attributes and build, draw, and use geometric models to solve problems in other areas of mathematics, such as number and measurement.

4. **Measurement**—Students in grades K–2 should recognize and compare objects according to length, volume, weight, area, and time; measure with

multiple copies of units of the same size; and use common measurement tools. Students in grades 3–5 should understand length, area, weight, volume, and degree of angle and select the appropriate type of unit for measuring; carry out simple unit conversions; and develop strategies for estimating the perimeters, areas, and volumes of irregular shapes.

5. **Data Analysis and Probability**—Students in grades K–2 should sort and classify objects according to their attributes and organize data about the objects using concrete objects, pictures, and graphs. Students in grades 3–5 should collect data using observations, surveys, and experiments; represent data using tables and graphs; and recognize the differences in representing categorical and numerical data.

Process Standards

1. **Problem-solving** emphasizes the use of problem-solving strategies to help students build their mathematical knowledge and to solve problems in other contexts as well.

2. **Reasoning and proof** involves logical thinking during problem solving and considering whether an answer makes sense.

3. **Communication** refers to talking about, describing, explaining, and writing about mathematics in a clear and organized manner.

4. **Connections** refers to relating mathematical ideas to other mathematical ideas, curricular areas, and real-world situations.

5. **Representation** refers to expressing math concepts through charts, graphs, symbols, diagrams, and manipulatives.

Together, these 10 standards define the basic mathematics that all students should have the opportunity to learn, and these standards reflect the increased demand for higher achievement and proficiency of students in mathematics. As a result, mathematics content is becoming more complex for younger students.

Zemelman, Daniels, and Hyde (1998) write,

> Mathematics is not a set of isolated topics but, rather, a science of patterns and relationships. Realizing, understanding, and using these patterns are a major part of mathematical power. Students need to see the connections between concepts and applications of general principles to several areas and relevance to solving problems in real life. (p. 90)

In other words, math is needed for science, social studies, and the arts. Students also need to see that math is necessary for everyday life. Concepts can be introduced by using real-life examples and motivating situations by dividing a pizza or equal pieces of paper or candy. You can ask questions such as, "Can you guess how much the answer will be? Can you draw a picture to show what is happening in the problem?" Encourage students to put their thinking on paper by writing about how they arrived at the answer—a skill frequently required on standardized tests. Manipulatives can be used to help visualize the solutions to problems and relate things that come in sets, such as four quarters in a dollar, four legs on a dog, five fingers on a hand, five days in a school week. You also must model and teach the strategies for solving word problems, or story problems. These are often difficult for students because they not only require reading but they also require an extra step: The problem must be read and understood, then transformed into a numerical equation. The skills needed to understand story problems are basically the same skills used for reading comprehension. Story problems should be used for reading instruction as well as for mathematics.

Integrating Mathematics With Trade Books

There is no textbook series or single textbook at a particular grade level that comprehensively addresses the NCTM standards, although virtually all publishers have attempted to move toward the standards. The textbook is the basis of instruction, however, and can be supplemented with appropriate trade books and activities to provide students with varied experiences in mathematics. Once you present a skill or concept, trade books can provide a different perspective or further explanation. Often, the use of a colorful trade book will increase student enthusiasm and interest. Although there are relatively few studies on the benefits of using literature in mathematics, Hong (1996) exposed kindergartners to story-related mathematics, and they exhibited a greater preference and aptitude for mathematics activities than did those in a comparison group. Wilde (1998) also found that children's literature can deepen mathematical understanding. Teaching and supplementing mathematics with children's trade books motivates students to learn in new ways, encourages them to think and reason mathematically, and builds student appreciation of both mathematics and literature.

One of the major elements of mathematics instruction emphasized in recent years has been to teach children problem-solving skills. Literature is a wonderful tool for supporting problem-solving learning. In *The Doorbell Rang* (Hutchins,

1986), children are trying to divide a batch of cookies among themselves. More friends arrive, and they must continually figure out how many cookies each one gets. Charlesbridge and Scholastic publish many trade books on mathematics (on topics such as shapes, addition, subtraction, multiplication, division, and fractions) featuring different candies or cereal with which most children are familiar. Many of these math books provide other learning opportunities, focusing on colors, wildlife, nutrition, and so forth, as well. *The Crayon Counting Book* (Ryan & Pallotta, 1996) counts up to 24, showing both numerals and number words, discusses odd and even numbers, and counts by 2s. But, it also names colors and explains primary, binary, and shades of colors. *1, 2, 3 Moose* (Helman, 1996) is a counting book, featuring photographs of the Pacific Northwest. While counting, young children can learn about wildlife and nature in Alaska, Oregon, Washington, and British Columbia. *Circle-Time Poetry Math* (Simpson, 2005), although not a trade book, includes 20 poems to use as springboards for mathematics lessons, as well as for language arts activities. Intended for grades K–1, each poem is accompanied by an activity, literature links, and reproducibles for games or patterns, and each lesson connects to the NCTM standards. When using *The Hershey's Milk Chocolate Multiplication Book* (Pallotta, 2002) with third graders, bring in one of the candy bars mentioned and have children read the label to find out how many calories and/or grams of sugar are in each piece. Students can then compare the candy with other foods that might have more nutritional value.

Cooking and recipes can be used for science lessons on nutrition, but mathematics is required for measuring and purchasing ingredients. When studying machinery in science, mathematics is used to compute the price of fuel and how much it would cost to get from one place to another or to run for a certain length of time. Ages of historical figures and characters in books are computed using mathematics. Maps, money, travel, and weather offer many ways to integrate mathematics with other subjects. Because much of science involves measurement, it is almost impossible to separate the two. And don't forget that numbers are an integral part of many folk tales, fairy tales, and nursery rhymes.

The ability to sequence is necessary to be able to solve algebraic and other step-by-step equations. Sequencing skills are also used in other content areas (reading, social studies, science, music, and art) so integration can occur. Additional mathematics skills that span content areas include using multi-step procedures, recognition and use of patterns, and the ability to count in multiples of numbers (2-4-6-8). Rhythm in music directly correlates to counting and fractions.

In the primary grades, there are many teachable moments related to children's literature that occur within the course of a school day (Whitin, 1994). Calendar time, birthdays, daily schedules, attendance, and lunch count are all daily activities which are overflowing with math concepts. For older students, computing calories expended during exercise, measuring and converting distances run in physical education class or on the playground, keeping score at athletic events, and graphing books read or how the class compares to others in various school contests all require mathematics. There is a vast array of children's literature which supports these parts of the school day, too.

Writing is integrated into mathematics through story problems, explaining how answers are reached, and recording the steps required to solve a problem. Math journals provide a way for students to express their thoughts about mathematics, and they allow the teacher to see if students understand what has been presented. Suggestions for journals include "Today I learned about (or how to)..."; "The most important ideas I learned today are..."; "The steps I used to solve this problem were..."; "I could use this type of problem solving to..."; and "One math activity I really enjoy is _____ because...."

Kindergarten teacher Maureen Akins celebrates the 100th day of school with her pupils, a practice that has become increasingly popular over the past few years. The 100th day usually occurs sometime in February. Students begin counting on the first day of school and write numerals on a chart, anticipating the 100th day. Weather and special events are also recorded on the chart. Students not only are learning how to count, but they also are learning about length of time and waiting, often a difficult concept for young children to grasp. As each day is recorded, it is easy to integrate other subject areas. Halloween is usually between the 40th and 50th day of school, which invites art, writing, and reading activities. For the 50th day, Mrs. Akins points out that there are 50 stars in the U.S. flag, which the class salutes each morning. This is also close to Veterans' Day, which invites a social studies lesson. Christmas and Hanukkah activities are done around the 70th day. Students also count how many days are in winter vacation and understand why those days won't count toward the 100 days. In winter, the class records snowfall and temperatures, shares books on snow, and makes snowflakes. As the 100th day approaches, Mrs. Akins has the class cut out 100 footprints. She then tapes them to the floor in a line, throughout the school, usually ending at the main office. Throughout the 100th day, students are allowed to walk the 100 steps, counting as they go; students count as others jump 100 times; beans or squares of paper are counted out in groups of twos, fives, tens, and so forth to make 100; and a celebration is held with 100 pieces of candy or other treat, divided among the class. Mrs. Akins also reads *Emily's First 100 Days of School* (2000) by Rosemary Wells on the 100th day, and the class compares their experiences with those of Emily.

Choosing Appropriate Trade Books for Math Instruction

Trade books for mathematics must contain factual information, be appealing and appropriate to the age and/or reading level of the students, and represent the mathematical skill or concept to be taught. Further, it is usually helpful if the mathematical skill or concept has already been introduced. In other words, using trade books in mathematics is a way of further explaining or illustrating, showing a new perspective, or reinforcing what has already been learned, although they can sometimes be used as an introduction to a lesson. Older students lacking basic skills in mathematics can often benefit from trade books. Many of the books available can provide the extra help that these students need. For instance, a fifth grader lacking basic addition or subtraction skills might gain confidence by reading one of the M&M's books published by Charlesbridge. And, when older students help younger ones by reading a mathematics trade book to them, they are also reinforcing their own skills.

Good books can promote the process standards by incorporating a variety of representations of mathematics in interdisciplinary contexts and, most important, inviting children to talk, reason, and solve problems in multiple ways. Trade books must convey sound and accurate content and promote healthy attitudes and dispositions about mathematics. Whitin and Whitin (2004) identified the following criteria for selecting good trade books for use in mathematics:

- Mathematical integrity: Fiction, as well as nonfiction, requires that the mathematics components be accurate, mathematic concepts or examples must be used in believable contexts, and the ideas and concepts should be obvious in the text and illustrations.
- Potential for varied response: The tone of the book invites the reader to think and respond in several ways.
- An aesthetic dimension: The book is pleasing to the eye, with informational graphics complementing the text.

For many years, most trade books dealing with mathematics were counting or concept books for the very young. But over the past few years, there have been more good books that deal with mathematics intended for older students. For instance, books by Japanese author and illustrator Mitsumasa Anno deal with subjects studied in the middle grades, such as factorials, logic, permutations, and combinations. There are several books written for children about the common frustrations about mathematics. Carl Sandburg's poem *Arithmetic* (1993) captures the feelings children sometimes have when "numbers fly like pigeons in and out of their head" (n.p.). *Math Curse* (Scieszka, 1995) is about the math that surrounds us. Fortunately, these books are intended to persuade the reader that mathematics is not so bad. *The I Hate Mathematics! Book* (Burns, 1975) promises to change the reader from a mathematical weakling to a mathematical heavyweight. Author Greg Tang has been described as an "unexpected math missionary" (Pierpont, 2006, p. 46) since the publication of his first book for children, *The Grapes of Math* (2001). Tang, who believes that math should be fun and that every child can be good at math, employs tricks and techniques in his books, such as looking at groups of items, counting by fives, and looking for pairs and patterns, to make math relevant to children.

For years there has been concern about "math anxiety," especially among girls. Tobias (1993) defines "math anxiety" as tension and anxiety when required to manipulate numbers or solve mathematical problems. Most people recognize that it is often caused by an unpleasant experience or lack of confidence and is sometimes transferred to children from parents who also are anxious about mathematics. Karp, Brown, Allen, and Allen (1998) examined the use of role models in children's literature to promote conceptual understanding and passion for mathematics among girls. I was one of those girls who was convinced I could not excel in mathematics. But I continue to see connections when I share good books with children and am often surprised when I am able to understand mathematical concepts and see relationships between mathematics and everyday activities. I truly believe that if the current trade books had been available when I was in elementary school, I could have avoided years of math phobia!

As with social studies and science, many publishing companies offer affordable and appealing sets of books dealing with mathematics at various reading levels. Weekly Reader publishes Math Monsters, a guided reading set for grades 2–5. This series is based on the *Math Monsters* public television show developed in cooperation with NCTM and is designed to meet and support NCTM standards. National Geographic's Windows on Literacy series offers sets of books for math in science and math in social studies, from emergent to fluent-plus reading levels. Sundance offers Little Readers Twin Texts with a mathematics focus, and Children's Press has Rookie Read-About Math for grades 1–2. Sadlier-Oxford's content area readers for grades K–2 include math words, a picture glossary, directions for a math project, an index, and suggestions for parents. Content includes patterns, numbers, time, measurement, and money. National Geographic Reading Expeditions has a Math Behind the Science series for grades 3–5.

When choosing trade books to use within your state/provincial curriculum guidelines, you might also consider the NCTM math standards (2000), noted earlier in this chapter. Many math textbooks and kits contain lists of trade books to accompany lessons, and there are also websites devoted to children's literature in mathematics instruction (see Appendix). Look for books that are visually appealing, deal with subjects of interest to children, and above all, contain factual information.

Sample Lesson Plans

Teaching About Measurement (Grades K–1)

OBJECTIVE: Students will understand that an inch is a standard unit for measuring length. Students will be able to measure objects to the nearest inch using a ruler (NCTM Standard 4).

INSTRUCTIONAL MATERIALS

- *Inch by Inch* (Lionni, 1995)
- *How Long Is It?* (Loughran, 2004)
- *Inchworm and a Half* (Pinczes, 2001)
- Inchworms (one-inch strips of tag board) for each child or one-inch blocks or cubes
- Rulers
- Objects to measure

TIME: 3 days. Each lesson will take from 20–30 minutes, depending on how much time is given for measuring objects.

DAY 1

1. Read aloud *Inch by Inch*, a fictionalized account of an inchworm who can measure anything (see Figure 20 for additional trade book suggestions for this topic).

2. Ask students how the inchworm measured the birds. Explain that inchworms are approximately one inch in length.

3. Distribute at least eight "inchworms" or one-inch blocks or cubes to each student or pair of students. Tell students that the inch is a standard unit of length and that their inchworm or each edge of their blocks is one inch long.

4. Have students find at least one object in the classroom that is one inch long, such as a paper clip.

5. Have students measure objects on and around their desks, such as a book, paper, pencil, etc., by laying a row of inchworms or cubes next to the object and then counting them. Demonstrate this on the overhead projector, too, explaining that the edge of the first inchworm or square should align with one end of the object.

6. Have students work in pairs, measuring at least four short objects that have not yet been measured (crayons, crayon box, scissors, etc.). They should record the measurements in their math journals. Entries can be drawn; pictures of objects should be shown in relation to the inchworm. More capable students can add words or a sentence about their measurements.

DAY 2

1. Read aloud *How Long Is It?*, a picture book that explains inches, feet, and rulers and compares the size of common objects found in a classroom.

2. Explain that students are going to learn to measure using rulers like the ones featured in the book.

FIGURE 20. Other Books to Use to Study Measurement, Grades K–1

Faulkner, K. (2000). *So Big! My First Measuring Book*. (S. Hinton, Illus.). New York: Simon & Schuster.
Hirschmann, K. (2007). *Is a Paw a Foot? All About Measurement*. New York: Scholastic.
Verdahl, E.J. (2004). *Eric the Inchworm*. Victoria, BC: Trafford.

---

3. Distribute 12-inch rulers to the class. (If you or the students do not have rulers, you can make rulers from tag board as long as they are labeled in inches and marked in half-inches. Many math series textbooks provide a master that can be used.)

4. On the overhead, display an object that is shorter than one foot. Demonstrate how to use a ruler to measure the object. Explain that this is like lining objects up side by side to measure, and review the previous day's "inchworm" lesson.

5. Stress that the zero mark on the ruler must align with the edge of what is being measured.

6. Instruct students to find the inch mark nearest the other end of the object, using the mark halfway between whole inches to help you decide. Explain that this is measuring to the nearest inch.

7. Allow time for students to practice measuring. Walk around the room to check to make sure students are lining up the end of the object with the zero mark on the ruler. Also, check to see if anyone has difficulty reading to the nearest inch.

8. Have students record their measurements in math journals. Again, entries can be drawn or written, depending on the ability of the students.

DAY 3

1. Read aloud *Inchworm and a Half*, the story of an inchworm who measures a bean and has a little left over. Smaller inchworms (called short worms) then come to help explain fractions.

2. Ask students what the short worms in the story were (fractions of an inch).

3. Display a ruler on the overhead. Ask students if they can guess what the smaller marks are on the ruler (half inches). Explain that the mark is halfway between the inch marks.

4. Some children may be ready to measure to the nearest half inch. For those who are not, have them continue measuring to the nearest inch.

5. Provide time for groups or individuals to measure objects and record in their math journals. As in previous lessons, entries can be drawn or written, depending on the ability of the students. Or, you can provide a worksheet of objects or lines to measure.

VARIATIONS

- Teach children the song "The Inch Worm" (Loesser, 1951).

- Have students make and illustrate a chart of things that are about one inch, three inches, six inches, and one foot.

ASSESSMENT

Student math journals should have correct measurements or drawings showing appropriate size. After students have had ample time to practice measuring and recording their measurements, you may want to provide a worksheet or quiz of items and/or lines to measure.

Teaching About Adding and Subtracting Money (Grades 2–3)

Note: This unit should be presented after students have a basic understanding of addition and subtraction. It is easily adaptable to use with Canadian currency as well.

OBJECTIVE: Students will understand that they can count money in their head by counting by fives, tens, and hundreds. Students will also understand that amounts of money may be written in several different ways and that adding and subtracting money is the same as adding and subtracting with decimals (NCTM Standard 1).

INSTRUCTIONAL MATERIALS

- *The Coin Counting Book* (Williams, 2001)

- *Counting Money* (Dalton, 2006)

- *Let's Subtract Money* (Doudna, 2003)

- *Pigs Will Be Pigs: Fun With Math and Money* (Axelrod, 1997)

- Coins that can be manipulated on an overhead projector. These often come with math texts or kits or can be purchased at most school supply stores.

- Coins for students to have at their desks. This "play money" is often included with math series or can be purchased at school supply stores.

TIME: 4 days. This lesson will take approximately 30 minutes each day. Depending on the ability of the students, several days might be needed on each skill.

DAY 1

1. Read aloud *The Coin Counting Book*, a rhyming text with photographs of actual coins (see Figure 21 for additional trade book suggestions for this topic).

2. Go back over the story page by page so that all students can see the coins and problems. Write the equations from each page on the overhead or board.

3. Using coins on the overhead, demonstrate how combinations of different coins can equal the same amount. You may want to have students manipulate coins at their desks as you do on the overhead.

4. When you get to the pages featuring half-dollar and dollar coins, explain that they are rarely used in the United States. However, if you can obtain some, you may want to show them to students.

5. Remind students that it is easier to count the number of nickels by fives to find out how many cents they equal. For dimes, count by tens and for dollars, by hundreds.

6. Explain to students that they are going to count in their heads to find out how many cents are in four dimes, five nickels, and four pennies. They will count by tens for the dimes; then starting at that total, count by fives for the nickels; and then continue counting by ones for the pennies.

7. Using the appropriate coins on the overhead, count aloud with the students:

       Four dimes—10, 20, 30, 40
       Five nickels—45, 50, 55, 60, 65
       Four pennies—66, 67, 68, 69
       Answer: 69 cents

FIGURE 21. Other Books to Use to Study Adding and Subtracting Money, Grades 2–3

Dalton, J. (2006). *Making Change at the Fair*. New York: Children's Press.
Doudna, K. (2002). *Let's Subtract Bills*. Edina, MN: ABDO Publishing.
Doudna, K. (2002). *Let's Subtract Coins*. Edina, MN: ABDO Publishing.
Hill, M. (2005). *Dollars*. New York: Children's Press.
Hill, M. (2005). *Quarters*. New York: Children's Press.
Rosinsky, N.M. (2003). *All About Money*. Mankato, MN: Compass Point.

---

8. Then write the equation on the board, explaining that cents are always written to the right of the decimal point.

$0.40
  0.25
+0.04
─────
  0.69

9. Do several similar problems with the students before asking them to complete problems on their own (see Figure 22 for additional sample coin problems).

FIGURE 22. Additional Sample Coin Problems

One quarter, two dimes, seven nickels, and three pennies.

One quarter—25
Two dimes—35, 45
Seven nickels—50, 55, 60, 65, 70, 75, 80
Three pennies—81, 82, 83
Answer—83 cents

$0.25
  0.20
  0.35
+ 0.03
─────
$0.83

Two dollars, one quarter, three dimes, four nickels, and seven pennies.

Two dollars—100, 200
One quarter—225
Three dimes—235, 245, 255
Four nickels—260, 265, 270, 275
Seven pennies—276, 277, 278, 279, 280, 281, 282
Answer—$2.82

$2.00
  0.25
  0.30
  0.20
+ 0.07
─────
$2.82

DAY 2

1. Read aloud *Counting Money*, a colorful picture book that explains how money is counted.

2. Remind students that a penny is worth 1 cent, a nickel 5 cents, a dime 10 cents, a quarter 25 cents, and a dollar is worth 100 cents.

3. Working together as in Day 1, find out how many cents you have if you have four dollars, one quarter, three dimes, two nickels, and three pennies.

   > Four dollars—100, 200, 300, 400
   > One quarter—425
   > Three dimes—435, 445, 455
   > Two nickels—460, 465
   > Three pennies—466, 467, 468

4. Remind students that the "4" in the hundreds column represents the dollars, and the tens and ones columns represent the cents. Write $4.68 on the overhead, reminding students that the dollars and cents are separated by the decimal point and the dollar sign appears before the top and bottom number.

5. Check work by writing the equation and adding:

   $$
   \begin{array}{r}
   \$4.00 \\
   0.25 \\
   0.30 \\
   0.10 \\
   + \ 0.03 \\
   \hline
   \$4.68
   \end{array}
   $$

6. Ask students how they can find out how many cents are in six dollars, two quarters, two dimes, one nickel, and two pennies. (Students should tell you to count the dollars, quarters, etc.). Then, demonstrate this on the overhead:

   > Six dollars—100, 200, 300, 400, 500, 600
   > Two quarters—625, 650
   > Two dimes—660, 670
   > One nickel—675
   > Two pennies—676, 677

7. Ask students how 677 cents can be written to show dollars and cents. ($6.77)

8. Have students write the equation:

$$\begin{array}{r} \$6.00 \\ 0.50 \\ 0.20 \\ 0.05 \\ + 0.02 \\ \hline \$6.77 \end{array}$$

9. Provide additional samples as needed until you feel all students have grasped the concepts.

DAY 3 (or whenever students have grasped the concept of adding money)

1. Read aloud *Let's Subtract Money*, which demonstrates subtracting money with colorful visuals and contains a word list.

2. Explain that subtracting money involves subtracting the amounts, keeping the decimal points lined up, and placing the proper sign in the answer. Subtracting money is just like subtracting other numbers.

3. Do the following sample problems with students on the overhead or board.

- You have $3.00. If you spend $2.40, how much money do you have left?

$$\begin{array}{r} \$3.00 \\ - 2.40 \\ \hline \$\,.60 \end{array}$$

- If you have $5.43 and need $7.00, how much more do you need?

$$\begin{array}{r} \$7.00 \\ - 5.43 \\ \hline \$1.57 \end{array}$$

- You got $10.00 for your birthday. You want a toy that costs $8.99. How much money will you have left?

$$\begin{array}{r} \$10.00 \\ - 8.99 \\ \hline \$\,1.01 \end{array}$$

4. Provide additional samples as needed, until you feel comfortable that students have grasped the concept. This is a good time to use problems from your math textbook, too.

DAY 4

1. Read *Pigs Will Be Pigs: Fun With Math and Money*, a hilarious story about hungry pigs who hunt for money, then spend it at a Mexican restaurant.

2. Review addition and subtraction of money on the overhead or board. Do several problems together with students to reinforce the concept.

ASSESSMENTS

When most of the class seems familiar with adding and subtracting money, you may wish to use an informal test from your math textbook or give oral and written problems such as the following:

1. You found two dimes, three nickels, and six pennies in your coat pocket. Count to find out how much money you have.

2. Using the least number of coins, how could you show $0.72?

3. You have one dollar, one quarter, five dimes, and seven nickels. You need $2.00 to buy a snack. Do you have enough?

4. You have $3.00. You want to buy three candy bars for you and your friends. Each candy bar costs $0.69. Do you have enough money? If yes, how much will you have left? If no, how much more do you need?

5. You need $5.00 for a field trip. You only have $3.46. How much more do you need?

For advanced students, give problems such as the following:

1. Billy has $0.82 cents. What are the possible combinations of coins he might have?

2. Jane has three quarters and a dime. Don has three dimes, a quarter, and a nickel. Ben has six nickels, three dimes, one quarter, and three pennies. Who has the most money? How much more than the others does that person have?

3. Mike's dad told him he would give him five coins for mowing the lawn. What is the most money he can get? (Mike's dad has at least two different kinds of coins, but no silver dollars.)

Teaching About Circumference (Grades 4–5)

Note: The ideal time to use this lesson is a day or two after introducing circumference.

OBJECTIVE: Students will understand how to measure the circumference and area of a circle and be able to write equations to find circumference and area (NCTM Standards 2, 3, 4).

INSTRUCTIONAL MATERIALS

- *Sir Cumference and the First Round Table* (Neuschwander, 1997)
- *Sir Cumference and the Dragon of Pi* (Neuschwander, 1999).
- Calculators (unless you want to reinforce multiplying and division using decimals)
- Worksheets on circumference and area of circles from math series or teacher made

TIME: This lesson will take between 45 and 60 minutes over a 2- or 3-day period.

DAY 1

1. Ask students if they have ever heard of the Knights of the Round Table and why the table was round. If they have not, explain that the legend claims that King Arthur devised the round table to promote equality among his knights.
2. Ask students how they could measure around the outside of a circle. Students should respond with $C = \pi \times$ diameter. Students should at least know the terms *circumference*, *diameter*, and *radius*. Explain that you are going to read a fictional story about King Arthur and the round table that also explains circumference. Instruct students to listen for all the math words in the story.
3. Read aloud *Sir Cumference and the First Round Table* (see Figure 23 for additional trade book suggestions for this topic). In this fanciful story, Sir Cumference, assisted by his wife, Lady Di Ameter, and their son Radius find the perfect shape for King Arthur's table.
4. Ask students to describe the shapes of each table and why, according to the story, the other shapes were unsatisfactory.

> **FIGURE 23.** Other Books to Use to Study Circumference, Grades 4–5
>
> Blatner, D. (1997). *The Joy of Pi*. New York: Walker & Company.
> Green, R.L. (1953). *King Arthur and His Knights of the Round Table*. New York: Penguin.
> Long, L. (2003). *Groovy Geometry: Games And Activities That Make Math Easy and Fun*. New York: Wiley.
> Ross, C.S. (1993). *Circles: Fun Ideas for Getting A-Round in Math*. Reading, MA: Addison-Wesley.
> Sutcliff, R. (1981). *The Sword and the Circle: King Arthur and the Knights of the Round Table*. New York: Dutton.
> Williams, M. (1996). *King Arthur and the Knights of the Round Table*. Cambridge, MA: Candlewick.

5. Ask students to name some of the math words in the story. If necessary, reread some parts of the story. Some of the words include: *Sir Cumference* (circumference), *Lady Di from Ameter* (diameter), *Radius, rectangle, equal, feet, half, sides, square, diagonally, diagram, parallelogram, diamond, triangles, octagon, oval, equal,* and *area.*

6. Going back to page 8, ask students to measure the perimeter of the rectangular table (50 feet) and the square table (40 feet). Have a student write the equations on the board or have all students write them at their desks. $(20 + 5 + 20 + 5 = 50$ or $25 \times 2 = 50$; $10 + 10 + 10 + 10 = 40$ or $10 \times 4 = 40)$. Ask them if the area is the same (yes, 100). Have them write the equations $(5 \times 20 = 100$; $10 \times 10 = 100)$.

7. Depending on the ability of the students, you may want to skip the perimeter and area of the parallelogram and octagon, and certainly that of the oval (ellipse). However, students could be assigned to measure the parallelogram for extra credit or homework (perimeter = side a + side b + side a + side b or $2a + 2b$; area = $b \times h$, where b is the length of the base and h is the corresponding height).

8. Tell students that they are now going to measure the circumference of the round table. Since you don't know the dimensions, you can assume that the diameter is 8 feet (in the book, Lady Di's reach is the diameter). Write the following equations on the board or overhead projector: $C = \pi \times 8$; $C = 3.14 \times 8$; $C = 25.12$.

9. Ask students if the circumference is more or less than the perimeter of the rectangular table (less) and the square table (less).

10. Ask students to find the radius of the round table (d = 2r; 8 = 2r; r = 8 ÷ 2; r = 4)

11. Tell students you are now going to find the area of the round table. Explain that the area of a circle is found by multiplying π (3.14) by the square of the radius. The square is found by multiplying the number by itself, so the square of the radius (4) is $4 \times 4 = 16$. Write the following equation on the board or overhead: $3.14 \times 16 = 50.24$.

12. Ask students if the area of the round table is more or less than the rectangular table (less) and the square table (less). This might follow with a discussion about the small size of the round table. Legend says that it was much larger, but in the story, Lady Di's reach was the diameter.

13. For extra practice, consider assigning some problems, such as the following or problems from the textbook, for homework:

> Problem: The diameter of a tablecloth is three feet. What is the circumference?
> Solution: $3 \text{ feet} \times 3.14 = 9.42 \text{ feet}$

> Problem: The radius of a circular rug is five feet. What is the circumference?
> Solution: $10 \text{ feet} \times 3.14 = 31.4 \text{ feet}$

> Problem: If the circumference of a flower bed is 40 feet, what is the radius and diameter?
> Solution: Diameter = $40 \text{ feet} \div 3.14 = 12.74 \text{ feet}$.
> Radius = diameter ÷ 2 = $12.74 \text{ feet} \div 2 = 6.37 \text{ feet}$.

DAY 2

1. Review the previous day's lesson by asking students to give the formula for circumference ($C = d \times 3.14$). Write the equation on the board or overhead.

2. Read aloud *Sir Cumference and the Dragon of Pi*, explaining that this is the sequel to the book you read the previous day and it contains the same characters. In this book, Radius must find the magic number (pi) to save his father. Ask students to look and listen for things pertaining to math and also to find similarities and differences with the previous day's story.

3. Ask students the name of the carpenter (Geo of Metry).

4. Have students look at page 17 (you may have to reproduce this page and put it on the overhead). What do the strips on the pie represent? (diameter)

5. How did Radius know that the magic number was more than three? (Three strips weren't enough to go around and an additional eighth of a strip was almost right.)

6. Reread pages 18 and 19. Ask students what $3^1/_7$ must represent (pi). How do they know? (Each time Radius divided the circumference by the diameter, he got around $3^1/_7$.)

7. Now review page 21, or put a reproduction of the page on the overhead. Ask students to write an equation for the onion slice ($11 \div 3^1/_2 = 3.14$), the basket ($22 \div 7 = 3.14$), the bowl ($44 \div 14 = 3.14$), and the cheese ($55 \div 17.5 = 3.14$).

8. Reread pages 24, 25, and 26. Have students write the equation for the dragon circle ($22 \div 7 = 3.14$).

9. Ask students why Sir Cumference decided to name the number for all things round *pi*. (Radius used pie to solve the mystery.)

VARIATIONS

• Have students relate some of the similarities of the two Sir Cumference books (about circles, diameter, radius, and circumference; some of the same characters; Radius solves the problem in both) and differences (only circles in the second book; other shapes in the first one).

• For extra practice, consider assigning some questions, such as the following or problems from the textbook, for homework: Have students measure the diameter of several objects (i.e., plate, Frisbee, stool, compact disc), then write the equation and find the circumference. Have students find the area of the same objects.

ASSESSMENT

When given a test on radius, diameter, and circumference (from math text or teacher made), students should understand the following concepts:

• If you know the diameter, multiply it by 3.14 to find circumference.

• If you know the radius, find the diameter (r × 2), then multiply by 3.14 to find circumference.

- If you know the circumference, you can find the diameter and radius (circumference ÷ 3.14 = diameter; diameter ÷ 2 = radius).

Conclusion

Mathematics instruction can be enhanced by the use of trade books, which are no longer limited to counting books for young children. Nearly every area of mathematics is represented in both fiction and nonfiction children's literature. After initial instruction using a textbook or mathematics program, trade books can provide additional information or explanation, or they show a new way to apply the concept just learned. They also can provide a review of skills. Because many mathematical skills (such as sequencing, patterns, and measurement) apply to other content areas, it is relatively easy to integrate math with other subjects, especially science, music, and art.

ANNOTATED BIBLIOGRAPHY—MATHEMATICS

The following titles are organized by the NCTM Content Standards (NCTM, 2000).

Numbers & Operations

Adler, David A. (1995). *Calculator Riddles*. (Cynthia Fisher, Illus.). New York: Holiday House.

> A calculator is used to solve the math problems. When the calculator is turned upside down, the answer to the math problem becomes the answer to the riddle. (Grades 3–5)

Drobot, Eve. (2004). *Money, Money, Money: Where It Comes From, How to Save It, Spend It, and Make It*. Toronto, ON: Maple Tree Press.

> Colorful illustrations, photographs, and reproductions accompany information about the history of money, banking, and saving. (Grades 4–6)

Ewing, Susan. (2005). *Ten Rowdy Ravens*. (Evon Zerbetz, Illus.). Portland, OR: Alaska Northwest.

> Rhyming text counts down the rowdy ravens. *The Daily Kaw*, an appended feature that gives true news from around the raven world, provides lots of scientific information about ravens. (Grades K–3)

Geisert, Arthur. (1996). *Roman Numerals I to MM*. Boston: Houghton Mifflin.
Readers learn Roman numerals by counting the pigs in the illustrations.
(Grades 3–5)

Hutchings, Amy, & Hutchings, Richard. (1997). *The Gummy Candy Counting Book*. New York: Scholastic.
Young readers count from 1 to 12 with gummy bears, using rhyming text and colors. (Grades K–1)

Leedy, Loreen. (2000). *Subtraction Action*. New York: Holiday House.
Subtraction vocabulary as well as story problems and equations are explained in this fun picture book. Leedy also wrote *Mission: Addition*. (Grades 1–2)

Long, Lynette. (1996). *Domino Addition*. Watertown, MA: Charlesbridge.
Addition problems are illustrated with dominoes. The numbers on the top and bottom of the dominoes correspond to the addends in the problem. (Grades 1–2)

McGrath, Barbara Barbieri. (1994). *The M&M's Counting Book*. Watertown, MA: Charlesbridge.
M&M's candies are used to count from 1 to 12, but sets and numerical equations are also included, as well as geometric shapes. (Grades K–2)

McGrath, Barbara Barbieri. (2003). *The M&M's Count to One Hundred Book*. Watertown, MA: Charlesbridge.
This book explains how to count up to 100 by ones, twos, fives, and tens. (Grades K–2)

Merriam, Eve. (1993). *12 Ways to Get to 11*. (Bernie Karlin, Illus.). New York: Simon & Schuster.
Objects familiar to young children are presented in combinations equaling 11. (Grades K–1)

Nagda, Ann Whitehead. (2004). *Polar Bear Math*. (Cindy Bickel, Illus.). New York: Henry Holt.
Klondike and Snow, newborn polar bear cubs, are abandoned by their mother at the Denver Zoo. A photographic journal of their first year is

presented to the reader, who learns about fractions while seeing how the zoo staff figured out how to care for the cubs. (Grades 3–5)

Pallotta, Jerry. (1999). *The Hershey's Milk Chocolate Fractions Book*. (Rob Bolster, Illus.). New York: Scholastic.

A Hershey's candy bar is used to show fractions. Numerical equations, number words, and conversions accompany each example. Addition and subtraction problems using fractions are also included. (Grades 3–5)

Pallotta, Jerry. (2001). *Twizzlers Percentages Book*. (Rob Bolster, Illus.). New York: Scholastic.

Licorice sticks are used to illustrate the relationship between fractions, decimals, and percentage. (Grades 3–5)

Pallotta, Jerry. (2002). *Apple Fractions*. (Rob Bolster, Illus.). New York: Scholastic.

Different varieties of apples are described using fractions. (Grades 3–4)

Pallotta, Jerry. (2002). *The Hershey's Kisses Subtraction Book*. (Rob Bolster, Illus.). New York: Scholastic.

Subtraction vocabulary (minus, equal, difference, remainder, minuend, subtrahend) is explained, and both vertical and horizontal equations are shown. (Grades 1–3)

Pallotta, Jerry. (2003). *The Hershey's Kisses Multiplication and Division Book*. (Rob Bolster, Illus.). New York: Scholastic.

Vocabulary and equations are shown in this fun, colorful book, as well as multiplication and division tables. (Grades 3–5)

Pallotta, Jerry. (2004). *Hershey's Chocolate Math From Addition to Multiplication*. (Rob Bolster, Illus.). New York: Scholastic.

Tables, grids, arrays, graphs, place value, four-digit carrying, and factors are all addressed in this colorful picture book. (Grades 3–5)

Pinczes, Elinor J. (1993). *One Hundred Hungry Ants*. (Bonnie MacKain, Illus.). Boston: Houghton Mifflin.

One hundred hungry ants march to a picnic, experimenting with divisions of 100. (Grades K–2)

Wells, Rosemary. (1997). *Bunny Money*. New York: Dial.

> Max and Ruby learn a lesson about saving and spending money. (Grades K–1)

Algebra

Anno, Mitsumasa. (1989). *Anno's Math Games*. New York: Philomel.

> In this bright and appealing picture book, Anno starts out with the concept of comparison and difference, then moves to proximity, combining disparate objects, sequence, hierarchy, and orientation. (Grades 2–5)

Anno, Mitsumasa. (1995). *Anno's Magic Seeds*. New York: Philomel.

> A wizard gives Jack two seeds with simple instructions. Each year seeds develop plants and more seeds. Readers are challenged to predict how many seeds and plants there will be each year. This book provides a good lesson in connecting math to the real world. (Grades K–4)

Anno, Masaichiro, & Anno, Mitsumasa. (1999). *Anno's Mysterious Multiplying Jar*. New York: Putnam.

> Simple text and beautiful pictures introduce the mathematical concept of factorials in this picture book. Younger students can count, while older ones explore multiplying skills as well as factorials. (Grades K–5)

Birch, David. (1988). *The King's Chessboard*. (Devis Grebu, Illus.). New York: Dial.

> This parable about a proud king and a wise man uses the familiar mathematical puzzle of a chessboard. (Grades 2–5)

Choos, Ramona G. (2003). *Sorting*. Lancaster, PA: Childcraft Education.

> Colorful photographs of everyday objects require the reader to find ways to sort them. (Grades K–2)

Cohen, Donald. (1989). *Calculus by and for Young People*. Champaign, IL: Author.

> Cohen and his students solve problems that involve infinite sequence, functions, graphs, algebra, and other mathematical ideas. (Grades 2–5)

McGrath, Barbara Barbieri. (2002). *The M&M's Brand Color Pattern Book.* (Roger Glass, Illus.). Watertown, MA: Charlesbridge.

> Colored candies are used to illustrate patterns from two-color to complicated six-color arrangements. (Grades K–2)

Pallotta, Jerry. (2000). *Reese's Pieces Count by Fives.* (Rob Bolster, Illus.). New York: Scholastic.

> Machinery at a construction site picks up and moves the Reese's pieces first by counting to ten by ones, then by counting to one hundred by fives. (Grades 1–2)

Tompert, Ann. (1998). *Grandfather Tang's Story.* (Robert Andrew Parker, Illus.). New York: Random House.

> Tangrams are arranged into patterns to tell a folktale. The constantly changing tangrams add a novel touch. (Grades K–4)

Geometry

Blackstone, Stella. (1998). *Bear in a Square.* (Debbie Harter, Illus.). New York: Scholastic.

> This colorful picture book features geometric shapes and also offers counting practice to the reader. (Grades K–1)

Burns, Marilyn. (1994). *The Greedy Triangle.* (Gordon Silveria, Illus.). New York: Scholastic.

> This picture book introduces shapes to young readers. (Grades K–2)

Burns, Marilyn. (1997). *Spaghetti and Meatballs for All! A Mathematical Story.* (Debbie Tilley, Illus.). New York: Scholastic.

> Each time the number of people coming to the family reunion changes, Mrs. Comfort must use area and perimeter to accommodate the seating plan. (Grades 2–4)

Ellis, Julie. (2004). *What's Your Angle, Pythagorus? A Math Adventure.* (Phyllis Hornung, Illus.). Watertown, MA: Charlesbridge.

> In this fictionalized account, Pythagorus discovers his famous theorem. (Grades 2–4)

Hoban, Tana. (2000). *Cubes, Cones, Cylinders, & Spheres*. New York: Greenwillow.

Photographs of familiar objects depict geometric shapes in this wordless book. (Grades K–3)

Murphy, Stuart J. (2001). *Captain Invincible and the Space Shapes*. (Rémy Simard, Illus.). New York: HarperCollins.

Captain Invincible uses three-dimensional shapes to help him get back to Earth. (Grades K–3)

Neuschwander, Cindy. (2003). *Sir Cumference and the Sword in the Cone*. (Wayne Geehan, Illus.). Watertown, MA: Charlesbridge.

Sir Cumference, Radius, and Sir Vertex search for Edgecalibur, the sword that King Arthur has hidden in a geometric solid. (Grades 3–5)

Neuschwander, Cindy. (2005). *Mummy Math: An Adventure in Geometry*. (Bryan Langdo, Illus.). New York: Henry Holt.

On a trip to Egypt, Matt and Bibi are accidentally trapped in a pyramid. They use hieroglyphics and their knowledge of geometric solids to get out. (Grades 1–4)

Neuschwander, Cindy. (2006). *Sir Cumference and the Isle of Immeter*. (Wayne Geehan, Illus). Watertown, MA: Charlesbridge.

This tale introduces a new character, Per, who visits Sir Cumference and becomes involved in a mystery. The solution explains the concepts of perimeter and area. (Grades 3–5)

Pallotta, Jerry. (2002). *Twizzlers Shapes and Patterns*. (Rob Bolster, Illus.). New York: Scholastic.

Angles, shapes, and parallel lines are demonstrated with strawberry twist candies. (Grades K–3)

Measurement

Adler, David A. (1999). *How Tall, How Short, How Far Away?* (Nancy Tobin, Illus.). New York: Holiday House.

Adler explains the development of systems of measurement; the standardization of these systems; the origin of the metric system; and the methods of measuring length, height, and distance. Simple text and bold illustrations make ideas clear and easy to understand. (Grades 2–4)

Allen, Pamela. (1980). *Mr. Archimedes' Bath*. New York: Lothrop, Lee & Shepard.

> The Law of Archimedes is explained in this humorous picture book. (Grades K–2)

Hightower, Susan. (1997). *Twelve Snails to One Lizard: A Tale of Mischief and Measurement*. (Matt Novak, Illus.). New York: Simon & Schuster.

> Inches, feet, and yards are explained in this story about a beaver and a frog trying to rebuild a dam. (Grades K–2)

Kaye, Marilyn. (1992). *A Day With No Math*. (Tim Bowers, Illus.). San Diego, CA: Harcourt.

> Kaye shows the reader how time, measurement, money, and mathematics are used in daily life. This is the perfect book for students who wonder how they are really going to use math. (Grades 2–5)

Keenan, Sheila. (1999). *What Time Is It? A Book of Math Riddles*. (Kayne Jacobs, Illus.). New York: Scholastic.

> Riddles and questions are answered with demonstrations of how to tell time. (Grades K–2)

Kensler, Chris. (2003). *Secret Treasures and Magical Measures: Adventures in Measuring Time, Temperature, Length, Weight, Volume, Angles, Shapes and Money*. New York: Kaplan.

> Tennessee Toledo must find a magic potion to return the Flung family back to normal size. He and the wise man, Punfucius, learn how to use important measuring tools to concoct the reversal formula. (Grades K–3)

Koscielniak, Bruce. (2004). *About Time: A First Look at Time and Clocks*. Boston: Houghton Mifflin.

> The beginning of time-keeping and the origins of the Gregorian calendar are explained in this instructive, yet entertaining, book. Sundials, water clocks, and timepieces through the ages are included. (Grades 3–5)

Leedy, Loreen. (1997). *Measuring Penny*. New York: Henry Holt.

> For a homework assignment, Lisa uses various units to measure her dog. Height, weight, volume, time, and temperature are included. (Grades 2–4)

Murphy, Stuart J. (2002). *Bigger, Better, Best!* (Marsha Winborn, Illus.). New York: HarperCollins.

> When they move to a new home, Jenny and Jeff quibble over whose room is the best and the biggest. By measuring, they find that, although their rooms and windows are different shapes, they are exactly the same size. (Grades 2–4)

Myller, Rolf. (1962). *How Big Is a Foot?* New York: Atheneum.

> The king wants to give the queen a bed for a birthday present. But how will they know how big to make it? (Grades K–1)

Nagda, Ann Whitehead. (2002). *Chimp Math: Learning About Time From a Baby Chimpanzee.* (Cindy Bickel, Illus.). New York: Henry Holt.

> A baby chimpanzee, ignored by its mother, is raised by staff at a Wichita zoo. His eating, learning, and growth are shown with timelines, charts, clocks, and calendars on the left page, including information on how to interpret the data. Accompanying text and photographs are on the right pages. (Grades 1–5)

Pallotta, Jerry. (2002). *Hershey's Milk Chocolate Weights and Measures.* (Rob Bolster, Illus.). New York: Scholastic.

> Measurement and weight are illustrated and explained in both the American system and the metric system, using candy as the reference. (Grades 2–4)

Ulmer, M. (2006). *Loonies and Toonies: A Canadian Number Book.* (Melanie Rose, Illus.). Chelsea, MI: Sleeping Bear Press.

> The title refers to the nicknames of Canadian one and two dollar coins. Metric system is explained, along with past and present Canadian history. (Grades K–6)

Data Analysis and Probability

Anno, Mitsumasa, & Nozaki, Akihiro. (1985). *Anno's Hat Tricks.* New York: Philomel.

> Three children, using the concept of binary logic, try to guess the color of the hats on their head. (Grades K–3)

Ball, Johnny. (2005). *Go Figure! A Totally Cool Book About Numbers*. New York: Dorling Kindersley.

> Four sections (where do numbers come from, magic numbers, shaping up, and the world of math) address the history of counting, zero, number theory, pi, chance, logics, and fractals. (Grades 4–5)

Cushman, Jean. (1991). *Do You Wanna Bet? Your Chance to Find Out About Probability*. (Martha Weston, Illus.). New York: Clarion.

> With brief stories, the laws of chance through coin tossing, spinner and card games, and weather are introduced. (Grades 4–5)

Gardner, Martin. (1969). *Perplexing Puzzles and Tantalizing Teasers*. (Laszlo Kubinyi, Illus.). New York: Simon & Schuster.

> Many classic brainteasers, including riddles, palindromes, and mazes, challenge readers to think in different ways to solve the problems. (Grades 4–5)

Hopkins, Lee Bennett. (1997). *Marvelous Math: A Book of Poems*. (Karen Barbour, Illus.). New York: Simon & Schuster.

> Poems about the significance of math and numbers were chosen to entice the reader. (Grades 3–5)

McGrath, Barbara Barbieri. (1998). *More M&M's Math*. (Roger Glass, Illus.). Watertown, MA: Charlesbridge.

> Math topics included in this picture book include estimation, graphs, factoring, and problem solving, as well as multiplication and division. (Grades 2–5)

Murphy, Stuart J. (1997). *Just Enough Carrots*. (Frank Remkiewicz, Illus.). New York: HarperCollins.

> Little Rabbit and his mother compare amounts of carrots while on a shopping trip. The concept of more and fewer is explained, and there are accompanying activities at the end. (Grades K–1)

Nagda, Ann Whitehead. (2002). *Tiger Math: Learning to Graph From a Baby Tiger*. (Cindy Bickel, Illus.). New York: Henry Holt.

> An orphaned Siberian tiger cub at the Denver Zoo is raised by the veterinary staff. The story (on the right-hand page) is accompanied by

circle, bar, and line graph (on the left-hand page) to chart his growth. (Grades 3–5)

Schwartz, David M. (1989). *If You Made a Million.* (Steven Kellogg, Illus.). New York: Lothrop, Lee & Shepard.

> Abstract, numerical concepts are put in terms that most students can understand. Not only are large sums of money discussed but interest, income tax, and loans are also explained. (Grades 3–5)

Schwartz, David M. (1998). *G Is for Googol: A Math Alphabet Book.* (Marissa Moss, Illus.). Berkeley, CA: Tricycle Press.

> Terms and ideas from mathematics (abacus, binary, cubit, diamond, etc.) represent each letter of the alphabet. (Grades 4–5)

Tang, Greg. (2005). *Math Potatoes: Mind-Stretching Brain Food.* (Harry Briggs, Illus.). New York: Scholastic.

> Rhyming verse challenges readers to combine numbers in smart ways by grouping rather than memorizing formulas. (Grades 3–5)

CHAPTER 6

Using Literature to Teach the Arts

In any of the arts, you never stop learning.

—CLAIRE BLOOM

Although the visual arts and music have traditionally received the most attention in elementary school, all four art disciplines—music, dance, drama, and visual arts—are essential to a well-rounded education. The arts offer a dimension to cognition that no other subject can. Eisner (1981) points out that learning is a sensory experience. Therefore, it is important that we help students develop and refine their senses. This is the role of the arts. By studying the arts, students discover how human beings communicate not only through words but also through music, dance, drama, and visual arts.

In addition to contributing to the development of a complete education, the arts offer the means to reach the diverse populations of our schools. With the variety of cultural, social, and economic backgrounds in schools today, there are varied ways of thinking, learning, and behaving. The arts offer especially valuable tools to facilitate learning for those who are primarily visual and kinesthetic learners, in addition to making it possible for all students to learn more effectively, retain what they have learned, and apply their learning in a variety of contexts.

The *National Standards for Arts Education: What Every Young American Should Know and Be Able to Do in the Arts* (1994) was the work of the Consortium of National Arts Education Associations, which included representatives from the American Alliance for Theatre and Education, National Art Education Association, Music Educators National Conference, and National Dance Association. The published standards are discipline-specific to music, dance, drama, and the visual arts, yet one standard is common to all the arts disciplines: *The student understands connections among the various art forms and other disciplines.* Trade books can be used to describe and study the individual arts and can also emphasize these connections.

According to the *Arts Education in Public Elementary Schools* survey (National Center for Education Statistics [NCES], 1995), music and visual arts are "almost universally included in the educational programs of public elementary schools in the United States" (p. 3). More than half of the elementary schools offering music included general, instrumental, and vocal music in their instructional programs. About two-thirds of schools reported that music is taught by specialists only, while another 22% indicated that both specialists and classroom teachers provide the instruction, with only 8% of the schools leaving music instruction totally up to the classroom teachers. A higher percentage (28%) of elementary schools relied solely on classroom teachers to provide visual arts instruction, however. In general, students received an average of 75 minutes of separate instruction in music and 78 minutes in visual arts per week. Schools where music or visual arts instruction was provided only by specialists offered more instruction time than those in which such instruction was provided only by classroom teachers. In this 1995 survey, dance and drama instruction did not receive the kind of commitment from schools that music and art did, however. Dance instruction was generally offered by physical education teachers and most schools included drama, such as enacting stories or plays, within the language arts curriculum.

During the 1999–2000 school year, as a follow-up to the 1995 survey, data was collected from elementary school arts specialists and classroom teachers (NCES, 2002). Results indicated that music and visual arts instruction were available in most of the nation's public elementary schools (94% and 87%, respectively). Dance and drama/theatre, however, were available in less than one third of elementary schools (20% and 19%, respectively).

One must realize that the first study was done in 1995, and the inclusion of music and visual art seemed to be growing in the 1999–2000 study. But, as stated in the Preface, the advent of the No Child Left Behind Act of 2001 (NCLB) has drastically changed things in some schools. With schools devoting more resources and attention to upgrading students' basic skills in reading, writing, and mathematics, cultural enrichment courses, such as music and art, are marginalized (von Zastrow & Janc, 2004).

It is interesting to note, however, that NCLB reaffirms the arts as a core academic subject that all schools should teach, putting the arts on equal footing with the other designated core subjects. In a letter to school superintendents, former U.S. Secretary of Education Rod Paige (2004) stated that the arts were included as a core academic subject in NCLB because of their importance to a child's education. He went on to explain that NCLB expects teachers of the arts to be highly qualified, just as it does teachers of other subjects. Paige acknowledged that arts education programs are endangered but argued that it is because some schools, administrators, and states interpret NCLB narrowly.

A few days later, an article by Karen MacPherson (2004) appeared in the *Pittsburgh Post-Gazette*, reporting that although the arts were declared a core academic subject under NCLB, educators were concerned that the arts are suffering in schools. School districts across the country have cut classroom time and funding for the arts. School officials say they need to focus attention and money on reading and math because students are tested annually on these subjects under NCLB law. In addition, a 2004 report by the Council for Basic Education found that while the amount of instructional time devoted to reading, writing, and math has increased, schools are spending substantially less time on the arts since NCLB went into effect (von Zastrow & Janc, 2004). This shifting of priorities, combined with budget cuts, is causing the study of the arts to quietly disappear from many public schools (Ruppert, 2006). When visiting schools, Dr. Ernest Boyer of the Carnegie Foundation for the Advancement of Teaching found the arts to be shamefully neglected, stating "Courses in the arts were the last to come and the first to go" (Dickinson, 2002, p. 1).

In 2007, Congress will begin the process of reauthorizing NCLB for another five years. Although there are 10 core subjects, NCLB currently requires schools to report student achievement test results for only reading and mathematics. Because of the demands on student achievement in these two subjects, there are many reports of decreasing instruction time for other subjects, such as the arts. The Council on Educational Policy recently completed a report, *From the Capital to the Classroom: Year Four of the No Child Left Behind Act* (2006), which finds a majority of school leaders report gains in achievement, but 71% reported having reduced instructional time in at least one other subject to make more time for reading and mathematics. Elementary school leaders report a 22% decline in art and music instruction time because of NCLB. This is why it is so important to find ways to integrate arts instruction into other classroom areas.

Integrating the Arts

Instruction in the arts can enhance learning in other academic subjects through interdisciplinary instruction, but schools can also subsume the arts within programs in other instruction. Gardner's (1982) theory of multiple intelligences claims that through music, dance, drama, and visual arts, most students will not only find the means for communication and self-expression but also the tools to construct meaning and learn almost any subject effectively. This is especially true when the arts are not only taught as separate subjects but integrated throughout the curriculum at every level.

The Arizona Board of Regents reported in *Schools, Communities, and the Arts: A Research Compendium* (1995) that using arts processes to teach academic subjects resulted in not only improved understanding of content, but it also greatly improves self-regulatory behavior. Integrated arts lessons in all major subject areas were observed in 14 New York City elementary schools. Student behavior improved strikingly in such areas as taking risks, cooperating, solving problems, taking initiative for learning, and being prepared. Content-related achievement also rose. Arts processes were extremely powerful for students who struggled with curriculum and instruction based primarily on verbal proficiency. New York's Educational Priorities Panel (Connell, 1996) studied a group of struggling inner-city elementary schools that raised their standardized test scores dramatically and got off the city's academic probation list. Panel researchers made a surprising discovery: Although probation status focused attention on reading and math, many of the schools that got off the list were distinguished by a strong arts program that was infused throughout the instructional program and included most of the students in the school. The panel concluded that the arts do matter, not only as worthwhile experiences in their own right but also as instruments of cognitive growth and development and as agents of motivation for school success.

For example, certain types of music instruction help develop the capacity for spatial–temporal reasoning, or the ability to understand the relationship of ideas and objects in space and time, which is integral to the acquisition of important mathematics skills. Studies of first and second graders have shown strong evidence that sequential, skill-building instruction in art and music, integrated with the rest of the curriculum, greatly improved performance in reading and math (Gardiner, Fox, Knowles, & Jeffrey, 1996). Students can also learn to decode through movement and rhythm found in dance. Many children who struggle with reading have difficulty with mid-line crossing skills, which are necessary for left to right tracking while reading. Large motor activities using wave streamers in a figure-eight pattern for a Chinese ribbon dance or dancing a grapevine step help establish fluid mid-line crossing skills, which can transfer to fluid eye movement for reading (Marshall, 1999). Further, the relationship between drama and literacy skills is well documented. Goodman (2002) found that the development of literacy skills among prekindergarteners was fostered when the children were allowed to act out their favorite stories. Drama can also be an effective method to develop and improve the quality of children's narrative writing. As a warm-up writing exercise, second- and third-grade students used poetry, games, movement, and improvisation to act out their story ideas, which contributed to their improved performance (Moore & Caldwell, 2002). Visual arts instruction can be vital to literacy learning, as well. Kolakowski (1995) describes parallels between paintings and story elements. She sees portraits and imagines them as characters, landscapes as story settings, and genre paintings as plots. Writing activities can focus on descriptions in order to depict a work of art using words.

An added advantage of integrating the arts into other subject areas is that it often bridges the cultural and economic differences among students. Nearly all students lack background knowledge in the arts, yet the arts celebrate the uniqueness of individuals. Also, the arts can be a powerful motivator for some students. We have all taught students who struggle with academics but are extremely talented in the arts. By allowing these students to shine through music, dance, drama, or visual arts, we recognize and celebrate their strengths, but we must also find ways to help them use their strengths to achieve in other areas. Often, a trade book about a student's area of expertise can be the catalyst for study in a content area. For example, a reluctant reader who is artistic is likely to read a book about art; a budding musician might be persuaded to read about music or write a song, poem, or rap. A child who takes dance lessons or admires modern dance forms is apt to read about dancers or types of dance. Many children will jump at the chance to perform in some way, but performance requires reading and sometimes research in order to portray a character correctly. There are many good trade books for children that feature the arts or artists. For younger students, there are picture biographies of famous artists, musicians, dancers, and actors. Others tell the story of one masterpiece or performance. There are also picture books and biographies for older students, as well as novels with characters involved in the arts.

Integrating Music Instruction With Trade Books and Songs

In 2004, the U.S. House of Representatives approved a resolution supporting school-based music education, stating that music instruction "is an important component of a well-rounded academic curriculum and should be available to every student in every school" (House Concurrent Resolution 380, n.p.). In response to this resolution, Mary Luehren, executive director of the International Foundation for Music Research, stated,

> there is a misperception that music education is a discretionary cost to a school and the reality is, one could not find a more efficient or effective conveyor of skills and knowledge than a music program in a school.... There is no doubt that the "accountability" pressures of the current educational climate are challenging access to quality music education programs in schools.... Intuitive knowledge and established research tell us that kids who are engaged with music do well in school. (Delisio, 2005, p. 2)

In the United States, the National Standards for Arts Education—Music (1994) were developed after the Consortium of National Arts Education Associations received grant money to develop national standards for each of the four art disciplines. These nine voluntary standards describe the knowledge, skills, and understanding that all students should acquire in the arts, providing a basis for development of curricula:

1. Singing
2. Performing on instruments
3. Improvising melodies, variations, and accompaniments
4. Composing and arranging music
5. Reading and notating music
6. Listening to, analyzing, and describing simple forms of music
7. Evaluating music and performance
8. Understanding relationships between music, the other arts, and disciplines outside the arts
9. Understanding music in relation to history and culture

The Canadian Music Educators Association has its own standards, *Achieving Musical Understanding—Concepts and Skills for Pre-Kindergarten to Grade 8* (2000), which are similar but more comprehensive, calling for integration with reading/writing, mathematics, history, and science. Most states and provinces have their own standards, as well, which are usually based on national standards.

Music can be integrated into your classroom in simple, daily ways. Music can be a powerful means for creating a mood, motivating, and inspiring. It is also useful for alerting, signaling, and transitioning. Many teachers use music to set the tone in their classroom. For instance, a lively march invites physical activity, while a soothing lullaby signals rest or "wind down" time. Piano, cello, or violin music has a calming effect and can help to mask "white noise" (hum of lights, voices in adjacent classrooms). Most Baroque music closely matches the human heart beat at rest (60–80 beats per minute) in an optimal learning condition, and when used as background music, it can facilitate student work. To calm down a noisy group, choose music at 40–50 beats per minute (Sousa, 2001).

Language is symbolic, as is music. Children need to learn to decode in order to read, and music is rich with opportunities to decode and interpret. Rhythm is essential to music. Good readers need good rhythm, too. Articulation, proper breathing, posture, and expression are essential to musicians; they are also important to readers. Several studies have compared the effects of music activities on the reading ability of primary-grade children. Hurwitz, Wolff, Bortnick, and Kodas (1975) matched two groups of first graders, one that received music training using a Kodaly-based curriculum and one that had no musical training. When tested for reading ability, the music instruction group performed more effectively on reading tests than students not receiving the instruction. Furthermore, this same achievement was found in higher grades when the music program continued. In another first-grade study, Turnipseed (1976) studied the effects of explicit instruction in listening skills using classical music on student achievement in reading and language arts. After students received the instruction on how and what to listen for in music, these students scored significantly higher in the discrimination sections of reading and language arts tests.

The use of children's literature in the music classroom is growing as educators become more accustomed to integrating music across the curriculum. Music teachers often tie their instruction to what students are learning in other curricular areas. The trade book *Mozart Finds a Melody* (Constanza, 2004) introduces young readers to the composer in a fictionalized account of how he wrote a famous piano concerto after experiencing writer's block, and *The Jazz of Our Street* (Shaik, 1998) describes a jazz parade in New Orleans. Award-winning actor John Lithgow has written a number of best-selling children's books that deal with artistic themes and have a hidden lesson, particularly about arts education. He wrote *The Remarkable Farkle McBride* (2000) to educate readers about orchestras. Lithgow also has written a series of reading primers, the Lithgow Palooza Readers, that feature characters from his books and introduce students in grades 1–3 to music, dance, and other artistic endeavors.

Using trade books such as *The Star-Spangled Banner* (Spier, 1973) and *O Canada* (Harrison, 1992) can teach these important songs while enhancing a social studies lesson. Hearing the music and analyzing the lyrics can give insight into the history, beliefs, and traditions of the United States and Canada. Also, orchestral arrangements have introductions, themes, development, bridges, and codas, which parallel story structure. Further, rehearsing for a musical performance can teach students to critique, edit, and revise their work, just as they do with their writing.

Besides fiction and nonfiction stories, nursery rhymes, folk tales, fables, myths, and poetry can bring music to children through trade books. As with all good books, the most important criteria are that it has literary merit, is appealing, and is appropriate for the intended age level of the child. There are many good trade books available that feature music, composers, and artists. *What Charlie Heard* (Gerstein, 2004) is a biographical picture book about U.S. composer Charles Ives; *Sing, Sophie!* (Dodds, 1997) features a main character with a song in her heart and a loud voice; percussion instruments and rhyme are featured in *Soon Baboon Soon* (Horowitz, 2005); and readers are introduced to jazz and the saxophone in *Charlie Parker Played Be Bop* (Raschka, 1992). Integrating music and children's literature can make music instruction more relevant and more comprehensive. It also can make music learning more collaborative and creative for children.

Sample Lesson Plan

Teaching Music (Grades K–5)

OBJECTIVE: Students will be able to listen to music and then write or draw their interpretations of the music.

INSTRUCTIONAL MATERIALS
- "Rodeo" (Copland, 1942)
- *Rodeo* (Bellville, 1985) for grades K–2
- *Welcome to the Rodeo!* (Sherman, 2001) for grades 3–5
- Music journal or notebook (can be spiral bound or teacher/student made)

TIME: 1–2 days

DAY 1

1. Play a recording of "Rodeo" and ask students to picture in their minds what the music suggests. Use questions such as, What does this music make you think of? and What kind of pictures do you see in your mind? Encourage students to write down their thoughts (brief listing or words) or draw a picture in their music journal as they listen. You may want to play an excerpt from each of the movements in "Rodeo" and continue playing them throughout the lesson.

2. Ask the class to share their thoughts. They will probably list things like sounds of hoof beats, hoedown or square dance music, horses whinnying; or they may draw pictures of cowboys and/or animals on a ranch or at a rodeo.

3. Explain to students that "Rodeo," written by American composer Aaron Copland, is a ballet that tells a story through music and dance of a tomboy who is as adept as her male counterparts as a rodeo rider. The work consists of four parts: Buckaroo Holiday, Corral Nocturne, Saturday Night Waltz, and Hoedown. Many of the melodies are based on American folk songs, and the score features fiddling and honky-tonk piano.

4. Read one of the books, *Rodeo* or *Welcome to the Rodeo!* (see Figure 24 for additional trade book suggestions for this topic), while playing the recording softly in the background. *Rodeo* is an introduction to rodeo events for K–2 students; *Welcome to the Rodeo!* focuses on the rodeo's history, the animals, and the people, including cowgirls, and is intended for older students.

5. Ask students to identify parts in the score that make them think of different events at a rodeo.

6. Have students write a reflection of how the music made them feel, what they liked or didn't like about it, or what it reminded them of. Or they could draw a picture in their music journal of what the music suggested to them.

FIGURE 24. Other Books to Use to Study Copland's "Rodeo," Grades K–5

Brett, J. (1995). *Armadillo Rodeo*. New York: Putnam.
Gibbons, G. (1998). *Yippee-Yay! A Book About Cowboys and Cowgirls*. New York: Little, Brown.
Rice, J. (1992). *Cowboy Rodeo*. Gretna, LA: Pelican.
Toriseva, J. (1994). *Rodeo Day*. (R. Casilla, Illus.). New York: Macmillan.

You could use this lesson plan with the following recordings and books:

- Seasons—Recording: *The Four Seasons* (Vivaldi, 1726). Books: *What Makes the Seasons?* (Cash, 2003); *Four Seasons Make a Year* (Rockwell, 2004); *Our Seasons* (Lin & McNeally, 2006).

- Typewriters—Recording: *The Typewriter* (Anderson, 1950). Books: *Click, Clack, Moo: Cows That Type* (Cronin, 2000); *Miss Tibbett's Typewriter* (Merriam, 1966); *The Little Typewriter* (Harrison, 1963).

- World War II—Recording: Songs performed by Glenn Miller. Books: *Children of the World War II Home Front* (Whitman, 2000); *Growing Up in World War II: 1941 to 1945* (Josephson, 2002).

- Abraham Lincoln—Recording of *Lincoln Portrait* (Copland, 1942). Books: *Meet Abraham Lincoln* (Cary, 2001); *Abraham Lincoln: A Life of Respect* (Rivera, 2006); *Abraham Lincoln* (Usel, 2006).

- Grand Canyon—Recording of *Grand Canyon Suite* (Grofe, 1931). Books: *Grand Canyon: Exploring a Natural Wonder* (Minor, 2000); *In Search of the Grand Canyon: Down the Colorado With John Wesley Powell* (Fraser, 1995).

ASSESSMENT

Students should contribute to class discussion. There are no "right" or "wrong" answers because this is a lesson in interpretation, but students should participate and show an understanding that composers, as well as writers and artists, intend for their works to convey a message.

Integrating Dance Instruction With Trade Books

Dance is an art form characterized by using the human body as a vehicle of expression (Overby, 1992). Dance found its home in education within physical education programs, but over time it has become recognized in schools as an art form comparable to music, drama, and the visual arts, and equally worthy of study (Carter, 1984). The AMERICA 2000 Arts Partnership (1992) recognizes dance in its nationwide initiative to encourage arts education in the schools. However, it has been observed that, of all the arts, dance is experienced the least (Dimondstein, 1990). Several states now have elementary school curriculum standards for dance, although some refer to dance as "movement." However, there are still many states that do not include dance in the arts curriculum (ArtsWork, 2005).

The National Standards for Arts Education—Dance (Consortium of National Arts Education Associations, 1994) state that children need to become literate in the language of dance as a means of communication and self-expression and as a way of responding to the expression of others. The seven standards are as follows:

1. Identifying and demonstrating movement elements and skills in performing dance

2. Understanding choreographic principles, processes, and structures

3. Understanding dance as a way to create and communicate meaning

4. Applying and demonstrating critical and creative thinking skills in dance

5. Demonstrating and understanding dance in various cultures and historical periods

6. Making connections between dance and healthful living

7. Making connections between dance and other disciplines

By 1990, at least 15 states had developed dance curriculum guidelines (Hilsendager, 1990). In Canada, only Saskatchewan (Saskatchewan Ministry of Education, 2006) and British Columbia (British Columbia Ministry of Education, 1998) have a dance curriculum, although a draft framework for dance is currently under development in Manitoba (Manitoba Education, Citizenship, and Youth, 2003). Ontario combines dance with drama (Ontario Ministry of Education, 1998).

In many schools, the music specialist works with the physical education teacher on units dealing with folk and square dancing. This is a natural and valid connection and should not be discouraged, but it should not be the only exposure to dance. Dance also has a place in drama activities. Many choral and dramatic performances in elementary schools incorporate some kind of dancing. And dance can be used as a means of interpretation in most content areas.

Gilbert (2002) believes that movement is the key to learning. This third-grade teacher taught her students spelling words by forming letters and punctuation marks with their bodies. They learned multiplication by moving in sets of threes and fours, discovered the difference between lunar and solar eclipses through planet dances, and choreographed their way across the Oregon Trail. While training teachers at the University of Washington, Gilbert studied 250 students from four elementary schools in the Seattle (Washington) Public Schools as they practiced language arts concepts through movement and dance activities for 20 weeks. The third-grade students increased their scores on the district test by 13% from fall to spring, while the district-wide average showed a decrease of 2%. Most significant was the relationship between the amount of movement the classroom teacher used and the percentage increase of student test scores: the more movement in the classroom, the higher the test scores.

Dance education programs include opportunities for the development of critical thinking and analytical skills, cooperation and teamwork, self-expression and self-esteem, organization and problem solving, cultural literacy, and communicating emotions through movement. Dance elements also can be integrated into other subject areas, which may increase the likelihood of dance being included in the school curriculum (Burke-Walker, 1989). Hanna (1992) provides an example of a science class in which principles of momentum, force, velocity, and energy are applied to dance to illustrate these science terms. And infused in the study of dance is the recognition and realization that dance contributes to a healthy lifestyle, as well as the development of individual and social skills. Other examples of integrating dance throughout the curriculum include an elementary teacher who takes students to see an art exhibit, then has them choose music appropriate to the painting and create a dance to express its mood; a first-grade class dancing the "water cycle"; a fourth-grade class choreographing a dance of the solar system to the music of Gustav Holst; and an elementary school studying cultures as each class learns and performs a dance of a different country (Dickinson, 2002).

There are many good trade books available, both fiction and nonfiction, that feature dance or dancers. Some relate to the origin and history of specific dances, such as *José! Born to Dance* (Reich, 2005), which tells the story of José Limón from his birth in Mexico to his transition from a struggling painter to a successful dancer and choreographer, as he deals with the Mexican Revolution and faces numerous obstacles as an immigrant to the United States. Others describe people or characters who dance. *Mikhail Baryshnikov: Dance Genius* (Glassman, 2001) is a biography of the famous Russian star of the Kirov Ballet who defected to the United States and joined the American Ballet Theatre. *Knockin' on Wood* (Barasch, 2004) tells the story of the famous tap dancer, Peg Leg Bates, who lost his leg in a mill accident when he was 12 years old. Often, fanciful fiction books about dance can serve as an introduction to nonfiction. A fiction book like *Angelina Ballerina* (Holabird, 1983) can spark interest in one like *The Illustrated Book of Ballet Stories* (Newman, 2005), which tells the stories of five famous ballets and includes a glossary, index, ballet basics, and steps for each ballet. This, of course, directly ties in to the music of the ballets and the composers.

When choosing books to complement social studies, try to select books that portray dances of a certain era or country, making sure that all content is accurate, such as *10 Go Tango* (Dorros, 2000), a counting book that highlights 10 different dances. Biographies of famous dancers and choreographers, such as *Martha Graham: A Dancer's Life* (Freedman, 1998), offer insight into how much work and talent is required to be successful. Many books describe a behind-the-scenes view of performance, too. It is important that books on dance convey a message that, although anyone can enjoy many kinds of dance, professional dancers (like musicians, artists, and athletes) are dedicated individuals who often work from childhood to achieve greatness. And, of course, illustrations are crucial to books about dance because the illustrations portray the dance itself.

Sample Lesson Plan

Teaching Dance (Grades K–5)

OBJECTIVE: Students will listen to a variety of books and music and explore the movements described in the book.

INSTRUCTIONAL MATERIALS

- Recordings of "Havah Nagila" and other Jewish folk dance songs
- *Dance Away* (Shannon, 1982)
- *Jewish Kids' Catalog* (Burstein, 1993)

TIME: 1–3 Days

DAY 1

1. Read aloud *Dance Away*, a fanciful story about a little rabbit that loves to dance (see Figure 25 for additional trade book suggestions for this topic).
2. Have students stand in rows or in a circle. Reread page 4. Demonstrating the steps, have children dance "left two three kick, right two three kick, left skip,

> **FIGURE 25.** Other Books to Use to Study Dance, Grades K–5
>
> Andrews, S. (2001). *Dancing in My Bones*. (E. Mueller, Illus.). New York: HarperFestival.
> McDonough, A. (2001). *Do the Hokey Pokey*. (J. Urbanovic, Illus.). Peterborough, NH: Cricket Books.
> Thomas, M. (2000). *African Dancing*. New York: Children's Press.
> Walton, R. (2001). *How Can You Dance?* (A. Lopez-Escriva, Illus.). New York: Putnam.
> Wheeler, L. (2006). *Hokey Pokey: Another Prickly Love Story*. (J. Bynum, Illus.). New York: Little, Brown.

right skip, turn around." Remind students that every time Rabbit danced, he smiled a big smile.

3. When students are comfortable with the steps, dance them to music. Most songs in 4/4 time will work. You can either play a recording or sing. For example, use the tune to "Skip to My Lou."

4. Reread the book, stopping at each page where Rabbit dances, giving students time to dance and sing the movements.

DAY 2

1. Tell students they are going to perform the book as a musical play. Assign parts of narrators and Rabbits for each page.

2. Have a different narrator read each page. For instance, on page one the narrator will read, "He danced in the morning," and the student who is Rabbit will do the dance. On page five, the narrator will read, "When he saw his friends, he would begin to dance with them," and all the students will do the dance.

3. This will end the lesson for younger children. Older students may continue to Day 3.

DAY 3

1. Have students stand in a circle and review the dance from previous days. Tell them that the first part of the dance ("left two three kick, right two three kick") is often referred to as a grapevine step and is used in many folk dances, including the Hora and Mayim.

2. Read the sections on the Hora and Mayim from the *Jewish Kids' Catalog*, which contains a wealth of information about Jewish customs, history, and so forth. Chapter 13 highlights music, songs, and dances. You also may want to read page 189, which includes the music for "Havah Nagila."

3. Have students dance both the Hora and Mayim.

VARIATIONS

- You may lead a reflection by asking if any of the students can tell what they did in dance class.

- Older students may research either the Hora or Mayim for a written or oral report.

ASSESSMENT

Students should be able to follow directions, participate, and perform the dances.

Integrating Drama Instruction With Trade Books

The National Standards for Arts Education—Drama (Consortium of National Arts Education Associations, 1994) assume that drama education will start with and have a strong emphasis on improvisation, which is the basis of social pretend play. These standards call for instruction that integrates several aspects of the art form: script writing, acting, designing, directing, researching and comparing art forms, analyzing and critiquing, and understanding contexts. In the elementary school, the teacher should be actively involved with the students' planning, playing, and evaluating, but students should be guided to develop group skills so that more independence is possible. The eight standards include the following:

1. Script writing by planning and recording improvisations based on personal experience and heritage, imagination, literature, and history

2. Acting by assuming roles and interacting in improvisations

3. Designing by visualizing and arranging environments for classroom dramatizations

4. Directing by planning classroom dramatizations

5. Researching by finding information to support classroom dramatizations

6. Comparing and connecting art forms by describing theatre, dramatic media (film, television, and electronic), and other art forms

7. Analyzing and explaining personal preferences and constructing meanings from classroom dramatizations and from theatre, film, television, and electronic media productions

8. Understanding context by recognizing the role of theatre, film, television, and electronic media in daily life

Dramatic arts education is an important means of stimulating creativity in problem solving. It can challenge students' perceptions about their world and about themselves. Dramatic exploration can provide students with an outlet for emotions, thoughts, and dreams that they might not otherwise have means to express. At the center of all drama is communication. Students who participate in dramatic activities are likely to have less difficulty speaking in public; be more persuasive in their written and oral communications; be better able to relate to others; and have a more positive, confident self image (Buchanan, 1985). And perhaps most important of all, drama can be a powerful motivator. In my classroom, for instance, when I introduced a play or Readers Theatre selection from the basal reader or some other source, there was great excitement. Even the most reluctant and apathetic students anticipated performing.

There are many ways to integrate drama into other subject areas. Young children engage in dramatic activities through imaginative and role play long before they come to school, but acting out nursery rhymes and folk tales is often the first school dramatic experience for children. This common practice in the primary grades develops comprehension, language skills, interpretation, and characterization. Because folk tales are inherently memorable, children can perform them without a script. Repetition helps young children to recall what has already happened and to predict what will happen next. And the goal-orientation of folk tales helps children improvise drama. For example, if one character is pursuing a goal and another resists or pursues a competing goal, interesting dialogue will almost always ensue. The folk tales you choose for classroom drama must meet three criteria: (1) They must appeal to the group leader (student director or teacher); (2) they must appeal to the students; and (3) because folk tales were never intended to be acted out by a group, they must be selected for their adaptability to the limitations of theater (Sierra, 2004). For example, folk tales such as The Three Little Pigs and The Gingerbread Man are easily acted out, yet Anansi the Spider and Sleeping Beauty do not lend themselves nearly as well to dramatization.

Because communication and empathy are central to drama, a student who has been exposed to dramatic arts activities will be better able to understand ideas in history and current events (Buchanan, 1985). Drama is a rich and direct method to express stories. In *creative drama*, students listen to or read a story or poem, hear a piece of music, or see a painting and plan how to interpret it dramatically. As with most learning, modeling is essential. You must model the authenticity necessary to be in role (Mantione & Smead, 2003). *Process drama* is a style that can be embedded in the curriculum and does not focus on actual performance. It tends to be very short; students become characters from text, creating their own dialogue and movement in response to the situation presented, creating meaning, not just receiving information. Process drama is especially useful for children struggling to understand a new language (Mantione & Smead, 2003). A *tableau* is a frozen frame or photo from a scene that focuses on one idea, event, or even a word. Students focus on gesture, composition, facial expression, and the overall message they want to send the viewer. In a *dramatic interview*, students become characters from text and may involve one character or a group of characters in an interview. Questions must relate to the text.

These types of drama study all aid reading comprehension. DuPont (1992) studied fifth-grade remedial readers who received opportunities for creative drama in conjunction with reading instruction. She found that the students in the control group scored consistently higher on the Metropolitan Reading Comprehension test than those in the other group.

In a *group playwriting project* (Buchanan, n.d.), after reading or hearing a new or familiar story, ask the class the following questions: "Who are the characters? What are the settings? What are the events?" The first session results in a list of characters, a list of settings, and a rough outline of the plot. The next session is spent on improvising. When the first scene (or event) is written on the board, students are chosen to act out the scene. As the group performs, the class brainstorms ways to refine the plot. Repeat this process for each event, which may take several sessions to complete. The third step is dialogue. Taking the scenes one at a time, the class brainstorms about who speaks and what, exactly, each character should say. All the dialogue is recorded on the board or on an overhead transparency so it can be adjusted. Once a scene is finished, selected students act it out to see if the dialogue works. This is done with every scene which may take several days. The result is a finished script. Because this activity centers on writing a play, an actual performance is not necessary, although most students will want to present it.

Readers Theatre is a means for groups of students to use their reading voices to perform a story or script for an audience. It can be used with fiction, nonfiction, or poetry and requires no sets, costumes, props, or memorized lines. Performers read a script aloud (after practice), enabling the audience to visualize the action. Performers bring the text alive by using voice and facial expressions. Readers Theatre has been used most often in the language arts to teach fluency and comprehension, but it is also useful in other content areas. There are many Readers Theatre scripts available in basal readers, magazines, and collections. And there are many children's books written in such a way that makes them perfect for a Readers Theatre presentation (Opitz & Rasinski, 1998). For example, books with lots of dialogue lend themselves to Readers Theatre, or for science or social studies nonfiction, facts can be read by different students. Because it is not necessary to use a piece of literature in its entirety, excerpts can be used very effectively, as can picture books. For example, *So You Want to Be President?* (St. George, 2000) can be performed by any number of narrators, each reading three or four lines from the story. *The Egg* (Gill, 2001) is a picture book about embryology with a short amount of text on each page, which can be performed by students. The same is true of *Polar Bears* (Gibbons, 2001).

There are a few publishing companies that offer sets of books to be used as group or class scripts for drama. Rigby offers Tales & Plays for grades 2 and 3. Steck-Vaughn offers Fluency Theater for grades 3 to 5, designed to build fluency, vocabulary, and comprehension. There are many resources available for scripts suitable for elementary school children. Scholastic produces Read Aloud Plays for grades 4 and 5 on the Civil War, Revolutionary War, Colonial America, and American History, which are useful in social studies. An Internet search for "elementary school plays" will provide many suggestions, too.

Good trade books are available about plays, theater, and actors who are appealing to children. *Will Smith* (Doeden, 2006) is a title about the popular actor in the Just the Facts Biography series, while *Christopher Reeve: Triumph Over Tragedy* (Alter, 2000) focuses more on the actor's personal struggle following the equestrian accident that left him paralyzed. Books can give information about putting on a play, such as *Show Time! Music, Dance, and Drama Activities for Kids* (Bany-Winters, 2000), which gives a brief history of musical theater and has scripts and activities for young performers. *Francine the Superstar* (Brown, 2000) and *Amazing Grace* (Hoffman, 1991) describe the responsibilities and performance expectations involved in taking a role. A number of fiction trade books feature characters who are in classroom or school plays. In *Junie B., First Grader: Shipwrecked* (Park, 2004), Junie has the starring role in the Columbus Day play for Parents' Night. Friendship is put to the test in *Pinky and Rex and the School Play* (Howe, 1998) when Pinky and Rex both want the lead in the class play. Trade books can serve as an introduction to theater and also provide an important message to children. In many of these books, the main character wants the "starring role," but often the lesson learned is about the importance of all characters in a play. Children need to know that they may not always get the part they want but that all roles are important to the play. This is another reason why Readers Theatre is so useful in the classroom: All parts are usually equal.

Sample Lesson Plan

Teaching Drama (Grades K–5)

OBJECTIVE: After hearing and seeing a picture book story, students will be able to plan and act out the story. Older students may also write a script for the dramatization.

INSTRUCTIONAL MATERIAL
Tuesday (Wiesner, 1991)

TIME: 1–2 days

DAY 1

1. Share the picture book *Tuesday* (see Figure 26 for additional trade book suggestions for this topic). This book, which contains very few words, depicts an invasion of frogs. You may want to reproduce some of the illustrations and display them on the overhead projector so all students can see.

2. As you show each page, ask students what they think is happening in the story or what the man might be thinking or saying. You can record answers for younger students on a chart and have older students take notes on their own.

3. Using the Group Playwriting Project technique described earlier in this chapter, ask students, "Who are the characters? What is the setting? What are the events?" Record answers.

DAY 2

1. Assign parts as follows: 1–2 narrators, man, old woman, dog, police officers, TV reporters. All other students will play frogs.

2. Ask students to act out first event as a scene. As they perform, brainstorm as a class ways to refine the scene. You may need to coach the group with questions like, "Do you think he's saying anything?" "What do you think the frogs are doing?" Repeat this process for each event.

3. For younger students, record the dialogue; for older students, assign a student or group of students to record. When refined, this will become the script.

4. Students should rehearse before performing the play for another class or parents.

VARIATION

Ask students to look at the last two pages of the book and create a play about flying pigs.

ASSESSMENT

Students should follow the sequence of illustrations in the story when creating their play.

Integrating Visual Arts Instruction With Trade Books

The visual arts include painting, sculpture, drawing, murals, pottery, photography, design, architecture, film, video, and folk art. They also include the study of art history, visual artists, and the study of the visual arts of different cultures. Discipline-

Based Art Education (DBAE), developed and formalized in the early 1980s by the Getty Center for Arts Education, is not an original theory, but a conceptual framework that advocates the development of critical thinking and cognitive skills through the study of art production, art history, art criticism, and aesthetics. According to Walling (2001), the aim of DBAE is to develop mature students who are comfortable and familiar with major aspects of the disciplines of art.

Since the National Standards for Arts Education—Visual Arts (Consortium of National Arts Education Associations, 1994) were established, the emphasis has switched to student acquisition of the most important and enduring ideas, concepts, issues, dilemmas, and knowledge offered by the visual arts, including the development of new techniques, approaches, and habits for applying knowledge and skills in the visual arts to the world beyond school. To meet the standards, students must learn vocabularies and concepts associated with various types of work in the visual arts and must exhibit their competence at various levels in visual, oral, and written form. In the elementary grades, this includes experimentation with art materials and investigation of ideas presented through visual arts. The six content standards include the following:

1. Understanding and applying media, techniques, and processes
2. Using knowledge of structures and functions
3. Choosing and evaluating a range of subject matter, symbols, and ideas
4. Understanding the visual arts in relation to history and cultures
5. Reflecting upon and assessing the characteristics and merits of their work and the work of others
6. Making connections between visual arts and other disciplines

Because the Canadian constitution states that education is a matter of provincial jurisdiction, there are no national standards, but each province has visual arts standards. They are similar to the U.S. National Standards and the standards for each state.

Children today are growing up in a highly visual world, surrounded by television, videos, advertising, and other media. The human brain has a visual cortex that is five times larger than the auditory cortex. Is it any wonder that students respond so positively when they have opportunities to learn through the visual arts? The discipline of understanding how to take an idea from its inception into a final visual product is itself a worthwhile learning experience (Dickinson, 2002). The visual arts not only provide these experiences but also offer opportunities to learn to use the tools of art, to observe carefully, and to express one's ideas visually.

The visual arts provide opportunities for students to be involved in divergent thinking and creative design. Van Buren (1986) states that communication and self-expression are two goals that are common to art, reading, and writing.

Seeing connections, identifying patterns, and building meaning through observation, identifying symbols, and problem solving while observing art, parallel the steps used in reading comprehension (Richardson, Sacks, & Ayers, 2003). Tishman, MacGillivray, and Palmer (2002) trained a group of third and fourth graders to look closely at works of art and reason about what they saw. Results showed that the ability to draw inferences about artwork transferred to their reasoning about images in science. Picture biographies of famous artists can accompany social studies lessons on specific countries. Multicultural studies can be introduced or supported through art. Brookes (1996) noticed that the motivation to read expanded when students drew characters and subjects from books. Drawing the content of science, geography, and social studies lessons resulted in noticeable differences in speed of learning and retention.

Reading a picture book engages children in both the visual and the language arts. Picture books are "bicultural, in that they share qualities of books and the visual arts" (Hammond et al., 1994, p. 11). Children's picture books can be used to stimulate learning in the visual arts. The illustrations in children's books are visual forms, created by artists. These images can be compared to images found in fine art, and using them to stimulate learning can help children develop skills in the areas of art criticism, aesthetics, art history, and studio production (Miller-Hewes, 1994). Students should explore the illustrations in picture books to see how they influence understanding and interpretation of content.

Many trade books feature famous artists, both past and present, and their artwork, such as *Camille and the Sunflowers* (Anholt, 1994), which is based on an actual encounter with Vincent van Gogh, or *Picasso and Minou* (Maltbie, 2005), which explains Picasso's Blue Period. Other books feature fictional characters who draw or are influenced by art in some way, such as *Dream Carver* (Cohn, 2002), a fiction picture book inspired by Oaxacan woodcarver Manual Jimenez, that conveys the message of the importance of following dreams. Instruction or "how-to" books on various art styles and media, such as *Dragonart: How to Draw and Paint Fantasy Creatures* (Peffer, 2005) and *How to Draw Faces* (Levy, 2003), are favorites of most children. Some books feature poetry about colors, which form the basis for many art lessons. *Hailstones and Halibut Bones*, a classic by Mary O'Neill (1961), includes poems about colors, defining color through words, objects, and feelings. When trade books contain reproductions of art work, it is important to look for high quality images so the art itself can be studied. *Norman Rockwell: Storyteller With a Brush* (Gherman, 2000) includes both photographs of the artist and his family and reproductions of Rockwell's work. Similarly, *Come Look With Me: Art in Early America* (Osofsky, 2002) introduces children to 12 magnificent works of art.

To integrate art books within other content areas, look for those that correspond to periods in history (social studies), such as *Hokusi: The Man Who Painted a Mountain* (Roy, 2001), a picture biography that tells the story of one of Japan's most prolific artists and also gives information about the life of peasants in eighteenth century Japan; feature shapes and patterns (mathematics), such as *Shape and Pattern* (Clemson & Clemson, 2002), which features games, puzzles, and craft activities; and describe different media (science), such as *Mixed Media* (Robins, 2006), which introduces young readers to ideas and techniques, and *Science Arts: Discovering Science Through Art Experiences* (Kohl & Potter, 1993), which uses art projects to teach science principles.

There are a number of publishers who offer sets of books for studying visual arts. Children's Press publishes Getting to Know the World's Greatest Artists, with 47 titles, showing both the actual work of artists such as Picasso, Warhol, Kahlo, and Lawrence, along with cartoon-like illustrations. Although the reading level is around 2.5, they are suitable for grades 2–5. Lickle Publishing, a division of Charlesbridge, offers the Come Look With Me series which features quality reproductions and introduces artists often overlooked. Titles include *Women in Art*, *Discovering African American Art for Children*, *Art in Early America*, and *Exploring Modern Art*, intended for grades 1–5. Watson-Guptill Publishing has the Art Explorers series (grades 1–5), which encourages children to interpret what they see in famous works of art and then try the techniques themselves, and the Kids Draw series, which offers instruction in drawing different objects. Houghton Mifflin's Little Readers series and Invitations to Literacy series and Sundance's Alphakids series, all have books on colors for primary students.

Sample Lesson Plan

Teaching Visual Arts (Grades K–5)

OBJECTIVE: Students will be able to identify paintings by Vincent van Gogh;

describe the techniques used by van Gogh; and, using oil pastels, create a version of one of van Gogh's paintings.

INSTRUCTIONAL MATERIALS

- *The First Starry Night* (Isom, 1997)
- *What Makes a van Gogh a van Gogh?* (Mühlberger, 2002)
- *Vincent's Colors* (van Gogh, 2005)
- *The Starry Night* (Waldman, 1999)
- Art paper
- Oil pastels

TIME: 3 days

DAY 1

1. Read aloud *The First Starry Night*, a story about an orphan who becomes friends with van Gogh (see Figure 27 for additional trade book suggestions for this topic). The boy's favorite painting is *The Starry Night*.

2. Read aloud *What Makes a van Gogh a van Gogh?*, which features 12 paintings, with analysis of composition, line, color, and subject matter. Emphasize the portraits, interiors, landscapes, and flower paintings, which represent the artist's techniques and uses of color.

3. If they are available, show students several reproductions of van Gogh's works, including *The Starry Night*. (Many schools and districts have reproductions of the masters' art available. Check with your building or district curriculum coordinator, or access one of the many websites for van Gogh's work, such as http://www.vangoghgallery.com.)

FIGURE 27. Other Books to Use to Study Visual Arts, Grades K–5

Breunesse, C. (1997). *Visiting Vincent van Gogh*. New York: Prestel.
Bucks, B., & Holub, J. (2001). *Vincent van Gogh: Sunflowers and Swirly Stars*. New York: Grosset & Dunlap.
Dionetti, M. (1996). *Painting the Wind*. (K. Hawkes, Illus.). New York: Little, Brown.
Green, J. (2002). *Vincent van Gogh*. New York: Franklin Watts.
Merberg, J., & Bober, S. (2002). *In the Garden With van Gogh*. San Francisco: Chronicle.

---

4. Ask students to compare the reproductions (or the illustrations in the Mühlberger book) with the illustrations in the Isom book, which has many van Gogh-like illustrations, although none is actually a copy of a particular work. Students should recognize elements of van Gogh's style, such as impasto, haloes, and discrete brush strokes, which are terms explained in *The First Starry Night*.

5. Have students compare the subject matter in the reproductions to that in the Isom book's illustrations (i.e., cornfield, snow, sunflower, narrow red bed, flowering trees).

6. Ask students to describe the colors most often used by van Gogh (orange, blue, red, purple).

DAY 2

1. Read aloud *Vincent's Colors*. The text in this picture book is pulled directly from the letters van Gogh wrote to his brother describing his paintings, and reproductions include *Sunflowers*, *The Bedroom*, and *The Starry Night*.

2. Ask students to recall the characteristics of van Gogh's paintings (brilliant colors and brush strokes, thick layers of paint).

3. Show students several reproductions of paintings by famous artists, including some by van Gogh. Ask students to identify those by van Gogh and have them explain their choices.

4. Distribute art paper and oil pastels. Have students practice van Gogh's technique. At this point it is okay to copy.

DAY 3

1. Read aloud *The Starry Night*. In this fiction book, Vincent van Gogh pops up in contemporary Manhattan, New York. Waldman's paintings cleverly imitate van Gogh's style.

2. Ask students how Waldman's paintings are similar to van Gogh's (brush strokes, color).

3. Invite students to create their own version of a star-filled night, using oil pastels to generate the effect of arcs of warm and cool colors on a dark background. Older students may want to use their own hometown area as a background (cityscape, mountains, prairie, etc.).

- Use this lesson plan with the book *Katie and the Sunflowers* (Mayhew, 2001) to explore van Gogh's *Sunflowers* painting.

- For first or second graders, introduce this lesson by reading together *Henry and Mudge and the Starry Night* (Rylant, 1998).

- Use this lesson plan to study the work of Monet, using the books *Linnea in Monet's Garden* (Bjork, 1985), *The Magical Garden of Claude Monet* (Anholt, 2003), *A Picnic With Monet* (Merberg & Bober, 2003), *What Makes a Monet a Monet?* (Mühlberger, 2002), and *Philippe in Monet's Garden* (Carmack, 1998).

ASSESSMENT

Students should be able to contribute orally in class and distinguish the works of van Gogh from other artists. Student work should represent the style of van Gogh (i.e., broad brush strokes, vivid color).

Conclusion

Music should be an important part of every child's education, whether it is for performance or development of an appreciation. Many elementary schools have music specialists who teach music as a separate subject, but it is becoming more common for the specialist and/or classroom teacher to integrate music with other subject areas. Dance, once relegated to a few lessons as part of physical education class, is now recognized as one of the four major arts areas. However, it is given the least amount of time, if any, in most schools. Creative drama can be integrated into the curriculum in many ways. Students can act out folk tales, as well as stories from the basal reader or content area trade books. Many stories and texts lend themselves to Readers Theatre and can be performed. In visual arts, the emphasis has shifted from student-created arts and crafts to a more comprehensive study and appreciation of art history, artists, critical thinking, and aesthetics, as well as having students experiment with various art mediums and techniques. Students also can make connections among the illustrations in their books, in fine art, and in their own art work.

Using children's books to motivate learning in the arts can be especially effective. By reading about musicians, dancers, actors, and artists, children gain information that many might otherwise miss. Trade books are especially important to the arts because few schools have textbooks for teaching the arts. Also, because classroom teachers are the ones who offer instruction in most of the arts, trade books can provide the impetus for a lesson. There are many books, both fiction and nonfiction, that cover a wide variety of the arts, and they should be a part of every classroom and school library.

Performance can be a powerful motivator for many children. For children who don't have the benefit of receiving private music, dance, drama, or art lessons, school provides their only experience with the arts. The highlight of many students' lives may be the opportunity to take part in a play, musical, or other school performance. Experiencing the process of rehearsing until the desired outcome is achieved helps instill responsibility and a sense of accomplishment in students.

ANNOTATED BIBLIOGRAPHY—THE ARTS

Music

The following titles are organized into five areas that address most of the strands of the National Standards for Music.

Singing and Songs

Anderson, Derek. (2005). *Over the River: A Turkey's Tale*. New York: Simon & Schuster.

> A new version of Lydia Maria Child's popular Thanksgiving song, this picture book illustrates each line of text. The actual music appears on the final pages. (Grades K–3)

Guthrie, Woody. (2002). *This Land Is Your Land*. (Kathy Jakobsen, Illus.). New York: Little, Brown.

> Guthrie's familiar song is accompanied by Jakobsen's oil paintings of the 1920s and 1930s. Also included are a short biography of the songwriter, information about other folk singers of the era, and the musical score. This book is a perfect link to the Dust Bowl, Depression, and geography. (Grades 1–5)

Heyward, Dubose. (1999). *Summertime: From Porgy and Bess*. (Mike Wimmer, Illus.). New York: Simon & Schuster.

> This picture book, with the lyrics to the song, captures the charm of summer life in rural United States. (Grades K–5)

Jacobs, Paul Dubois, & Swender, Jennifer. (2005). *Children's Songbag*. Salt Lake City, UT: Gibbs Smith.

> This collection includes music and lyrics to 50 children's songs. Each selection includes a "learn more about it" section that gives some information about the song or suggests an activity to accompany it. (Grades K–5)

Kovalski, Maryann. (1992). *Take Me Out to the Ballgame*. Richmond Hill, ON: North Winds.

> Their fun-loving grandmother takes Jenny and Joanna to a baseball game. Whimsical illustrations accompany the song lyrics. (Grades K–3)

Zane, Alex. (2005). *The Wheels on the Race Car*. (James Warhola, Illus.). New York: Orchard.

> An updated version of the familiar song "The Wheels on the Bus," this book illustrates and invites innovations. For example, students might write "The Wings on the Plane." (Grades K–1)

Instruments

Baer, Gene. (1989). *Thump, Thump, Rat-a-Tat-Tat*. (Lois Ehlert, Illus.). New York: HarperCollins.

> The marching band comes and goes, and the sound gets bigger and smaller. (Grades K–1)

Cutler, Jane. (1999). *The Cello of Mr. O*. (Greg Couch, Illus.). New York: Dutton.

> When the relief truck bringing supplies to a war-torn area is blown up, Mr. O. tries to restore hope by playing his cello. (Grades 2–4)

Garriel, Barbara S. (2004). *I Know a Shy Fellow Who Swallowed a Cello*. (John O'Brien, Illus.). Honesdale, PA: Boyds Mills Press.

> This musical adaptation of the popular folk rhyme "I Know an Old Lady Who Swallowed a Fly" features musical instruments. (Grades K–4)

Koscielniak, Bruce. (2000). *The Story of the Incredible Orchestra*. Boston: Houghton Mifflin.

> Expressive language and watercolor illustrations complement the text, a vast collection of facts about the history of orchestral instruments and music from the 1600s to the present. (Grades 3–5)

Madison, Alan. (2005). *Pecorino's First Concert*. (AnnaLaura Cantone, Illus.). New York: Atheneum.

> A zany musical adventure about the silliest boy in the world, heading off to his first concert, this book also offers musical terminology and information about instruments. (Grades 2–5)

Composers

Anderson, M.T. (2001). *Handel, Who Knew What He Liked*. (Kevin Hawkes, Illus.). Cambridge, MA: Candlewick.

> A picture biography of the composer who did what he wanted despite the consequences. Illustrations depict the first performance of "Water Music," "Messiah," and "Music for the Royal Fireworks." (Grades 3–5)

Austin, Patricia. (2001). *The Cat Who Loved Mozart*. (Henri Sorenson, Illus.). New York: Holiday House.

> Jennifer wishes that her cat Amadeus would be friendlier. Then she discovers that he loves hearing her play Mozart on the piano. The "Author's Notes" include information about the composer as well as recommended books about Mozart. (Grades 3–5)

Krull, Kathleen. (1993). *Lives of the Musicians: Good Times, Bad Times (And What the Neighbors Thought)*. (Kathryn Hewitt, Illus.). San Diego, CA: Harcourt.

> The lives of 19 composers, from Vivaldi to Woody Guthrie, are featured in this humorous book. There are "musical notes" about each composer's work at the end of each chapter and a section on musical terms at the end of the book. (Grades 4–5)

Streissguth, Thomas. (1994). *Say It With Music: A Story About Irving Berlin*. (Jennifer Hagerman, Illus.). Minneapolis, MN: Carolrhoda.

> Through this biography of the famous composer of popular musicals and songs, readers can gain understanding of the music business as well as the

difficulties experienced by immigrants at the turn of the century. (Grades 3–5)

Venezia, Mike. (1999). *Johannes Brahms*. New York: Children's Press.

A combination of fact and fun gives readers a more personal look at Brahms's interesting and full life. (Grades 3–5)

Winter, Jeanette. (1999). *Sebastian: A Book About Bach*. San Diego, CA: Harcourt.

Delightful illustrations and simple text provide an introduction to Bach, his family, and his music. (Grades K–2)

Musical Artists

Bustard, Anne. (2005). *Buddy: The Story of Buddy Holly*. (Kurt Cyrus, Illus.). New York: Simon & Schuster.

From the time he was born until he got his first guitar in sixth grade, Buddy Holly was a musician. His part in the birth of rock 'n' roll is portrayed through rollicking text and illustrations. (Grades 2–5)

Konieczny, Vladimir. (2004). *Struggling for Perfection: The Story of Glenn Gould*. Toronto, ON: Napoleon.

This biography of Canada's most famous musical genius, concert pianist Glenn Gould, includes a timeline and photographs, as well as a look at his endearing, yet eccentric, personality and his musical achievements. (Grades 4–5)

Orgill, Roxanne. (1997). *If Only I Had a Horn: Young Louis Armstrong*. (Leonard Jenkins, Illus.). Boston: Houghton Mifflin.

This picture biography tells of the early life of Louis Armstrong and how he overcame odds to achieve his dream. (Grades K–3)

Pinkney, Andrea Davis. (2002). *Ella Fitzgerald: The Tale of a Vocal Virtuosa*. (Brian Pinkney, Illus.). New York: Hyperion.

Ella's life and "scat" singing are described in this biography. (Grades 1–5)

Troupe, Quincy. (2005). *Little Stevie Wonder*. (Lisa Cohen, Illus.). Boston: Houghton Mifflin.

This picture biography not only tells the story of Stevie's childhood and his passion for music, but the text references his well-known lyrics. The book also includes a CD of his music. (Grades 1–4)

Musical Genre

Chernaik, Judith (Ed.). (1998). *Carnival of the Animals*. (Satoshi Kitamura, Illus.). New York: Henry Holt.

> One-hundred fifty years ago, a famous French composer was commissioned to write a "musical joke" for children. Through colorful illustrations and simple text, each of the 14 sections of this famous musical work is described, as well as why certain instruments were used for distinct animal sounds. This book includes a CD to be played during the reading. (Grades K–2)

Izen, Marshall, & West, Jim. (2004). *The Dog Who Sang at the Opera*. (Erika Oller, Illus.). New York: Harry N. Abrams.

> This picture book about a dog who upstaged the diva at an opera performance was inspired by a true incident. Also featured is the colorful world of the opera and the many people behind the scenes. (Grades 2–5)

Krull, Kathleen. (2003). *M Is for Music*. (Stacy Innerst, Illus.). San Diego, CA: Harcourt.

> Innovative illustrations accompany words to describe something or someone musical for each letter of the alphabet. The chosen words are explained at the end of the book. (Grades 4–5)

Marsalis, Wynton. (2005). *Jazz ABZ*. (Paul Rogers, Illus.). Cambridge, MA: Candlewick.

> A jazz legend represents every letter of the alphabet, each with a poem. Brief biographies of each artist appear at the end of the book, as well as an explanation of the poetic forms used. (Grades 4–5)

Purdy, Carol. (1994). *Mrs. Merriwether's Musical Cat*. (Petra Mathers, Illus.). New York: Putnam.

> Alliteration, composers, and names all relate to music in this fiction picture book. Mrs. Merriwether's piano students disturb the neighbors until her cat Beethoven's tail works like a metronome. (Grades 1–5)

Siberell, Anne. (2001). *Bravo! Brava! A Night at the Opera*. New York: Oxford University Press.

> Lively illustrations accompany text about composers, cast, and crew, as well as the origin of the opera, vocal ranges, and opera terms. (Grades 3–5)

Dance

The following titles are organized into three areas that address most of the strands of the National Standards for Dance.

Dance Performance

Ackerman, Karen. (1988). *Song and Dance Man*. (Stephen Gammell, Illus.). New York: Knopf.

> Grandpa entertains the kids by re-creating his past as a song and dance man in vaudeville. (Grades K–2)

Barboza, Steven. (1992). *I Feel Like Dancing: A Year With Jacques d'Amboise and the National Dance Institute*. (Carolyn George d'Amboise, Illus.). New York: Crown.

> Featuring dance star Jacques d'Amboise, founder of the National Dance Institute in New York City, the text and color photographs chronicle tryouts and rehearsals that lead to a production featuring students and professional dancers. (Because the production is *Chakra: A Celebration of India*, this can tie in to a social studies unit.) (Grades 3–5)

Fonteyn, Margot. (1998). *Coppélia*. (Steve Johnson & Lou Fancher, Illus.). San Diego, CA: Harcourt.

> Prima ballerina Margot Fonteyn tells the tale of the mysterious doll maker whose creation comes to life. (Grades 1–3)

Maybarduk, Linda. (2004). *James the Dancing Dog*. (Gillian Johnson, Illus.). Toronto, ON: Tundra.

> Based on a real dog that was part of the National Ballet of Canada, James wants to play the part of the hunting dog in *Giselle*. (Grades 1–3)

Dancers

Dillon, Leo, & Dillon, Diane. (2002). *Rap a Tap Tap: Think of That!* New York: Blue Sky Press.

The story of African American tap dancer Bill "Bojangles" Robinson is
told through simple rhyming text in this picture book. The afterword
gives additional information about Robinson. (Grades K–2)

Duvall, Jill D. (1997). *Meet Rory Hohenstein: A Professional Dancer*. (Lili
Duvall, Illus.). New York: Children's Press.

Photographs help tell the story of a teenager in New York who is a
professional dancer. (Grades K–2)

Govenar, Alan. (2006). *Stompin' at the Savoy: The Story of Norma Miller*.
(Martin French, Illus.). Cambridge, MA: Candlewick.

This biography of a "Lindy Hopper" from the Harlem Renaissance was
written from interviews with Norma Miller, the subject of the book.
(Grades 3–5)

O'Connor, Barbara. (1994). *Barefoot Dancer: The Story of Isadora Duncan*.
Minneapolis, MN: Carolrhoda.

This is a biography of modern dancer Isadora Duncan, from her
childhood in 19th-century San Francisco to her travels and career in
both Europe and the United States. (Grades 4–5)

Pavlova, Anna. (2001). *I Dreamed I Was a Ballerina*. (Edgar Degas, Illus.). New
York: Atheneum.

Told in the Russian prima ballerina's own words, this picture book is
accompanied by the art of French impressionist Edgar Degas. (Grades
K–3)

Pinkney, Andrea Davis. (1995). *Alvin Ailey*. (Brian Pinkney, Illus.). New York:
Hyperion.

This is a picture biography of the famous dancer and choreographer
whose dance company lives on today. (Grades K–3)

Tallchief, Maria, & Wells, Rosemary. (1999). *Tallchief: America's Prima
Ballerina*. (Gary Kelley, Illus.). New York: Viking.

This picture autobiography tells the story of Maria, an Osage Indian,
from birth to age 17, when she arrived in New York as an aspiring
ballerina. (Grades 2–4)

Types of Dance

Ancona, George. (1998). *Let's Dance!* New York: William Morrow.

> Styles, costumes, and occasions for dances around the world are shown through photographs and text in this picture book. (Grades K–2)

Auch, Mary Jane. (1993). *Peeping Beauty.* New York: Holiday House.

> A parody of Sleeping Beauty, this fiction picture book features Poulette, a chicken who believes the fox is a talent scout and will make her a ballerina. Ballet terms and the original story of Sleeping Beauty are included. (Grades 1–4)

Auch, Mary Jane (1995). *Hen Lake.* New York: Holiday House.

> Full of puns about ballet, this picture book tells the story of Poulette, the aspiring ballerina who talks the other chickens into performing *Hen Lake* (their version of *Swan Lake*) for a talent show. (Grades 1–4)

Bray-Moffat, Naia. (2003). *Ballet School.* (David Handley, Illus.). New York: Dorling Kindersley.

> Beautiful photographs and easy-to-understand text make this a perfect introduction to ballet for young children. Warm-up, bending and stretching, barre, leaping and jumping, and ballet positions are described. Also included is an index with pronunciation guide. (Grades K–3)

Burgard, Anna Marlis. (2005). *Flying Feet: A Story of Irish Dance.* (Leighanne Dees, Illus.). San Francisco: Chronicle.

> Based on a true incident, this picture book tells the story of two champion dancers, both determined to be the dance master in Ballyconneely. More information about Irish dance appears at the end of the book, as well as a pronunciation guide for Gaelic words, and a bibliography for further reading. (Grades 1–3)

Edwards, Patricia Duncan. (2000). *Bravo, Livingstone Mouse!* (Henry Cole, Illus.). New York: Hyperion.

> Livingstone Mouse comes to the rescue and provides the rhythm when the creatures of Wild Wood can't get their dance performance quite right. I have taught students to fox-trot and twist after reading this book. (Grades K–2)

Hebach, Susan. (2001). *Tap Dancing*. New York: Children's Press.

> Part of the High Interest book series at an easier reading level, photographs accompany the text that includes styles of tap dancing, vocabulary, and famous tap dancers. (Grades 4–5)

Smith, Cynthia Leitich. (2000). *Jingle Dancer*. (Cornelius Van Wright & Ying-Hwa Hu, Illus.). New York: William Morrow.

> Jenna, of Muscogee and Ojibway descent, practices the jingle dance by watching a video of her grandmother. She must earn money to get enough tin jingles to dance at the powwow. (Grades 1–3)

Drama

The following titles are organized into three areas that address most of the strands of the National Standards for Drama.

Plays and Productions

Alexander, Sue. (1977). *Small Plays for Special Days: Holiday Plays for You and a Friend*. (Tom Huffman, Illus.). New York: Clarion.

> This book has seven plays (2–3 pages each) for two performers. (Grades 1–3)

Bany-Winters, Lisa. (1997). *On Stage: Theater Games and Activities for Kids*. Chicago: Chicago Review Press.

> Basic theater vocabulary, theater games, and pantomime are featured in this book, as well as play scripts. (Grades 3–5)

Davidson, Rebecca Piatt. (2003). *All the World's a Stage*. (Anita Lobel, Illus.). New York: Greenwillow.

> A tribute to Shakespeare told in cumulative verse, this picture book introduces nine of his well-known plays. (Grades 3–5)

Friedman, Lise. (2002). *Break a Leg! The Kids' Guide to Acting and Stagecraft*. New York: Workman.

> Photographs of school actors illustrate discussions of costumes, makeup, and props. Games and improvisations for young actors are also included. (Grades 4–5)

Littlesugar, Amy. (2001). *Tree of Hope*. (Floyd Cooper, Illus.). New York: Putnam.

This picture book describes the rebirth of African American theater in Harlem during the Great Depression. (Grades K–3)

Packer, Tina. (2004). *Tales From Shakespeare*. New York: Scholastic.

The author, who is President and Artistic Director of Shakespeare & Company in Massachusetts, retells 10 of Shakespeare's most popular works. Each of the plays is illustrated by an award-winning artist. (Grades 4–5)

Rowland-Warne, L. (2000). *Costume*. New York: Dorling Kindersley.

The history of clothes and fashion is shown through photographs of theatrical recreations of historic costumes, and this book includes an index. (Grades 3–5)

Biographies

Bankston, John. (2004). *Melissa Gilbert*. Bear, DE: Mitchell Lane.

This biography focuses on Gilbert's life as a child actor and combining rehearsals with school work. (Other Blue Banner Biographies include Sally Field, Mary-Kate and Ashley Olsen, Jodie Foster, and Daniel Radcliffe.) (Grades 4–5)

Bankston, John. (2004). *Shirley Temple*. Bear, DE: Mitchell Lane.

Although her later life is briefly covered, this biography emphasizes the child star's film career in the 1930s. (Grades 3–5)

Brown, Don. (2003). *Mack Made Movies*. Brookfield, CT: Roaring Brook Press.

Humorous illustrations enhance this delightful picture book biography of film pioneer Mack Sennett, perhaps most famous for the "Keystone Kops." (Grades 2–4)

Stanley, Diane, & Vennema, Peter. (1992). *Bard of Avon: The Story of William Shakespeare*. (Diane Stanley, Illus.). New York: William Morrow.

This biography of Shakespeare spans his early life in Stratford to his years in London. His major works are discussed, as well as the political changes in England during his lifetime. (Grades 3–5)

Fiction About Plays

Aliki. (2005). *A Play's the Thing*. New York: HarperCollins.

> Miss Brilliant uses a student-led performance of "Mary Had a Little Lamb" to help a student deal with his bullying behavior. (Grades 1–4)

Cecil, Randy. (2004). *One Dark and Dreadful Night*. New York: Henry Holt.

> The Wayward Orphans Theatre performs three tragic tales (also known as fractured fairy tales) with hilarious results. (Grades K–3)

dePaola, Tomie. (2005). *Stagestruck*. New York: Putnam.

> Tommy wants to be Peter Rabbit in the class play but is cast as Mopsy. When he "steals the show" he must face the consequences. (Grades K–2)

Ernst, Lisa Campbell. (2005). *Sylvia Jean, Drama Queen*. New York: Dutton.

> Sylvia Jean is always in costume, so why can't she come up with something to win the grand prize at the costume party? (Grades K–2)

Lithgow, John. (2005). *Marsupial Sue Presents "The Runaway Pancake."* (Jack E. Davis, Illus.). New York: Simon & Schuster.

> Sue and her friends present their own version of The Gingerbread Man for the neighborhood. This book includes a CD of Lithgow reading the text. (Grades K–3)

Mazer, Anne. (2000). *The Amazing Days of Abby Hayes: Reach for the Stars*. New York: Scholastic.

> In this novel, Abby's class is putting on a production of *Peter Pan*. Guess which character everyone wants to be? (Grades 3–4)

Palatini, Margie. (2003). *Mary Had a Little Ham*. (Guy Francis, Illus.). New York: Hyperion.

> Stanley Snoutowski heads to Broadway to get his name in lights. He is cast in *Pigmalion*, *The Pig and I*, *Hamadeus*, *The Loin King*, *Oinklahoma*, and *South Pigcific*. This zany picture book is full of puns, but most will have to be explained to young children. (Grades K–3)

Streatfeild, Noel. (1994). *Theater Shoes*. New York: Random House.
> During WWII in England, three children go to live with their grandmother in London. She then enrolls them in a theater school, which they hate until they find that they have talent. (Grades 4–5)

Visual Arts

The following titles are organized into four categories that address the National Standards for Visual Arts Education.

Colors

Ehlert, Lois. (1988). *Planting a Rainbow*. San Diego, CA: Harcourt.
> Flowers of different colors are grown in this "rainbow" garden. (Grades K–1)

Heller, Ruth. (1995). *Colors*. New York: Putnam.
> Heller celebrates color by describing color-producing instruments (pencils, markers, crayons, paints, chalk, and so forth). The examples are illustrated with four acetate overlays that demonstrate how color printing is done. (Grades K–5)

Jenkins, Jessica. (1992). *Thinking About Colors*. New York: Dutton.
> Vibrant colors and text explore objects, ideas, emotions, and expressions that have to do with colors. (Grades K–3)

Serfozo, Mary. (1988). *Who Said Red?* (Keiko Narahashi, Illus.). New York: Margaret K. McElderry.
> Simple rhyming text accompanies pictures of different colors. (Grades K–1)

Seuss, Dr. (1996). *My Many Colored Days*. (Steve Johnson & Lou Fancher, Illus.). New York: Scholastic.
> Rhymes describe colors in this picture book. The size and positioning of the words relate to the text. (Grades K–3)

Walsh, Ellen Stoll. (1989). *Mouse Paint*. San Diego, CA: Harcourt.
> Three mice find three jars of paint. By hopping in and out of jars of primary colors, they change colors, too. (Grades K–1)

Children as Artists

dePaola, Tomie. (1989). *The Art Lesson*. New York: Putnam.
> This book shares a classic story about creativity and individuality. (Grades K–3)

McDonnell, Patrick. (2006). *Art*. New York: Little, Brown.
> Wordplay and simple artwork illustrate the wonders of creativity and the relationship between words and pictures. (Grades K–3)

Reynolds, Peter H. (2003). *The Dot*. Cambridge, MA: Candlewick.
> Vashti just can't draw! But a patient and wise teacher helps her discover that everyone can be an artist. (Grades K–4)

Say, Allen. (1996). *Emma's Rug*. Boston: Houghton Mifflin.
> Emma has been drawing ever since she could hold a pencil. Then, when she loses a childhood blanket, she no longer draws. Beautiful illustrations portray Emma's discovery that creativity comes from within. (Grades K–5)

Ziefert, Harriet. (1994). *Pete's Chicken*. (Laura Rader, Illus.). New York: William Morrow.
> When the class draws chickens, Pete makes his special. But the others tease him because it is different. This book provides a classic lesson in creativity. (Grades K–2)

Art Genre

Freymann, Saxton, & Elffers, Joost. (2003). *Dog Food*. New York: Scholastic.
> Ingenious photographs and word play show dogs made of fruit and vegetables. (Grades K–5)

Gelman, Rita Golden. (2004). *Doodler Doodling*. (Paul O. Zelinsky, Illus.). New York: Greenwillow.
> Wordplay and simple artwork illustrate the wonders of creativity and the relationship between words and pictures. (Grades K–3)

Gibbons, Gail. (1997). *Click! A Book About Cameras and Taking Pictures*. New York: Little, Brown.

> Gibbons offers good information about cameras and taking pictures in this nonfiction picture book. Although it is somewhat outdated in this digital age, the section on composition and different types of pictures is valuable. (Grades 2–4)

Gonyea, Mark. (2005). *A Book About Design: Complicated Doesn't Make it Good*. New York: Henry Holt.

> Minimal text and simple graphics explain balance, contrast, and line in this book about the basic approach to design. (Grades 1–5)

Metropolitan Museum of Art. (2002). *Museum ABC*. New York: Little, Brown.

> Four works of art from different cultures and periods illustrate each letter of the alphabet. This book also includes an index. (Grades 3–5)

Pittman, Helena Clare. (1998). *Still-Life Stew*. (Victoria Raymond, Illus.). New York: Hyperion.

> Rosa's vegetable garden becomes a still-life painting and then a stew! (Grades K–3)

Raimondo, Joyce. (2005). *Express Yourself: Activities and Adventures in Expressionism*. New York: Watson-Guptill.

> A description of the genre, step-by-step projects, and student art samples accompany examples of the works of Munch, van Gogh, Kirchner, Kandinsky, deKooning, and Pollock. (Grades 1–5)

Scieszka, Jon. (2005). *Seen Art?* (Lane Smith, Illus.). New York: Viking.

> A young boy goes to meet his friend, Art, and ends up in New York City at the Museum of Modern Art. Each time he asks someone if they have "seen Art," he is shown a different exhibit. (Grades 4–5)

Thomson, David. (1991). *Visual Magic*. London: Murray.

> This collection of visual tricks and illusions involving colors, shapes, patterns, and perspective is sure to fascinate readers of all ages. Some illusions require the use of 3-D glasses, which are included with the book. (Grades K–5)

Artists

Andrews-Goebel, Nancy. (2002). *The Pot That Juan Built*. (David Diaz, Illus.). New York: Lee & Low.

> Told in the form of The House That Jack Built, this picture book tells the story of Juan Quezada, Mexico's premier potter. The rhyming text is on the left-hand page, and information about Juan and his art is on the right. (Grades K–5)

Byrd, Robert. (2003). *Leonardo: Beautiful Dreamer*. New York: Dutton.

> The life, work, and dreams of Leonardo da Vinci are featured in this book. A bibliography, timeline, and illustrations are included. (Grades 3–5)

Cocca-Leffler, Maryann. (2001). *Edgar Degas: Paintings That Dance*. New York: Grosset & Dunlap.

> Biographical information and reproductions of the paintings by French artist Degas are presented in the style of a school report. (Grades 1–3)

Everett, Gwen. (1994). *Li'l Sis and Uncle Willie: A Story Based on the Life and Paintings of William H. Johnson*. New York: Hyperion.

> Based on a true story, this book tells the story of African American painter William H. Johnson from the perspective of his young niece. Johnson's actual paintings provide the illustrations. (Grades 2–5)

Jacobson, Rick. (2004). *Picasso: Soul on Fire*. (Laura Fernandez & Rick Jacobson, Illus.). Toronto, ON: Tundra Books.

> This beautifully illustrated tribute to Picasso covers his famous Blue and Rose Periods, as well as the Cubist revolution to ceramics, collage, and sculpture. (Grades 3–5)

Marcus, Leonard S. (1998). *A Caldecott Celebration: Six Artists Share Their Paths to the Caldecott Medal*. New York: Walker & Company.

> The stories of six children's book illustrators and their medal-winning books are featured in this volume. (Grades 3–5)

Slaymaker, Melissa Eskridge. (2004). *Bottle Houses: The Creative World of Grandma Prisbrey*. (Julie Paschkis, Illus.). New York: Henry Holt.

> Illustrations and photographs of her "houses" accompany the story of Tressa Prisbey, who began building her bottle village in 1956. (Grades 2–5)

Stanley, Diane. (2000). *Michelangelo*. New York: HarperCollins.

> The artist's achievements as an architect, painter, and sculptor are featured in this beautifully illustrated biography. (Grades K–5)

How to Obtain Books
for the Classroom

We all know that teachers spend their own money to buy supplies and books for their classroom. Here are some suggestions for economical ways to get books:

- Bonus points from classroom book clubs
- Garage sales
- Used book stores
- Parent donations—Post your "teacher wish lists" when your school has a book fair
- Grants—Professional, parent, and community organizations often give small grants to teachers for purchasing books
- Book swaps
- eBay and Craigslist

Lists of Nonfiction Trade Books

American Library Association
http://www.ala.org/ala/booklist/youthseriesroundup/SeriesRoundup.htm
Reviews of nonfiction books

Book Links: Connecting Books, Libraries, and Classrooms
American Library Association
http://www.ala.org/ala/productsandpublications/periodicals/booklinks/book
links.htm

Bimonthly magazine that explores themes, many in science and social studies, and includes annotated book lists and teaching ideas

Carol Hurst's Children's Literature Site
http://www.carolhurst.com/subjects/curriculum.html
Contains information on related children's books (both nonfiction and fiction), activities, related professional books, and links to related sites for each curriculum area

Children's Choices and Teacher's Choices
International Reading Association
http://www.reading.org/resources/tools/choices.html
Includes informational books

The Kobrin Letter: Concerning Children's Book About Real People, Places, and Things
732 Greer Road
Palo Alto, CA 94303, USA
Newsletter reviews of both recent and older informational books on selected topics

Notable Books for Young People
National Council for the Social Studies
http://www.socialstudies.org/resources/notable/
Includes annotations and suggested grade levels; divided into social studies themes

Orbis Pictus Award for Outstanding Nonfiction for Children
National Council of Teachers of English
http://www.ncte.org/elem/awards/orbispictus/106877.htm
Includes honor books with annotations

Outstanding Science Trade Books for Students K–12
National Science Teachers Association
http://www.nsta.org/ostbc
Includes annotations and suggested grade levels

Robert F. Sibert Informational Book Award
American Library Association
http://www.ala.org/ala/alsc/awardsscholarships/literaryawds/sibertmedal/Sibert_
Medal.htm
Contains links to current and past winners of this prestigious award

School Library Journal/Curriculum Connections
http://www.slj.com
School Library Journal includes annotated reviews of nonfiction books
Curriculum Connections reviews only nonfiction, organized by subject area

Children's Magazines Featuring Informational Text

Appleseeds
Cobblestone Publishing
30 Grove Street, Suite C
Peterborough, NH 03458, USA
http://www.cobblestonepub.com
Focuses on a social studies theme in each issue (Grades 3–5)

ASK (ASK stands for Arts and Sciences for Kids)
Cobblestone Publishing
30 Grove Street, Suite C
Peterborough, NH 03458, USA
http://www.cobblestonepub.com
Focuses on a theme in each issue (Grades 1–4)

chickaDEE
25 Boxwood Lane
Buffalo, NY 14227-2707, USA
http://www.owlkids.com
Includes hands-on science activities (Grades 1–4)

OWL (in Canada)
PO Box 726
Markham Station, Markham
ON Canada L3P 7V9
Features amazing facts and the science behind how things work (Grades 4–5)

Kids Discover
149 Fifth Avenue
New York, NY 10010, USA
http://www.kidsdiscover.com
Covers one of the following subjects in depth in each issue—history, nature, science, and geography (Grades 1–5)

National Geographic for Kids
PO Box 6300
Tampa, FL 33663-3302, USA
http://www.nationalgeographic.com/education
Articles and photographs focus on geography, science, nature, and social studies (Grades 3–5)

Ranger Rick
National Wildlife Federation
PO Box 2038
Harlan, IA 51593, USA
http://www.nwf.org/kids
Provides children with insight on nature, with animal photographs, information, and stories (Grades 2–5)

YES Mag: Canada's Science Magazine for Kids
3968 Long Gun Place
Victoria, BC
Canada V8N 3A9
http://www.yesmag.bc.ca
Features general science, technology, engineering, and mathematics (Grades 3–5)

Zoobooks
Wildlife Education Ltd.
12233 Thatcher Court
Poway, CA 92064, USA
http://www.zoobooks.com
Facts and photographs about specific animals and animal groups (Grades K–5)

Publishers of Readers Theatre Scripts

Libraries Unlimited/Teacher Ideas Press (Grades K–5)
7730 East Belleview Avenue, Suite A200
Greenwood Village, CO 80111, USA
http://www.lu.com

Reader's Theater Fluency and Comprehension (Grades 1–5)
Benchmark Education Company
629 Fifth Avenue
Pelham, NY 10803-1251, USA
http://www.benchmarkeducation.com

Websites for Readers Theatre Scripts

Aaron Shepard's Home Page: Stories, Scripts, and More
http://www.aaronshep.com
Scripts and tips for Readers Theatre (Grades 2–5)

Scripts for Schools
http://www.scriptsforschools.com
Chorale speaking and Readers Theatre scripts (Grades K–5)

Story Cart
http://www.storycart.com
Free sample scripts for Readers Theatre; priced scripts and collections (Grades 1–5)

Readers Theatre K–3
http://www.readerstheatre.ecsd.net
Over 150 free small poems, stories, and chants (Grades K–3)

Reader's Theater Script and Plays
http://teachingheart.net/readerstheater.htm
Free scripts, both fiction and nonfiction (Grades 1–5)

Websites for Students

The Art Room
http://www.arts.ufl.edu/art/rt_room/
Includes a gallery, book list, facts about art and artists, and interactive activities (Grades 3–5)

ArtsAlive From the Canadian National Arts Center's Orchestra
http://www.artsalive.ca/en/mus/index.asp
Includes information about composers, instruments, and orchestra, as well as activities and games (Grades 3–5)

Ask Dr. Math
http://mathforum.org/dr.math
Answers to common questions; formulas and specifics for elementary school (Grades 1–5)

Cool Science for Curious Kids
http://www.hhmi.org/coolscience
Includes plants, air, critters, and butterflies on this interactive site (Grades 2–5)

Discovery Science Center
http://www.discoverycube.org/kids
Science experiments, fun facts, and brain teasers (Grades 3–5)

Math Playground
http://www.mathplayground.com
Skills, activities, and games (Grades 1–5)

Science Explorations
http://www.scholastic.com/scienceexplorations
In-depth investigations on six major science topics—Animals, Adaptations and the Galapagos Islands, Classify Insects, Journey into Space, Investigate Invertebrates, Beam Up with Bats, and Research with Reptiles—and includes a teacher's guide (Grades 2–5)

Social Studies for Kids
http://www.socialstudiesforkids.com
Includes current events, cultures, holidays, geography, government, history, and archaeology (Grades 2–5)

Time for Kids—Homework Helper/Rapid Research
http://www.timeforkids.com/TFK/hh/rapidresearch
Includes history, government and politics, geography, holidays, world culture, homework helper, and games (Grades 2–5)

Lesson Plans for Teachers

Discovery Education
http://school.discovery.com/lessonplans
Lesson plans for social studies, science, mathematics, and arts (Grades K–5)

NCTM
http://illuminations.nctm.org/lessons.aspx
Math lessons and activities (Grades K–5)

Nortel LearniT
http://www.nortellearnit.org/lessons
Lesson plans for social studies, science, mathematics, and arts (Grades 4–5)

Verizon Thinkfinity
http://www.thinkfinity.org
Lesson plans for reading, writing, math, geography, government, science, and the arts, with links to national education standards in each discipline (Grades K–5)

Professional Organizations

American Alliance for Theatre and Education
http://www.aate.com

American Library Association
http://www.ala.org

Canadian Social Studies Super Site
http://www.ualberta.ca/~jkirman

International Reading Association
http://www.reading.org

Music Educators National Conference
http://www.menc.org

National Art Education Association
http://www.naea-reston.org

National Council for the Social Studies
http://www.socialstudies.org

National Council of Teachers of English
http://www.ncte.org

National Council of Teachers of Mathematics
http://www.nctm.org

National Dance Association
http://www.aahperd.org/nda/

National Science Teachers Association
http://www.nsta.org

References

Afflerbach, P., & VanSledright, B. (2001). Hath! Doth! What? Middle graders reading innovative history text. *Journal of Adolescent & Adult Literacy, 44,* 696–707.

Akerson, V.L., & Young, T.A. (2005). Science the "write" way. *Science and Children, 43,* 38–41.

Alberta Government Online. (2004). Alberta students show strong results on international tests. Retrieved May, 22, 2005, from http://www.education.gov.ab.ca/news/2004/December/nr-IntlTests.asp

Albright, L.K., & Vardell, S.M. (2003). 1950 to 2000 in picture books. *Book Links, 13,* 21–25.

Allen, D.D., & Piersma, M.L. (1995). *Developing thematic units: Process and product.* Albany, NY: Delmar.

American Association for the Advancement of Science. (1989). *Science for all Americans: A Project 2061 report on literacy goals in science, mathematics, and technology.* Washington, DC: Author.

Anderson, E. (1998). Motivational and cognitive influences on conceptual knowledge: The combination of science observation and interesting texts. *Dissertation Abstracts International, 59*(06), 1913A.

Arizona Board of Regents. (1995). *Schools, communities, and the arts: A research compendium.* Phoenix, AZ: Author.

Armbruster, B.B., & Anderson, T.H. (1988). On selecting "considerate" content area textbooks. *Remedial and Special Education, 9,* 47–52.

Aronson, E. (1978). *The jigsaw classroom.* Beverly Hills, CA: Sage.

ArtsWork. (2005). *Herberger College of Fine Arts.* Arizona State University. Retrieved February 26, 2007, from http://artswork.asu.edu/

Ashcroft, M.H. (1994). *Human memory and cognition.* New York: HarperCollins.

Baker, L., & Wigfield, A. (1999). Dimensions of children's motivation for reading and their relations to reading activity and reading achievement. *Reading Research Quarterly, 34,* 452–477.

Barnes, D.R. (1992). *From communication to curriculum* (2nd ed.). Portsmouth, NH: Boynton/Cook.

Beck, I.L., & McKeown, M.G. (1991). Social studies texts are hard to understand: Mediating some of the difficulties. *Language Arts, 68,* 482–490.

Beck, I.L., McKeown, M.G., & Gromoll, E.W. (1989). Learning from social studies texts. *Cognition and Instruction, 6,* 99–158.

Beck, I.L., McKeown, M.G., Hamilton, R.L., & Kucan, L. (1997). *Questioning the author: An approach for enhancing student engagement with text.* Newark, DE: International Reading Association.

Bosma, B., & Brower, M. (1995). A first-grade literature-based science program. In B. Bosma & N.D. Guth (Eds.), *Children's literature in an integrated curriculum: The authentic voice* (pp. 14–26). New York: Teachers College Press; Newark, DE: International Reading Association.

Bosma, B., & Guth, N.D. (1995). Making the connections. In B. Bosma & N.D. Guth (Eds.), *Children's literature in an integrated curriculum: The authentic voice* (pp. 1–13). New York: Teachers College Press; Newark, DE: International Reading Association.

British Columbia Ministry of Education. (1998). *Fine arts K to 7*. Retrieved March 30, 2007, from http://www.bced.gov.bc.ca/irp/fak7/fak7toc.htm

Brookes, M. (1996). *Drawing with children: A creative method for adult beginners, too*. New York: Putnam.

Bruning, R., & Schweiger, B.M. (1997). Integrating science and literacy experiences to motivate student learning. In J.T. Guthrie & A. Wigfield (Eds.), *Reading engagement: Motivating readers through integrated instruction* (pp. 149–167). Newark, DE: International Reading Association.

Bryant, J.A., Jr. (2005). Teaching history: The fax about history. *Phi Delta Kappan, 86*, 754–756.

Buchanan, M. (1985). *Why teach drama? A defense of the craft*. Retrieved April 26, 2006, from http://www.childdrama.com/why.html

Buchanan, M. (n.d.). *Group playwriting project*. Retrieved March 4, 2007, from http://www.child drama.com

Buehl, D. (2001). *Classroom strategies for interactive learning* (2nd ed.). Newark, DE: International Reading Association.

Burke-Walker, D. (1989). An update on states' dance curricula: Idaho. *Journal of Physical Education, Recreation & Dance, 60*(5), 40–41.

Caine, R.N., & Caine, G. (1994). *Making connections: Teaching and the human brain*. Menlo Park, CA: Addison Wesley.

Calkins, L.M. (1994). *The art of teaching writing*. Portsmouth, NH: Heinemann.

Camp, D. (2000). It takes two: Teaching with twin texts of fact and fiction. *The Reading Teacher, 53*, 400–408.

Carter, C.L. (1984). The state of dance in education: Past and present. *Theory Into Practice, 23*, 293–299.

Casteel, C.P., & Isom, B.A. (1994). Reciprocal processes in science and literacy learning. *The Reading Teacher, 47*, 538–545.

Center on Education Policy. (2006). *From the capital to the classroom: Year four of the No Child Left Behind Act*. Washington, DC: Author.

Chall, J.S. (2000). *The academic achievement challenge: What really works in the classroom?* New York: Guilford.

Chappel, J.M.(1998). Literature circles in intermediate science. In S. Zemelman, H. Daniels, A. Hyde, & W. Varner (Eds.), *Best practice: New standards for teaching and learning in America's schools* (2nd ed., pp. 107–131). Portsmouth, NH: Heinemann.

Coalition for Music Education in Canada & Canadian Music Educators Association. (2000). *Achieving musical understanding—concepts and skills for pre-kindergarten to grade 8*. Agincourt, ON; Waterloo, ON: Authors.

Connell, N. (1996). *Getting off the list: School improvement in New York City*. New York: Education Priorities Panel. (ERIC Document Reproduction Service No. ED448212)

Consortium of National Arts Education Associations. (1994). *National standards for arts education: What every young American should know and be able to do in the arts*. Reston, VA: Music Educators National Conference.

Danielson, K.E., & LaBonty, J. (1994). *Integrating reading and writing through children's literature*. Boston: Allyn & Bacon.

Davis, J.C., & Palmer, J. (1992). A strategy for using children's literature to extend the social studies curriculum. *The Social Studies, 83*(3), 125–128.

DeLain, M.T. (1999). Equity and performance-based assessment: An insider's view. In S.J. Barrentine (Ed.), *Reading assessment: Principles and practices for elementary teachers* (pp. 109–112). Newark, DE: International Reading Association.

Delisio, E.R. (2005). Music's key role in helping students learn. *Education World*. Retrieved April 4, 2006, from http://www.education-world.com

Dewey, J. (1938). *Experience and education*. New York: Macmillan.

Dimondstein, G. (1990). Moving in the real and feeling worlds: A rationale for dance in education. In A.S. Akins & J. LaPointe-Crump (Eds.), *Encores II: Travels through the spectrum of dance* (pp. 48–50). Reston, VA: National Dance Association.

Dickinson, D. (2002). *Learning through the arts*. Seattle, WA: New Horizons for Learning. Retrieved April 10, 2006, from http://www.newhorizons.org/strategies/arts/dickinson_lrnarts.htm

Donovan, C.A., & Smolkin, L.B. (2001). Genre and other factors influencing teachers' book selections for science instruction. *Reading Research Quarterly, 36*, 412–440.

DuPont, S. (1992). The effectiveness of creative drama as an instructional strategy to enhance the reading comprehension skills of fifth-grade remedial readers. *Reading Research and Instruction, 31*, 41–52.

Eisner, E.W. (1981). The role of the arts in cognition and curriculum. *Phi Delta Kappan, 63*, 48–52.

Farstrup, A.E. (2005, June/July). A classic case of mixed feelings. *Reading Today, 22*, 7.

Fielding, L., & Roller, C. (1992). Making difficult books accessible and easy books acceptable. *The Reading Teacher, 45*, 678–685.

Fisher, D., Flood, J., Lapp, D., & Frey, N. (2004). Interactive read-alouds: Is there a common set of implementation practices? *The Reading Teacher, 58*, 8–17.

Fisher, D., Frey, N., & Williams, D. (2002). Seven literacy strategies that work. *Educational Leadership, 60*, 70–73.

Flood, J., & Lapp, D. (1991). Reading comprehension instruction. In J. Flood, J.M. Jensen, D. Lapp, & J.R. Squire (Eds.), *Handbook of research on teaching the English language arts* (pp. 732–742). New York: Macmillan.

Fogarty, R. (1991). *How to integrate the curricula*. Palatine, IL: Skylight.

Fogarty, R., Perkins, D., & Barell, J. (1992). *How to teach for transfer*. Palatine, IL: Skylight.

Forman, E.A., & Cazden, C.B. (1985). Exploring Vygotskian perspectives in education: The cognitive value of peer interaction. In J.V. Wertsch (Ed.), *Culture communication, and cognition: Vygotskian perspectives* (pp. 323–347). New York: Cambridge University Press.

Freeman, E.B. (1995). Supporting children's learning: Informational books across the curriculum. In M. Sorensen & B. Lehman (Eds.), *Teaching with children's books: Paths to literature-based instruction* (pp. 188–196). Urbana, IL: National Council of Teachers of English.

Fulwiler, T. (1980). Journals across the disciplines. *The English Journal, 69*(9), 14–19.

Galda, L., & Liang, L.A. (2003). Literature as experience or looking for facts: Stance in the classroom. *Reading Research Quarterly, 38*, 268–275.

Gardiner, M., Fox, A., Knowles, F., & Jeffrey, D. (1996). Learning improved by arts training. *Nature, 381*, 284.

Gardner, H. (1982). *Art, mind, and brain*. New York: Basic Books.

Gilbert, A.G. (2002). *Teaching the three R's through movement experiences: A handbook for teachers*. Bethesda, MD: National Dance Education Organization.

Goodman, J.R. (2002). A naturalistic study of the relationship between literacy development and dramatic play in five-year-old children. In R.J. Deasy (Ed.), *Critical links: Learning in the arts and student academic and social development* (pp. 26–27). Washington, DC: Arts Education Partnership.

Greeno, J.G., & Hall, R.P. (1997). Practicing representation: Learning with and about representational forms. *Phi Delta Kappan, 78*, 361–367.

Gregg, M., & Sekeres, D.C. (2006). Supporting children's reading of expository text in the geography classroom. *The Reading Teacher, 60*, 102–110.

Gunning, T.G. (2003). *Creating literacy instruction for all children* (4th ed.). Boston: Allyn & Bacon.

Guthrie, J.T. (1996). Educational contexts for engagement in literacy. *The Reading Teacher, 49*, 432–445.

Guthrie, J.T., & McCann, A.D. (1997). Characteristics of classrooms that promote motivations and strategies for learning. In J.T. Guthrie & A. Wigfield (Eds.), *Reading engagement: Motivating readers through integrated instruction* (pp. 128–148). Newark, DE: International Reading Association.

Guthrie, J.T., McGough, K., Bennett, L., & Rice, M.E. (1996). Concept-oriented reading instruction: An integrated curriculum to develop motivations and strategies for reading. In L. Baker, P. Afflerbach, & D. Reinking (Eds.), *Developing engaged readers in school and home communities* (pp. 165–190). Mahwah, NJ: Erlbaum.

Guthrie, J.T., Van Meter, P., & Mitchell, A. (1999). Performance assessments in reading and language arts. In S.J. Barrentine (Ed.), *Reading assessment: Principles and practices for elementary teachers* (pp. 100–108). Newark, DE: International Reading Association.

Hall, T. (2002). *Differentiated instruction*. Wakefield, MA: National Center on Accessing the General Curriculum. Retrieved July 19, 2005, from http://www.cast.org/publications/ncac/ncac_diffinstruc.html

Hammond, M., Howard, P., Marantz, K., Packard, M., Shaw, J., & Wilson, H.M. (1994). *The picture book: Source and resource for art education*. Reston, VA: National Art Educators Association.

Hanna, J.L. (1992). Connections: Arts, academics, and productive citizens. *Phi Delta Kappan, 73*, 601–607.

Harris, T.L., & Hodges, R.E. (Eds.). (1995). *The literacy dictionary: The vocabulary of reading and writing*. Newark, DE: International Reading Association.

Hawley, S.W., & Spillman, C.V. (2003). *Literacy and learning: An expeditionary discovery through children's literature*. Lanham, MD: Scarecrow.

Hepler, S. (1989). A literature program: Getting it together, keeping it going. In J. Hickman & B. Cullinan (Eds.), *Children's literature in the classroom: Weaving Charlotte's web* (pp. 201–219). Norwood, MA: Christopher-Gordon.

Hilsendager, S. (1990). In transition—American dance education. *Journal of Physical Education, Recreation, & Dance, 61*, 47, 49, 51.

Hoffman, J.V., Roser, N.L., & Battle, J. (1993). Reading aloud in classrooms: From the modal toward a "model." *The Reading Teacher, 46*, 496–503.

Hong, H. (1996). Effects of mathematics learning through children's literature on math achievement and dispositional outcomes. *Early Childhood Research Quarterly, 11*, 477–494.

Hurwitz, I., Wolff, P.H., Bortnick, B.D., & Kokas, K. (1975). Nonmusical effects of the Kodaly music curriculum in primary grade children. *Journal of Learning Disabilities, 8*, 167–174.

Jacobs, A., & Rak, S. (1997). Mathematics and literature—A winning combination. *Teaching Children Mathematics, 4*, 156–157.

Jacobs, V.A. (2002). Reading, writing, and understanding. *Educational Leadership, 60*, 58–61.

Jones, M.G., Jones, B.D., Hardin, B., Chapman, L., Yarbrough, T., & Davis, M. (1999). The impact of high-stakes testing on teachers and students in North Carolina. *Phi Delta Kappan, 81*, 199–203.

Jones, R.C., & Thomas, T.G. (2006). Leave no discipline behind. *The Reading Teacher, 60*, 58–64.

Karp, K., Brown, E.T., Allen, L., & Allen, C. (1998). *Feisty females: Inspiring girls to think mathematically.* Portsmouth, NH: Heinemann.

Kletzien, S.B., & Dreher, M.J. (2004). *Informational text in K–3 classrooms: Helping children read and write.* Newark, DE: International Reading Association.

Kolakowski, J.S. (1995). Reading and Rembrandt: An integrated study of artists and their works. In B. Bosma & N.D. Guth (Eds.), *Children's literature in an integrated curriculum: The authentic voice* (pp. 27–36). New York: Teachers College Press; Newark, DE: International Reading Association.

Lenski, S.D., Ehlers-Zavala, F., Daniel, M.C., & Sun-Irminger, X. (2006). Assessing English-language Learners in mainstream classrooms. *The Reading Teacher, 60*, 24–34.

Lipson, M.Y., Valencia, S.W., Wixson, K.K., & Peters, C.W. (1993). Integration and thematic teaching: Integration to improve teaching and learning. *Language Arts, 70*, 252–263.

MacLure, M. (1988). Oracy: Current trends in context. In M. MacLure, T. Phillips, & A. Wilkinson (Eds.), *Oracy matters: The development of talking and listening in education* (pp. 1–12). Buckingham, England: Open University Press.

MacPherson, K. (2004, July 12). Educators voice growing concern that schools leaving arts behind. *Pittsburgh Post-Gazette.* Retrieved March 9, 2007, from http://www.post-gazette.com/pg/04194/345166.stm

Manitoba Education, Citizenship, and Youth. (2003). *Arts education: Dance, dramatic arts, music, visual arts.* Retrieved March 20, 2007, from http://www.edu.gov.mb.ca/k12/cur/arts/dance.html

Mantione, R.D., & Smead, S. (2003). *Weaving through words: Using the arts to teach reading comprehension strategies.* Newark, DE: International Reading Association.

Manz, S.L. (2002). A strategy for previewing textbooks: Teaching readers to become THIEVES. *The Reading Teacher, 55*, 434–435.

Manzo, K.K. (2005). Social studies losing out to reading, math. *Education Week, 24* (27), 1, 16–17.

Marshall, C. (1999, Fall). Reading and writing and.... *Pennsylvania Music Educators Association News*, n.p.

Mayer, D.A. (1995). How can we best use literature in teaching science concepts? *Science and Children, 32*, 16–19, 43.

Meece, J.L., Blumenfeld, P.C., & Hoyle, R.H. (1988). Students' goal orientations and cognitive engagement in classroom activities. *Journal of Educational Psychology, 80*, 514–523.

Miller, W. (1997). *Reading & writing remediation kit: Ready-to-use strategies and activities to build content reading and writing skills*. Englewood Cliffs, NJ: Center for Applied Research in Education.

Miller-Hewes, K.A. (1994). Making the connection: Children's books and the visual arts. *School Arts, 94*(4), 34.

Mills, H., O'Keefe, T., & Jennings, L.B. (2004). *Looking closely and listening carefully: Learning literacy through inquiry*. Urbana, IL: National Council of Teachers of English.

Moje, E.B., Ciechanowski, K.M., Kramer, K., Ellis, L., Carrillo, R., & Collazo, T. (2004). Working toward third space in content area literacy: An examination of everyday funds of knowledge and discourse. *Reading Research Quarterly, 39*, 38–70.

Moore, B.H., & Caldwell, H. (2002). Drama and drawing for narrative writing in primary grades. In R.J. Deasy (Ed.), *Critical links: Learning in the arts and student academic and social development* (pp. 32–33). Washington, DC: Arts Education Partnership.

Morrow, L.M., Pressley, M., & Smith, J.K. (1995). *The effect of a literature-based program integrated into library and science instruction on achievement, use, and attitudes toward literacy and science* (Reading Research Report, No. 37). Athens, GA: National Reading Research Center.

Moss, B. (2003). *Exploring the literature of fact: Children's nonfiction trade books in the elementary classroom*. New York: Guilford.

Moss, B., Leone, S., & DiPillo, M.L. (1997). Exploring the literature of fact: Linking reading and writing through information trade books. *Language Arts, 74*, 418–429.

Murphy, S.J. (2000). Children's books about math: Trade books that teach. *New Advocate, 13*, 365–374.

National Center for Education Statistics. (1995). *Arts education in public elementary schools*. Retrieved April 11, 2006, from http://nces.ed.gov/surveys/frss/publications/95082/index.asp?sectionID=3

National Center for Education Statistics. (2002). *Arts education in public elementary and secondary schools*. Retrieved February 25, 2007, from http://nces.ed.gov/surveys/frss/publications/2002131

National Commission on Writing in America's Schools and Colleges. (2003). *The neglected "R": The need for a writing revolution*. New York: College Entrance Examination Board. Retrieved May 20, 2005, from http://www.writingcommission.org/prod_downloads/writingcom/neglectedr.pdf

National Council for the Social Studies. (1994). *Curriculum standards for social studies: Expectations of excellence*. Silver Spring, MD: Author.

National Council of Teachers of Mathematics. (2000). *Principles and standards for school mathematics*. Reston, VA: Author. Retrieved April 4, 2007, from http://standards.nctm.org/document/chapter2/index.htm

National Institute of Child Health and Human Development. (2000). *Report of the National Reading Panel. Teaching children to read: An evidence-based assessment of the scientific research literature on reading and its implications for reading instruction* (NIH Publication No. 00-4769). Washington, DC: U.S. Government Printing Office.

National Science Teachers Association. (1996). *National science education standards* (Position statement). Retrieved May 22, 2005, from http://www.nsta.org/about/positions/standards.aspx

National Science Teachers Association. (2002). *Elementary school science* (Position statement). Retrieved January 16, 2006, from http://www.nsta.org/positionstatement&psid=8

New arts partnership to support AMERICA 2000 communities. (1992). *America 2000 communities: Getting started*. Retrieved April 5, 2007, from http://www.eric.ed.gov/sitemap/html_0900000b8004e923.html

Nichols, J. (1980). Using paragraph frames to help remedial high school students with written assignments. *English Journal, 24*, 228–231.

Ogle, D. (1986). K-W-L: A teaching model that develops active reading of expository text. *The Reading Teacher, 39*, 564–570.

Ontario Ministry of Education. (1982). *Partners in action: The library resource centre in the school curriculum*. Toronto, ON: Author.

Ontario Ministry of Education. (1998). *The arts: Drama and dance*. Retrieved March 30, 2007, from http://www.edu.gov.on.ca/eng/curriculum/elementary/arts368ex/

Ontario Ministry of Education and Training. (1995). *Information literacy and equitable access: A framework for change*. Toronto, ON: Author.

Opitz, M.F., & Rasinski, T.V. (1998). *Good-bye round robin*. Portsmouth, NH: Heinemann.

Overby, L.Y. (1992). *Status of dance in education*. (ERIC Document Reproduction Service No. ED348368). Retrieved April 25, 2006, from http://www.vtaide.com/png/ERIC/Dance-in-Ed.htm

Palmer, R.G., & Stewart, R.A. (2003). Nonfiction trade book use in primary grades. *The Reading Teacher, 57*, 38–48.

Paige, R. (2004). Key Policy Letter, July, 2004. Retrieved February 22, 2007, from http://www.ed.gov/policy/elsec/guid/secletter/040701.html

Pate, P.E., McGinnis, K., & Homestead, E. (1995). Creating coherence through curriculum integration. In J.A. Beane (Ed.), *Toward a coherent curriculum* (1995 Yearbook of the Association for Supervision and Curriculum Development, pp. 62–70). Alexandria, VA: Association for Supervision and Curriculum Development.

Perkins-Gough, D. (2004). The eroding curriculum. *Educational Leadership, 62*(1), 84–85.

Person, D.G., & Cullinan, B.E. (1992). Windows through time: Literature of the social studies. In E.B. Freeman & D.G. Person (Eds.), *Using nonfiction trade books in the elementary classroom: From ants to zeppelins* (pp. 65–75). Urbana, IL: National Council of Teachers of English.

Piaget, J., & Inhelder, B. (1969). *The psychology of the child* (H. Weaver, Trans.). New York: Basic Books.

Pierpont, K. (2006). Greg Tang: Making math count. *Teaching preK–8, 36*(4), 46–48.

Reeves, D.B. (2000). *Accountability in action: A blueprint for learning organizations*. Denver, CO: Advanced Learning Press.

Reeves, D.B. (2002). *Reason to write: Student handbook*. New York: Kaplan.

Reeves, D.B. (2005). High performance in high-poverty schools: 90/90/90 and beyond. In J. Flood & P.L. Anders (Eds.), *Literacy development of students in urban schools: Research and policy* (pp. 362–388). Newark, DE: International Reading Association.

Regents of the University of California. (2005). *FOSS: Full option science system*. Nashua, NH: Delta Education.

Rice, D., & Rainsford, A. (1996). *Using children's trade books to teach science: Boon or boondoggle?* Paper presented at the annual meeting of the National Association for Research in Science Teaching, St. Louis, MO. (ERIC Document Reproduction Service No. ED393700)

Richardson, M.V., Sacks, M.K., & Ayers, M.N. (2003). Paths to reading and writing through the visual arts. *Reading Improvement, 40,* 113–116.

Roser, N.L., & Keehn, S. (2002). Fostering thought, talk, and inquiry: Linking literature and social studies. *The Reading Teacher, 55,* 416–426.

Routman, R. (2003). *Reading essentials: The specifics you need to teach reading well.* Portsmouth, NH: Heinemann.

Ruppert, S. (2006). *Critical evidence. How the ARTS benefit student achievement.* Washington, DC: National Assembly of State Arts Agencies in collaboration with the Arts Education Partnership.

Santa, C.M., Havens, L.T., & Maycumber, E.M. (1996). *Project CRISS: Creative independence through student-owned strategies* (2nd ed.). Dubuque, IA: Kendall/Hunt.

Santa, C.M. (1997). School change and literacy engagement: Preparing teaching and learning environments. In J.T. Guthrie & A. Wigfield (Eds.), *Reading engagement: Motivating readers through integrated instruction* (pp. 218–233). Newark, DE: International Reading Association.

Saskatchewan Ministry of Education. (2006). *Evergreen curriculum: Elementary level.* Retrieved March 30, 2007, from http://www.sasked.gov.sk.ca/branches/curr/evergreen/artsed.shtml

Schwartz, R.M., & Raphael, T.E. (1985). Concept of definition: A key to improving students' vocabulary. *The Reading Teacher, 39,* 198–205.

Sebesta, S.L. (1989). Literature across the curriculum. In J.W. Stewig & S.L. Sebesta (Eds.), *Using literature in the elementary classroom* (pp. 110–128). Urbana, IL: National Council of Teachers of English.

Sierra, J. (2004). "I'll be the monster!" Folk tales and classroom drama. In T.A. Young (Ed.), *Happily ever after: Sharing folk literature with elementary and middle school students* (pp. 282–292). Newark, DE: International Reading Association.

Simpson, J. (2005). *Circle-time poetry math.* New York: Scholastic.

Snow, C.E., Burns, M.S., & Griffin, P. (Eds.). (1998). *Preventing reading difficulties in young children.* Washington, DC: National Academy Press.

Sousa, D. (2001). *How the brain learns* (2nd ed.). Thousand Oaks, CA: Corwin Press.

Swift, J. (2005, November 1). Schools seek science WASL delay. *King County Journal.*

Tiedt, I.M. (2000). *Teaching with picture books in the middle school.* Newark, DE: International Reading Association.

Tishman, S., MacGillivray, D., & Palmer, P. (2002). Investigating the educational impact and potential of the Museum of Modern Art's Visual Thinking Curriculum: Final report. In R.J. Deasy (Ed.), *Critical links: Learning in the arts and student academic and social development* (pp. 142–143). Washington, DC: Arts Education Partnership.

Tobias, S. (1993). *Overcoming math anxiety.* New York: Norton.

Tomlinson, C.A. (2001). *How to differentiate instruction in mixed-ability classrooms* (2nd ed.). Alexandria, VA: Association for Supervision and Curriculum Development.

Turnipseed, J.P. (1976). *The effects of participation in structured classical music education programs on the total development of first grade children.* Paper presented at the Mid-South Educational Research Conference, New Orleans.

U.S. House of Representatives. (2004, May 4). House Congressional Resolution 380: Recognizing the benefits and importance of school-based music education.

Usnick, V., & McCarthy, J. (1998). Turning adolescents onto mathematics through literature. *Middle School Journal, 29*(4), 50–54.

Vacca, J.L., Vacca, R.T., Gove, M.K., Burkey, L.C., Lenhart, L.A., & McKeon, C.A. (2003). *Reading and learning to read* (5th ed.). Boston: Allyn & Bacon.

Vacca, R.T., & Vacca, J.L. (1996). *Content area reading* (5th ed.). New York: HarperCollins.

Van Buren, B. (1986). Improving reading skills through elementary art experiences. *Art Education, 39*(1), 56, 59, 61.

von Zastrow, C.E., & Janc, H. (2004). *Academic atrophy: The condition of the liberal arts in America's schools.* Washington, DC: Council for Basic Education.

Vygotsky, L.S. (1978). *Mind in society: The development of higher psychological processes* (M. Cole, V. John-Steiner, S. Scribner, & E. Souberman, Eds. & Trans.). Cambridge, MA: Harvard University Press. (Original work published 1934)

Walling, D.R. (2001). Rethinking visual arts education: A convergence of influences. *Phi Delta Kappan, 82,* 626–628.

Walpole, S. (1998/1999). Changing texts, changing thinking: Comprehension demands of new science textbooks *The Reading Teacher, 52,* 358–369.

Weaver, C. (1988). *Reading process and practice: From socio-psycholinguistics to whole language.* Portsmouth, NH: Heinemann.

Welchman-Tischler, R. (1992). *How to use children's literature to teach mathematics.* Reston, VA: National Council of Teachers of Mathematics.

Whitin, D.J. (1994). Literature and mathematics in preschool and primary: The right connection. *Young Children, 49*(2), 4–11.

Whitin, D.J., & Whitin, P. (2004). *New visions for linking literature and mathematics.* Urbana, IL: National Council of Teachers of English; Reston, VA: National Council of Teachers of Mathematics.

Wilde, S. (1998). Mathematical learning and exploration in nonfiction literature. In R. Bamford & J.V. Kristo (Eds.), *Making facts come alive: Choosing quality nonfiction literature K–8* (pp. 123–134). Norwood, MA: Christopher-Gordon.

Zemelman, S., Daniels, H., & Hyde, A. (1998). *Best practice: New standards for teaching and learning in America's schools* (2nd ed.). Portsmouth, NH: Heinemann.

LITERATURE CITED

Alter, J. (2000). *Christopher Reeve: Triumph over tragedy.* London: Franklin Watts.

Anholt, L. (1994). *Camille and the sunflowers: A story about Vincent van Gogh.* Hauppauge, NY: Barron's.

Anholt, L. (2003). *The magical garden of Claude Monet.* Hauppauge, NY: Barron's.

Avi. (1995). *Poppy.* (B. Floca, Illus.). New York: Avon.

Axelrod, A. (1997). *Pigs will be pigs: Fun with math and money.* (S. McGinley-Nally, Illus.). New York: Simon & Schuster.

Bannatyne-Cugnet, J. (1992). *A prairie alphabet.* (Y. Moore, Illus.). Toronto, ON: Tundra.

Bany-Winters, L. (2000). *Show time! Music, dance, and drama activities for kids.* Chicago: Chicago Review Press.

Barasch, L. (2004). *Knockin' on wood.* New York: Lee & Low.

Bellville, C.W. (1985). *Rodeo*. Minneapolis, MN: Carolrhoda.

Beard, D.B. (1999). *Twister*. (N. Carpenter, Illus.). New York: Farrar, Straus and Giroux.

Bentley, W.A., & Humphreys, W.J. (1962). *Snow crystals*. New York: Dover.

Birtha, B. (2005). *Grandmama's pride*. (C. Bootman, Illus.). Morton Grove, IL: Albert Whitman.

Bjork, C. (1985). *Linnea in Monet's garden*. (L. Anderson, Illus.). Stockholm, Sweden: Raben & Sjogren.

Brown, M. (2000). *Francine the superstar*. Boston: Little, Brown.

Bunting, E. (1999). *Butterfly house*. (G. Shed, Illus.). New York: Scholastic.

Burns, M. (1975). *The I hate mathematics! book*. (M. Weston, Illus.). Cambridge, England: Cambridge University Press.

Burstein, C.M. (1993). *Jewish kid's catalog*. Philadelphia: Jewish Publication Society.

Carle, E. (1990). *The very quiet cricket*. New York: Philomel.

Carle, E. (1969). *The very hungry caterpillar*. New York: Philomel.

Carmack, L.J. (1998). *Philippe in Monet's garden*. Boston: Museum of Fine Arts.

Cary, B. (2001). *Meet Abraham Lincoln*. New York: Random House.

Cash, M.M. (2003). *What makes the seasons?* New York: Viking.

Clemson, W., & Clemson, D. (2002). *Shape and pattern*. Minnetonka, MN: Two-Can.

Cohn, D. (2002). *Dream carver*. (A. Cordova, Illus.). San Francisco: Chronicle.

Collard, S.B., III. (1997). *Animal dads*. (S. Jenkins, Illus.). Boston: Houghton Mifflin.

Constanza, S. (2004). *Mozart finds a melody*. New York: Henry Holt.

Coughlan, C. (1999). *Beetles*. Mankato, MN: Capstone.

Cronin, D. (2000). *Click, clack, moo: Cows that type*. (B. Lewin, Illus.). New York: Simon & Schuster.

Dalton, J. (2006). *Counting money*. New York: Children's Press.

Davies, N. (2005). *Ice bear: In the steps of the polar bear*. (G. Blythe, Illus.). Cambridge, MA: Candlewick.

Demarest, C.L. (2006). *Hurricane hunters! Riders on the storm*. New York: Margaret K. McElderry.

dePaola, T. (1978). *The popcorn book*. New York: Holiday House.

Dodds, D.A. (1997). *Sing, Sophie!* (R. Litzinger, Illus.). Cambridge, MA: Candlewick.

Doeden, M. (2006). *Will Smith*. Minneapolis, MN: Lerner.

Dorros, A. (2000). *10 go tango*. (E.A. McCully, Illus.). New York: HarperCollins.

Doudna, K. (2003). *Let's subtract money*. Edina, MN: ABDO Publishing.

Ehlert, L. (2001). *Waiting for wings*. San Diego, CA: Harcourt.

Farndon, J. (1993). *Eyewitness question & answer book*. New York: Dorling Kindersley.

Fraser, M.A. (1995). *In search of the Grand Canyon: Down the Colorado with John Wesley Powell*. New York: Henry Holt.

Frattini, S. (2003). *Face-to-face with the cat*. (J.-L. Klein & M.-L. Hubert, Illus.). Watertown, MA: Charlesbridge.

Freedman, R. (1991). *The Wright brothers: How they invented the airplane*. (W. Wright & O. Wright, Illus.). New York: Holiday House.

Freedman, R. (1998). *Martha Graham: A dancer's life*. New York: Clarion.

Gerstein, M. (2002). *What Charlie heard*. New York: Farrar, Straus and Giroux.

Gherman, B. (2000). *Norman Rockwell: Storyteller with a brush*. New York: Atheneum.

Glassman, B. (2001). *Mikhail Baryshnikov: Dance genius*. Woodbridge, CT: Blackbirch.

Gibbons, G. (1990). *Beacons of light: Lighthouses*. New York: Scholastic.

Gibbons, G. (1992). *Recycle! A handbook for kids*. Boston: Little, Brown.

Gibbons, G. (1993). *Frogs*. New York: Holiday House.

Gibbons, G. (2001). *Polar bears*. New York: Holiday House.

Gibbons, G. (2003). *Grizzly bears*. New York: Holiday House.

Gill, S. (2001). *The egg*. (J.-E. Bosson, Illus.). Watertown, MA: Charlesbridge.

Harrison, H.H. (1963). *The little typewriter*. San Antonio, TX: Naylor.

Harrison, T. (1992). *O Canada*. Toronto, ON: Kids Can Press.

Helman, A. (1996). *1, 2, 3 moose: A Pacific Northwest counting book*. (A. Wolfe, Photo.). Seattle, WA: Sasquatch Books.

Himmelman, J. (1998). *A ladybug's life*. New York: Children's Press.

Hirschi, R. (1997). *Faces in the mountains*. (T.D. Mangelsen, Illus.). New York: Cobblehill.

Hodge, D. (1996). *Bears: Polar bears, black bears and grizzly bears*. (P. Stephens, Illus.). Toronto, ON: Kids Can Press.

Hoffman, M. (1991). *Amazing Grace*. (C. Binch, Illus.). New York: Dial.

Holabird, K. (1983). *Angelina ballerina*. (H. Craig, Illus.). New York: Crown.

Horowitz, D. (2005). *Soon Baboon soon*. New York: Putnam.

Houston, G. (1992). *But no candy*. (L. Bloom, Illus.). New York: Philomel.

Howe, J. (1998). *Pinky and Rex and the school play*. (M. Sweet, Illus.). New York: Atheneum.

Hutchins, P. (1986). *The doorbell rang*. New York: Scholastic.

Isom, J.S. (1997). *The first starry night*. Watertown, MA: Charlesbridge.

James, S. (1991). *Dear Mr. Blueberry*. New York: Margaret K. McElderry.

Josephson, J.P. (2002). *Growing up in World War II: 1941 to 1945*. Minneapolis, MN: Lerner.

Keys, J. (2002). *Animal families*. Littleton, MA: Sundance.

Kohl, M., & Potter, J. (1993). *Science arts: Discovering science through art experiences*. Bellingham, WA: Bright Ring.

Krishnaswami, U. (2003). *Monsoon*. (J. Akib, Illus.). New York: Farrar, Strauss and Giroux.

Krull, K. (1995). *V is for victory*. New York: Knopf.

Lang, A. (2001). *The adventures of baby bear*. (W. Lynch, Illus.). Markham, ON: Fitzhenry & Whiteside.

Langley, J. (1993). *Goldilocks and the three bears*. New York: HarperCollins.

Lester, H. (1988). *Tacky the penguin*. (L. Munsinger, Illus.). Boston: Houghton Mifflin.

Levy, B.S. (2003). *How to draw faces*. New York: Dover.

Lin, G., & McKneally, R.T. (2006). *Our seasons*. (G. Lin, Illus.). Watertown, MA: Charlesbridge.

Lithgow, J. (2000). *The remarkable Farkle McBride*. (C.F. Payne, Illus.). New York: Simon & Schuster.

Lionni, L. (1995). *Inch by inch*. New York: Mulberry.

Lobel, A. (1998). *No pretty pictures: A child of war*. New York: Greenwillow.

Loughran, D. (2004). *How long is it?* New York: Children's Press.

Machotka, H. (1991). *What neat feet!* New York: William Morrow.

Maltbie, P.I. (2005). *Picasso and Minou*. (P. Estrada, Illus.). Watertown, MA: Charlesbridge.

Markle, S. (2005). *A mother's journey*. (A. Marks, Illus.). Watertown, MA: Charlesbridge.

Martin, J.B. (1998). *Snowflake Bentley*. (M. Azarian, Illus.). Boston: Houghton Mifflin.

Marzollo, J. (1993). *Happy Birthday, Martin Luther King.* (J.B. Pinkney, Illus.). New York: Scholastic.

Mayhew, J. (2001). *Katie and the sunflowers.* New York: Orchard.

McSwigan, M. (1942). *Snow treasure.* New York: Scholastic.

Mellonie, B. (1983). *Lifetimes: The beautiful way to explain death to children.* (R. Ingpen, Illus.). New York: Bantam.

Merberg, J., & Bober, S. (2003). *A picnic with Monet.* San Francisco: Chronicle.

Merriam, E. (1966). *Miss Tibbett's typewriter.* (R. Schreiter, Illus.). New York: Knopf.

Minor, W. (2000). *Grand Canyon: Exploring a natural wonder.* New York: Scholastic.

Moss, M. (2001). *Brave Harriet.* (C.F. Payne, Illus.). San Diego, CA: Harcourt.

Murphy, J. (2003). *Inside the Alamo.* New York: Delacorte.

Mühlberger, R. (2002). *What makes a Monet a Monet?* New York: Viking.

Mühlberger, R. (2002). *What makes a van Gogh a van Gogh?* New York: Viking.

Neuschwander, C. (1997). *Sir Cumference and the first round table: A math adventure.* (W. Geehan, Illus.). Watertown, MA: Charlesbridge.

Neuschwander, C. (1999). *Sir Cumference and the dragon of pi: A math adventure.* (W. Geehan, Illus.). Watertown, MA: Charlesbridge.

Newman, B. (2005). *The illustrated book of ballet stories.* (G. Tomblin, Illus.). New York: Dorling Kindersley.

Nicholson, D.M. (2001). *Pearl Harbor warriors: The bugler, the pilot, the friendship.* (L. Nicholson, Illus.). Kansas City, MO: Woodson House.

O'Neill, M. (1961). *Hailstones and halibut bones.* (L. Weisgard, Illus.). Garden City, NY: Doubleday.

Osofsky, R. (2002). *Come look with me: Art in early America.* New York: Lickle.

Pallotta, J. (1986). *The icky bug alphabet book.* (R. Masiello, Illus.). Watertown, MA: Charlesbridge.

Pallotta, J. (2001). *The Hershey's Kisses addition book.* (R. Bolster, Illus.). New York: Scholastic.

Pallotta, J. (2002). *The Hershey's Milk Chocolate multiplication book.* (R. Bolster, Illus.). New York: Scholastic.

Pallotta, J. (2005). *Ocean counting: Odd numbers.* (S. Bersani, Illus.). Watertown, MA: Charlesbridge.

Park, B. (2004). *Junie B., first grader: Shipwrecked.* (D. Brunkus, Illus.). New York: Random House.

Peffer, J. (2005). *Dragonart: How to draw and paint fantasy creatures.* Cincinnati, OH: Impact.

Pinczes, E.J. (2001). *Inchworm and a half.* (R. Enos, Illus.). Boston: Houghton Mifflin.

Raschka, C. (1992). *Charlie Parker played be bop.* New York: Scholastic.

Reed, H. (2002). *The pond.* Littleton, MA: Sundance.

Reich, S. (2005). *José! Born to dance.* (R. Colón, Illus.). New York: Simon & Schuster.

Rinehart, S.C. (2004). *Eliza and the dragonfly.* (A.C. Hovemann, Illus.). Nevada City, CA: Dawn.

Rivera, S. (2006). *Abraham Lincoln: A life of respect.* Minneapolis, MN: Lerner.

Robins, D. (2006). *Mixed media.* Minnetonka, MN: Two-Can.

Rockwell, A. (2004). *Becoming butterflies.* (M. Halsey, Illus.). New York: Walker & Company.

Rockwell, A. (2004). *Four seasons make a year.* (M. Halsey, Illus.). New York: Walker & Company.

Rodman, M.A. (2004). *Yankee girl.* New York: Farrar, Straus and Giroux.

Roy, D.K. (2001). *Hokusai: The man who painted a mountain.* New York: Farrar, Straus and Giroux.

Ryan, P.M., & Pallotta, J. (1996). *The Crayon counting book*. (F. Mazzola, Jr., Illus.). Watertown, MA: Charlesbridge.

Rylant, C. (1998). *Henry and Mudge and the starry night*. (S. Stevenson, Illus.). New York: Simon & Schuster.

Sandburg, C. (1993). *Arithmetic*. (T. Rand, Illus.). San Diego, CA: Harcourt.

Scieszka, J. (1995). *Math curse*. (L. Smith, Illus.). New York: Viking.

Scillian, D. (2001). *A is for America: An American alphabet*. (P. Carroll, Illus.). Chelsea, MI: Sleeping Bear Press.

Schultz, J., & Sherwonit, B. (1993). *Iditarod: The great race to Nome*. Seattle, WA: Alaska Northwest Books.

Seuss, Dr. (1968). *The foot book*. New York: Random House.

Shaik, F. (1998). *The jazz of our street*. (E.B. Lewis, Illus.). New York: Dial.

Shannon, G. (1982). *Dance away*. (J. Aruego & A. Dewey, Illus.). New York: Greenwillow.

Sherman, J. (2001). *Welcome to the rodeo!* Portsmouth, NH: Heinemann.

Spier, P. (Illus.). (1973). *The star-spangled banner*. Garden City, NY: Doubleday.

St. George, J. (2000). *So you want to be president?* (D. Small, Illus.). New York: Philomel.

Sundance Little Reader Twin Texts. (2002). Littleton, MA: Sundance.

Swanson, D. (2003). *Welcome to the world of penguins*. North Vancouver, BC: Whitecap Books.

Tang, G. (2001). *The grapes of math*. (H. Briggs, Illus.). New York: Scholastic.

Taylor, T. (1995). *The bomb*. San Diego, CA: Harcourt.

Tunnell, M.O., & Chilcoat, G.W. (1996). *The children of Topaz: The story of a Japanese-American internment camp*. New York: Holiday House.

Ulmer, M. (2001). *M is for Maple: A Canadian alphabet*. (M. Rose, Illus.). Chelsea, MI: Sleeping Bear Press.

Usel, T.M. (2006). *Abraham Lincoln*. Mankato, MN: Capstone Press.

van Gogh, V. (2005). *Vincent's colors*. San Francisco: Chronicle.

Waldman, N. (1999). *The starry night*. Honesdale, PA: Boyds Mills Press.

Ward, K. (2003). *Born to be wild*. Santa Cruz, CA: WildLight.

Wells, R. (2000). *Emily's first 100 days of school*. New York: Hyperion Books for Children.

Whitman, S. (2000). *Children of the World War II home front*. Minneapolis, MN: Carolrhoda.

Wiesner, D. (1991). *Tuesday*. New York: Clarion.

Williams, R.L. (2001). *The coin counting book*. Watertown, MA: Charlesbridge.

MUSIC CITED

Anderson, L. (1950). The typewriter. Van Nuys, CA: Warner Brothers. Retrieved March 6, 2007, from http://www.leroyanderson.com/html/hearthemusic.htm

Copland, A. (1942). Lincoln portrait [Conducted by E. Kunzel, performed by Cincinnati Pops Orchestra & Katharine Hepburn]. On *Aaron Copland: Lincoln Portrait; Old American Songs* [CD]. Cincinnati, OH: Cincinnati Pops Orchestra. (1990)

Copland, A. (1942). Rodeo [Conducted by L. Bernstein, performed by New York Philharmonic Orchestra]. On *Bernstein Century—Copland: Appalachian Spring, Rodeo, etc.* [CD]. New York: New York Philharmonic Orchestra. (1997)

Grofe, F. (1931). Grand Canyon Suite [Conducted by W.T. Stromberg, performed by Bournemouth Sinfonietta]. On *American Classics: Grofé: Orchestral Works* [CD]. Franklin, TN: Naxos. (1999)

Loesser, F. (1951). The inch worm. On *Frank Sings Loesser* [CD]. New York: KOCH International Classics. (1995)

Vivaldi, A. (1726). The four seasons. Retrieved March 6, 2007, from http://www.baroque-music-club.com/19Web.html

Index

Note: Page numbers followed by *f* indicate figures.

I

IDENTITY: books on, 50–52

INDIVIDUALS: books on, 48–50, 52–54; in science, books on, 96–98

INFORMATION SEARCH MONITORING: questions for, 15–16, 15*f*

INFORMATIONAL TEXT: magazines with, 175–176

INFORMATIONAL TRADE BOOKS: in content area instruction, 7–8; definition of, 7; lists of, 173–175; precautions for, 69–70; reading instruction on, 8–12

INHELDER, B., 19

INQUIRY: science as, books on, 86–89

INSTITUTIONS: books on, 52–54

INSTRUMENTS: books on, 158–159

INTEGRATED CURRICULUM, 18–31; and arts, 133–135; definition of, 18–19; models of, 23–24; rationale for, 19–22; risks of, 22–23

ISOM, B.A., 2

ISOM, J.S., 154

J

JACOBS, A., xiii

JACOBS, V.A., 29

JAMES, S., 69

JANG, H., 132–133

JEFFREY, D., 134

JENNINGS, L.B., xi

JIGSAW STRATEGY, 22–23

JOHNS, JERRY L., vii–viii

JONES, B.D., ix

JONES, M.G., ix

JONES, R.C., 29–30, 32

JOSEPHSON, J.P., 140

JOURNALS: science, 67

K

KARP, K., 107

KEEHN, S., 2, 4

KEYS, J., 37

KLETZIEN, S.B., 7, 12–13, 15–16, 30, 35

KNOWLEDGE HANDICAPS, 27

KNOWLES, F., 134

KOHL, M., 153

KOKAS, K., 137

KOLAKOWSKI, J.S., 135

KRAMER, K., xii

KRISHNASWAMI, U., 80

KRULL, K., 22

KUCAN, L., 2

K-W-L STRATEGY, 9–10, 10*f*

PINCZES, E.J., 108
PISA. *See* Programme for International Student Assessment
PLACES: books on, 48–50
PLAYS: books on, 165–168
POTTER, J., 153
POWER: books on, 54–56
PRESSLEY, M., 20
PROBABILITY: books on, 128–130; instructional standards for, 102
PROBLEM-SOLVING SKILLS, 21; mathematics instruction and, 102; trade books and, 103–104
PROCESS DRAMA, 147
PROCESSES: scientific, books on, 85–86
PRODUCTION: books on, 57–58
PRODUCTS: differentiation of, 27
PROFESSIONAL ORGANIZATIONS, 179–180
PROGRAMME FOR INTERNATIONAL STUDENT ASSESSMENT (PISA), 20–21
PROOF: instructional standards for, 102

Q–R

QUESTIONS: for information search monitoring, 15–16, 15*f*; for weather research, 80*f*
RAINSFORD, A., 69
RAK, S., xiii
RAPHAEL, T.E., 11
RASCHKA, C., 137
RASINSKI, T.V., 148
READ-ALOUDS: trade books as, 4–5
READERS THEATRE, 148; script sources, 177
READING INSTRUCTION: trade books for, 5–6
REASONING: instructional standards for, 102
REED, H., 70
REEVES, D.B., 18–19, 21, 28–29
REGENTS OF THE UNIVERSITY OF CALIFORNIA, 67
REICH, S., 142
REPORT CHECKLIST, 29–31, 30*f*
REPRESENTATION: instructional standards for, 102
RESEARCH: on weather, questions for, 80*f*
RESOURCE-BASED MODEL, 20–21
RICE, D., 69
RICE, M.E., 20
RICHARDSON, M.V., 152
RINEHART, S.C., 7
RIVERA, S., 140
ROBINS, D., 153
ROCKWELL, A., 75, 140
RODMAN, M.A., 3
ROLLER, C., 27
ROSER, N.L., 2, 4
ROUTMAN, R., 19, 35